Markt- und Unternehmensentwicklung Markets and Organisations

Series Editors

Ralf Reichwald, HHL Leipzig Graduate School of Management, Leipzig, Sachsen, Germany

Egon Franck, University of Zurich, Zurich, Switzerland

Kathrin M. Möslein, HHL Leipzig Graduate School of Management, University of Erlangen-Nuremberg, Erlangen-Nuremberg, Bayern, Germany

Change of institutions, technology and competition drives the interplay of markets and organisations. The scientific series 'Markets and Organisations' addresses a magnitude of related questions, presents theoretic and empirical findings and discusses related concepts and models.

Maximilian Perez Mengual

Designing Physical Interaction Platforms

Springer Gabler

Maximilian Perez Mengual
Nürnberg, Germany

Dissertation Friedrich-Alexander-Universität Erlangen-Nürnberg/2022

ISSN 2945-879X ISSN 2945-8803 (electronic)
Markt- und Unternehmensentwicklung Markets and Organisations
ISBN 978-3-658-41919-6 ISBN 978-3-658-41920-2 (eBook)
https://doi.org/10.1007/978-3-658-41920-2

This Springer Gabler imprint is published by the registered company Springer Fachmedien Wiesbaden GmbH, part of Springer Nature.
The registered company address is: Abraham-Lincoln-Str. 46, 65189 Wiesbaden, Germany

Paper in this product is recyclable.

Foreword

What is the locus of innovation? Creating dedicated spaces to facilitate and foster ideation, experimentation and collaborative innovation is en vogue anywhere, from research to industry and administration. Maximilian Perez Mengual examines spaces like innovation labs, maker spaces and incubators from a novel perspective—he is considering them as interaction platforms. As platforms, these places create value by bringing actors together and by enabling the exchange of goods, services, and ideas (collaboration). To reflect such value creation, this thesis describes such spaces as Physical Interaction Platforms (PIPs).

Looking at PIPs, Maximilian Perez Mengual's work aims to understand how a sustainable PIP can be systematically designed. Four studies in this book, covering the lifecycle of a PIP, explore the structure and systematic design of PIPs. The first study explores the design dimensions of PIPs as a foundation for the design process. The second study delves into the design process of a PIP itself. The third study focuses on sustainable innovation in PIPs during later stages of their lifecycle. Lastly, the fourth study applies the findings and models from the previous three studies to a PIP design process and evaluates their effectiveness.

Building on an Action Research Design Approach, Maximilian Perez Mengual is one of the first to present not only theoretical insights but to focus on implementation. As a result, this book is a very valuable guideline for organizations and innovators thinking about using PIPs for their progress. It illustrates the development process of several PIPs, expressing the authors conviction to not only write about PIPs but also to experience and shape their creation first-hand and is therefore of high practical relevance. It was accepted as doctoral dissertation by the School of Business, Economics and Society at Friedrich-Alexander University Erlangen-Nuremberg.

This book is inviting readers from academia and practice, bridging the gap between theory and application. It is a valuable resource for PIP designers, as well as anyone interested in spaces for innovation and value creation. The models and knowledge generated contribute to scholarly understanding, while practitioners can learn from experiences and utilize the developed tools to create sustainable, successful, and engaging PIPs. Accordingly, this book should be widely disseminated in the academic community and management practice.

I wish Maximilian Perez Mengual all the best for his future and many inspiring PIP experiences. Congratulations on this compelling achievement.

Prof. Dr. Angela Roth

Contents

Abbreviations

AR	Action research
BM	Business model
BMI	Business model innovation
cf.	Confer (Lat.); compare
DR	Design research
e.g.	Exempli gratia (Lat.); for example
ENIQ	Energy Intelligence (name)
et al.	Et alii (Lat); and others
etc.	Et cetera (Lat.); and so forth
FRS	Future Retail Store (name)
GDL	Goods-dominant logic
i.e.	Id est (Lat.); that is
IS	Information systems
KPI	Key performance indicator
MSP	Multi-sided platform
OI	Open innovation
p.	Page
PIP	Physical interaction platform
SDL	Service-dominant logic
SLR	Systematic literature review

List of Figures

List of Tables

Part I
Introduction: About This Dissertation

Motivation

1

This chapter explains this dissertation's motivation, introducing the importance of spaces for physical interaction by providing historical and contemporary examples. Following this, the current research problem is formulated, and the concept of physical interaction platforms (PIPs) is put forward. Furthermore, the author's perspective and personal motivation for the dissertation are presented.

1.1 The Importance of Spaces for Physical Interaction

In terms of human interaction throughout history—from sharing thoughts, brainstorming, learning, and discussing to philosophising, creating new political movements, and innovating—physical places have been crystallisation points at which 'the new' has evolved. One outstanding example of such a crystallisation point is Madame Geoffrin's Paris Salon, which played an essential role during the French Enlightenment in the 18th century. Here, at the invitation of Madame Geoffrin, great thinkers of that generation met regularly. For Montesquieu, Jean-Jacques Rousseau, and Marshal Richelieu, this salon functioned as a social haven, forum for exchange, and hive of intellectual activity (Bessant, 2020). As a result, the salon has been attributed with a significant role in driving the French Enlightenment (Goodman, 1989).

In a different domain, consider Menlo Park, the world's first organised research and development site, founded by Thomas Alva Edison in 1876 (Stross, 2007). Edison and a large team of experts worked collaboratively to invent, experiment with, and implement technological innovations that would change the world: Menlo Park is the birthplace of sound recording (November 1877) as well as

M. Perez Mengual, *Designing Physical Interaction Platforms*,
Markt- und Unternehmensentwicklung Markets and Organisations,
https://doi.org/10.1007/978-3-658-41920-2_1

the world's first practical incandescent lamp-light bulb (October 1879) and suitable light switch. A total of 400 inventions materialised at Menlo Park, a place Edison proudly called his 'Invention Factory.'

Marketplaces and trade fairs comprise another type of physical space with impact on people and the economy. These places were and still are focal points where merchants and consumers meet and interact by trading both material supplies and immaterial goods like information. In addition to trading, these places fulfilled other purposes, such as the administration of justice, informing citizens, or, in darker medieval times, the use of the pillory. For example, the *Leipziger Messe* (German for 'Leipzig Trade Fair'), traces its rich history back almost nine hundred years (Leipziger Messe, 2022). As early as the 12th century, a fair was held in Leipzig, which led to the settlement of numerous merchants there. In the 18th century, Leipzig became the central marketplace for trade with Russian, Polish, and English merchants—called 'the marketplace of all Europe.' In its latest iteration today, the *Leipziger Messe* is a congress and exhibition centre.

Although such places for exchange and interaction have often been taken for granted, the 2020 COVID-19 pandemic has reminded the world of the importance of physical interaction among people. Even with the benefits of new digitised work environments, e-commerce, and data-driven digital innovation, people still need and want to be close to each other. Humans are social beings, and behaviour is shaped by nonverbal cues, emotional proximity, and togetherness. Thus, it is not surprising that physical spaces and direct interaction between individuals still play essential roles in the creation of all types of value, from opinion building to innovation to trade.

1.2 Modern Physical Interaction Spaces

The physical spaces of our today's everyday lives come in a wide variety—for example, (1) innovation activities are orchestrated in spaces such as start-up incubators or innovation labs; (2) new forms of work are taking place outside the traditional organisation in co-working spaces (3) and interaction and community building have become priorities in retail, with some stores hosting yoga sessions[1] and running groups. The common purpose of these spaces is to create value for heterogeneous groups in terms of offering services and experiences.

[1] Lululemon is a Canadian sportswear retailer specializing in yoga apparel. The brick-and-mortar stores blend traditional retail and yoga studio. (https://corporate.lululemon.com/our-business).

Looking into these modern physical spaces in more depth, we can see that spaces for innovation (1) are known by a variety of names—incubators, experience labs, innovation hubs, Living Labs, makerspaces, and FabLabs, among others (Hossain, Leminen, & Westerlund, 2019, Mortara & Parisot, 2018; Nevens et al., 2013). In particular, the rising complexity of innovative (i.e., digital) products and services creates a need to engage in collaborative innovation, including the exchange of experience, expertise, and technical knowledge among different disciplines (Chesbrough, 2003; Ketchen, Ireland, & Snow, 2007). Facilitating such exchange can be a challenge. Collaboration is sensitive to the interacting individuals and the context in which it occurs. It requires specific spaces and orchestration to allow for meaningful and sustained interaction between the various, often heterogeneous, actors (Bason, 2018). Designing dedicated physical spaces to facilitate collaborative innovation (Caccamo, 2020) in the tradition of Menlo Park is one approach to addressing this challenge. Prominent innovation spaces like Xerox PARC and the Bell Laboratories show how companies have been experimenting with different types of spaces and physical layouts (Ahuja, 2019; Caccamo, 2020). Physical spaces that facilitate interactive value creation are found in diverse domains, as depicted in Table 1.1.

When it comes to the office (2)—a workspace where employees have traditionally worked at assigned desks and met in dedicated break areas—the idea of 'new work' and permeable work organisation has transformed the locus of work. Many organisations have redesigned traditional offices into multifunctional, flexible work areas to break down intra- and inter-organisational barriers and foster exchange (Bouncken & Reuschl, 2018; Moriset, 2014). Co-working spaces have further dissolved the boundaries of traditional organisations. What began as affordable office and meeting spaces for freelancers, entrepreneurs, and start-ups have, in some cases, developed into a new form, where people from different organisations work in one office space, benefitting from diverse opportunities for exchange (Kraus, Bouncken, Görmar, González-Serrano, & Calabuig, 2022). Co-working operators like TNW[2] or WeWork[3] offer shared infrastructure, where meeting rooms and coffee kitchens are communal, and regular events actively promote interaction and networking among the tenants.

---

[2] TNW is a company that builds and operates curated workspaces for technology start-ups. Next to the provision of space, the company offers additional services (e.g., for hiring and networking) (https://thenextweb.com/spaces).

[3] WeWork is a real estate company that builds and provides shared workspaces for entrepreneurs, freelancers, and start-ups as well as services for other enterprises (https://www.wework.com/ideas/research-insights/expert-insights/creating-workspace-community).

In light of social change and digitalization, brick-and-mortar retail (3) has been—and still is—forced to re-think its traditional concept of 'selling things' towards creating new customer experiences and developing new partnerships (Olsson, Paredes, Johansson, Olander Roese, & Ritzén, 2019; Palmié, Miehé, Oghazi, Parida, & Wincent, 2022; Varadarajan et al., 2010; Wolpert & Roth, 2020). Many modern retail stores have blurred the boundaries between store, testbed, and co-creation space (Danzinger, Schmidt, Memmert, & Pichlbauer, 2020). Stores such as VAUND[4] and blaenk[5] are running new concepts like 'retail as a service.' Instead of selling goods as in traditional retail, these stores generate their revenue through monthly fees for presenting the products, offering consultation, and allowing customers to test the products. In this way, VAUND and blaenk are not only retail stores but also market research and experience centres, connecting companies and customers in new ways.

As diverse as these spaces for innovation, work or retail are, they all share a common characteristic—they serve as platforms, bringing together actors and facilitating the exchange of goods, services, or social currency such as information (Yablonsky, 2018). These spaces create value by enabling an ecosystem of networked actors to create value through their interaction (Peschl & Fundneider, 2014). As such, the underlying mechanism behind innovation labs, co-working spaces, and innovative retail concepts is the same: they are platforms where people meet, become inspired, and support each other in various pursuits (Bessant, 2020). Innovation labs, for example, serve as places for innovation, prototyping, and testing, connecting organisations with end users. Start-up incubators and co-working spaces provide infrastructure and establish networks from which ecosystem members benefit. In city centres, innovative retail concepts enrich interactions between sellers and buyers beyond the transaction—for example, by providing additional services. Just like digital platforms, these physical spaces operate according to the mechanisms of bringing together various actors and creating value through interaction (Ramaswamy & Ozcan, 2018). This dissertation thus refers to these spaces as *physical interaction platforms* (PIPs).

---

[4] VAUND is a multi-brand showroom. Instead of aiming at maximising transactions, focus is on the presentation of the products. The aim is to excite customers about the products and brands on display (https://vaund.de/).

[5] blaenk is a retail store offering a curated assortment of lifestyle products. blaenk wants to promote sustainable consumption and supports customers by displaying information on the products' sustainability and impact (https://blaenk.com/).

Table 1.1 Overview of PIP types

Type of Space	Purpose	Associated types of PIPs	Examples of PIPs	Selected References
"Innovation"	Facilitating user-led innovation of technology, products, and services	Open Innovation Labs, Living Labs, Corporate Innovation Labs, Innovation Hubs, Start-Up Incubators[6], Maker Spaces, Hacker Spaces, FabLabs	IKEA Space 10, Xerox PARC, Bell Laboratories; JOSEPHS	Bergvall-Kåreborn, Ihlström Eriksson, Ståhlbröst, & Svensson, 2009; Caccamo, 2020; Dell'Era & Landoni, 2014; Greve, Martinez, Jonas, Neely, & Möslein, 2016; Leminen, Westerlund, & Nyström, 2012; Mortara & Parisot, 2018; Roth, Fritzsche, Jonas, Danzinger, & Möslein, 2014; Weiblen & Chesbrough, 2015
"Workplace"	Collaboration, Networking, and Tinkering	Co-Working Spaces	Munich Urban Colab, TNW, WeWork, Workthere	Bouncken & Reuschl, 2018; Capdevila, 2019; Kraus et al., 2022; Lewis & Moultrie, 2005; Van Holm, 2015; W. You, Chen, Agyapong, & Mordi, 2020
"Retail"	Transaction of material goods	Pop-Up Stores, Innovative Retail Concepts	VAUND, blaenk	Alexander & Blazquez Cano, 2020; Danzinger et al., 2020; Warnaby & Shi, 2019

[6] Start-up incubators are listed as innovation spaces because their primary goal is innovation, i.e. the development of new products and services. However, many start-up incubators also facilitate collaboration and tinkering, similar to co-working spaces and fab labs.

1.3 A Review of Literature on PIPs

The various types of PIPs exemplified above are the subject of scholarly research and have sparked numerous publications. The following section briefly summarizes the current state of research on the three types of PIPs: innovation PIPs, workplace PIPs, and retail PIPs.

1.3.1 Literature review: Innovation PIPs

The growing amount of innovation PIPs has sparked many academic publications. This academic debate can be centred on five key topics: (1) concept definitions, (2) purpose and outcomes, (3) activities and interaction, (4) methods and tools, and (5) organization and business model.

(1) Numerous publications deal with the concept definition of innovation PIPs. The distinction between the different concepts (e.g., between "innovation labs" and "living labs") is not always apparent, and there are various, sometimes overlapping, definitions in existence (Westerlund, Leminen, & Rajahonka, 2018). In essence, these spaces are described as approaches to facilitate innovation (Bergvall-Kåreborn et al., 2009; Hossain, Leminen, & Westerlund, 2019; Leminen et al., 2012), education, learning, knowledge creation, and transfer, co-creation, and experimentation (Scholl & Kemp, 2016; Steen & van Bueren, 2017; Van Holm, 2015). (2) Closely intertwined with the various concept definitions is the academic discourse on the purpose and outcomes of innovation PIPs. Hossain et al. (2019) distinguish between tangible outcomes, including products and prototypes, and intangible outcomes, including concepts, ideas, knowledge, and services. In addition, the purpose with which the outcomes are generated is discussed—e.g., in the context of sustainability (Engels, Wentland, & Pfotenhauer, 2019; Zavratnik, Superina, & Duh, 2019), policy making (McGann, Blomkamp, & Lewis, 2018; Schuurman & Tõnurist, 2017), urban and regional development (Otto, 2019; Scholl & Kemp, 2016), entrepreneurship (Mortara & Parisot, 2018) and open innovation (Greve et al., 2016; Leminen et al., 2012). (3) Another topic in the literature focuses on activities and interaction at innovation PIPs. This stream explores what is taking place in innovation PIPs—how they foster creativity and collaborative innovation (Elmquist, Ollila, & Yström, 2016; Greve et al., 2016; Lewis & Moultrie, 2005; Peschl & Fundneider, 2014; Wycoff & Snead, 1999) and how they are used for the development, testing, and commercialization of innovations (Steen & van Bueren, 2017). (4) On a more practically oriented level, research has explored the mechanisms facilitating

these activities and interactions, such as tools and methods used in PIPs (Leminen & Westerlund, 2017; Perez Mengual, Jonas, Schmitt-Rüth, & Danzinger, 2018) that are required for high engagement of the participating stakeholders (Almirall, Lee, & Wareham, 2012; Dell'Era & Landoni, 2014). (5) The emphasis of research on innovation PIPs has recently been moving away from a conceptual focus to a more practical focus on organization and business model (Katzy, 2012; Westerlund et al., 2018). This research highlights the challenge that the sustained operation of innovation PIPs requires organization and continuous funding.

1.3.2 Literature Review: Workplace PIPs

Workplace PIPs have captured scholars' attention from various fields — e.g., management, business, architecture, and psychology. A recent review by Berbegal-Mirabent (2021) provides an overview of the literature around workplace PIPs identifying five main topics: (1) entrepreneurship, (2) urban geography, (3) sustainable cities, (4) information technologies, and (5) psychology of work.

(1) The first stream in the literature perceives and studies workplace PIPs as a tool to support entrepreneurship and new ventures (Bouncken & Aslam, 2019; Bouncken & Reuschl, 2018; Clayton, Feldman, & Lowe, 2018). These studies examine how co-working spaces can be adapted to support entrepreneurship, e.g., by embracing elements of start-up incubators or playing a more active role within an innovation ecosystem. (2) The urban geography stream in the literature is concerned with the role of workplace PIPs in shaping urban development and regional growth (Coll-Martínez & Méndez-Ortega, 2020; Fiorentino, 2019). (3) Closely related to urban geography is the topic of sustainable cities. In these studies, workplace PIPs are examined from the perspective of the sharing economy. The focus of these studies lies on the operating principles of workplace PIPs, e.g., how resources are shared and used efficiently (Cappellaro et al., 2019; Orel & Kubátová, 2019). (4) The branch of literature focusing on information technologies examines the lifestyle of employees in the context of future of work (e.g., digital nomads) and explores the technical requirements needed to facilitate this lifestyle (e.g., communication technologies, social networks) (Bouncken, Laudien, Fredrich, & Görmar, 2018; Orel, 2019). (5) Finally, the literature deals with the psychological component, linking workplace PIPs to productivity and corporate culture. The research explored the knowledge dynamics within PIPs (Cohendet, Grandadam, Simon, & Capdevila, 2014) and how they are shaped by participatory culture, serving as intermediaries facilitating engagement among people, ideas, and technologies (Capdevila, 2015; Osorio et al., 2019).

Further, it has been explored how they influence workplace culture (Shirahada & Hamazaki, 2013) and the social relationships of their users (Castilho & Quandt, 2017; Schmidt & Brinks, 2017).

1.3.3 Literature Review: Retail PIPs

Compared to the other two types of PIPs, retail PIPs have received little academic attention. The literature focuses mainly on (1) retail technologies, (2) digitization and changing business models, and (3) how to facilitate innovation in retail.

(1) Most publications on retail PIPs, the physical embodiments of retail, focus on technology. This means, the development and evaluation of technology used for direct customer interactions, such as e.g. augmented reality applications (Cruz et al., 2019). Following this, the research examines how the interactions in retail are transformed by this technology (Roggeveen & Sethuraman, 2020), how customers react toward technology (Inman & Nikolova, 2017; Meyer, Jonas, & Roth, 2020), and how retail technology can be classified (Grewal, Noble, Roggeveen, Nordfalt, & Noble, 2020; Wolpert & Roth, 2020). (2) Closely related to research on technology, academics are focusing on how digitization is changing retail. This literature stream explores (1) how digitization transforms the retail business model to achieve a competitive advantage, including communication channels and retail settings, products and services offered, and the actors participating in retailing (Hagberg, Sundstrom, & Egels-Zandén, 2016; Palmié et al., 2022; Varadarajan et al., 2010). Additionally, research focuses on (2) the development of the retail organization, identifying drivers and barriers to digitization as well as trigger points for digital development (Bollweg, Lackes, Siepermann, Sutaj, & Weber, 2016; Bollweg, Lackes, Siepermann, & Weber, 2020). (3) The third stream of literature deals with brick-and-mortar retail needing to innovate. It is argued that retail needs to utilize and integrate new technology to create novel, interactive retail concepts (Alexander & Blazquez Cano, 2020; Niehm, Fiore, Jeong, & Kim, 2007) and experiment with new store concepts such as pop-stores (Warnaby & Shi, 2019). However, this innovation must be implemented by retailers themselves. In this line, the research examines the climate for innovation and creativity in retail (Olsson et al., 2019) and explores the competencies of future retail designers (Quartier, Claes, & Vanrie, 2020).

1.4 Framing the Research Problem

The research problem of this dissertation is motivated by (1) a gap in the scholarly literature regarding the design process of PIPs and (2) a problem arising from the practice and implementation of PIPs regarding their sustainability.

(1) One issue arising from the scholarly research around the various types of PIPs is that there is little knowledge and research on how to design PIPs. The literature on innovation PIPs mainly focuses on defining the concept itself and exploring the interactions taking place there. Research on how such places can be designed and what is needed for sustainable operation is still in its infancy (Bloom & Faulkner, 2016; Matzner et al., 2018). For workplace PIPs, research is still maturing and has room for development (Kraus et al., 2022). Most scholarly contributions are concerned with defining the purpose of workplace PIPs and exploring their impact (i.e., their effect on people, organizations, and regions). However, the actual design of workplace PIPs and their business models have received little scholarly attention (Berbegal-Mirabent, 2021; Kraus et al., 2022). Finally, the literature on retail PIPs mainly concerns technology and digitization. The topic of how to facilitate innovation in retail, concerning designing retail PIPs and their business models, has only recently come into focus but is still under-investigated in academia (Olsson et al., 2019). All in all, the design process required to establish and open a PIP in the first place is still underexplored. This has been recognized by scholars raising the need for research such as 'how can we design living lab spaces for specific requirements of digitized organizations?' (Matzner et al., 2018, p. 16).

(2) PIPs are in vogue, and many of the organisations creating PIPs seem to hope that by simply building an interaction space, an ecosystem of users will "magically" form and generate value (e.g. in terms of innovative solutions, employee productivity or more revenue). However, reality shows that the value generated by many of these spaces does not go beyond opening enthusiasm or marketing purposes. Failure is far more prevalent than is commonly imagined (Di Fiore & Vetter, 2016; Narsalay, Kavathekar, & Light, 2016). This becomes particularly clear in the context of innovation spaces when companies try to measure the success of their innovation space through traditional methods of return on investment (Caccamo, 2020), and unfulfilled financial expectations make high levels of investment difficult to justify (Ahuja, 2019). Alternatively, spaces are launched as funded projects, and after the funding period, the space is terminated. Thus, despite their growing popularity, many innovation spaces fail to deliver on

their promises and are subsequently shut down. The cases of the Nordstrom innovation lab[7] and the BMW Guggenheim Lab[8] are just two examples of failure and declining commitment (Berengian, 2017). The reasons for failure can be manifold. Lack of alignment with the company's core business, no metrics to track success, a lack of strong leadership, or poor team composition are just a few to name (Ahuja, 2019; Berger & Brem, 2016).

Nevertheless, companies are still building PIPs, as the benefits are apparent. In innovation, PIPs bring together actors when there are persistent problems, when disruptive changes are imminent, or when close collaboration to find solutions is needed (Westley et al., 2014). They also serve as platforms for directing and orchestrating innovation efforts so that these can be addressed productively (Kuhlmann & Rip, 2018; Mazzucato, 2018). Workplace PIPs emphasize social interactions, facilitating the exchange of knowledge and ideas, transcending the mere sharing of workspace to entrepreneurship (Bouncken & Reuschl, 2018; Capdevila, 2015; You et al., 2020). In traditional retail, spaces evolve to appeal to changing consumer demands (Evans, 2011; Olsson et al., 2019).

Considering the advantages for an organisation and, at the same time, the difficulties in the design and implementation of PIP, an important question is, how can PIPs be systematically designed to increase the likelihood of sustainable functioning?

[7] Seattle-based brick-and-mortar retailer Nordstrom received widespread attention for having had the foresight to create an innovation lab, being a traditional brick-and-mortar retailer able to keep up with digitisation (Duryee, 2015). Their innovation lab was set up to develop innovative customer-focused solutions for the shop floor, such as an app to help customers choose appropriately fitting sunglasses (Catlin, Scanlan, & Willmott, 2015). After only four years, the innovation lab was dissolved for strategic reasons. The innovation activities formerly executed by the lab were internalised to the company and aligned with Nordstrom's core business, making innovation 'everyone's job' (Duryee, 2015).

[8] The BMW Guggenheim Lab was planned as a mobile laboratory traveling to various cities worldwide, part urban think tank, part community centre, and part meeting space. The lab was supposed to address and investigate issues of contemporary urban life via public dialogue (Grubbauer, 2013). It was a collaboration between the Solomon R. Guggenheim Foundation and the BMW Group between 2011 and 2013. Initially, the lab was scheduled to visit nine cities over the course of six years. In 2013, however, after visiting just three cities (Berlin, New York, and Mumbai), BMW terminated the financial support for strategic reasons, ending the project in 2014.

1.5 The Author's Motivation for the Thesis

Building on the theoretical perspective and need for research on PIP design processes, this dissertation is also motivated by the author's personal interest. The idea for this dissertation emerged at a time when PIPs were popular. It felt like every large corporation needed its own 'innovation space', taking on diverse forms, including incubators for start-ups, co-working spaces for employees, or testbeds for technology. At the time (2017), I was an employee of a PIP—JOSEPHS, an open innovation lab founded in 2014, where visitors can interactively engage with prototypes of products and services from various companies, thereby directly influencing the further development and design of the companies' offerings (cf. Roth et al., 2014).

As PIP operators, we were often asked by other aspiring PIP founders, 'How do I build a space like this?' It dawned on me that although we had significant tacit knowledge regarding how to operate a PIP, this question was difficult to answer. While systematic approaches toward design can be found in almost all disciplines—typically aiming to ensure the best possible function of the design object—this was not the case in the context of PIPs. Instead, several PIPs I visited during my career supposed that 'providing a physical space' is enough. Such spaces were imagined as 'breeding grounds', actively designed and animated by participating actors. But instead of being tailored explicitly towards their audience, the actors in a PIP were expected to figure out by themselves what value the space might create for them—or rather, what value propositions the space can represent for them. In practice, such an approach seldomly worked, with some spaces already failing to attract actors / the right actors to interact with them.

Thus, the question arose of how PIPs can be systematically designed to succeed and provide value to the participating actors. While there is a wide range of definitions of design, they all share three characteristics (Friedman, 2003): 'first, the word refers to a process; second, this process is goal-oriented, and third, the goal of design is solving problems, meeting needs, improving situations, or creating something new or useful' (p. 508). In this context, design is a purposeful problem-solving activity (Wetter-Edman, 2014).

Therefore, my research in this dissertation does not look at PIPs themselves or the activities that take place within them. Instead, *this dissertation examines how a physical interaction platform (PIP) can be designed in a systematic and structured way,* leading to prosperous and sustainably operating PIPs. For this research, I draw on practical experiences from real PIP design projects to permeate the multi-layered and complex nature of these PIPs as an engaged scholar. Throughout the life cycle of a PIP, this dissertation examines (1) what design elements are needed for value creation and sustainable operation. Furthermore, it illustrates (2) how a PIP can be systematically designed and implemented; and (3) explores how a PIP's design can be renewed when they reach or transcend maturity and must react to changing actor requirements.

Research Questions

2

Motivated both from a theoretical and a personal perspective, this dissertation explores *how a physical interaction platform (PIP) can be designed in a systematic and structured way*. In this explorative process, both scientific knowledge and specific recommendations for practical action are generated (Van De Ven & Johnson, 2006). To achieve the overall objective, the empirical research of the dissertation is divided into four steps, presented in Parts III, IV, V, and VI. The first three steps reflect the design and life cycle of a PIP, as shown in Figure 2.1. The final step, presented in Part VI, provides an evaluation of the findings from the previous parts. In addition to the theoretical knowledge gained, the empirical research aims to support designers in creating sustainable and successful PIPs. The four steps and associated research questions are therefore not solely based on research gaps identified in the literature but also on the challenges encountered by PIP designers.

M. Perez Mengual, *Designing Physical Interaction Platforms*,
Markt- und Unternehmensentwicklung Markets and Organisations,
https://doi.org/10.1007/978-3-658-41920-2_2

Step 1—Starting from scratch: Most existing research has focused on specific aspects of PIPs, e.g., the collaboration that takes place there (Greve et al., 2016) or how collaborative innovation is organised (Ollila & Yström, 2016). But for practitioners seeking to design PIPs, it remains unclear what dimensions are essential for their sustainable operation. If the design process is to be 'started from scratch,' where should it begin, and what decisions need to be made? To provide guidance regarding these issues, the following research questions were formulated and are addressed in Part III of this dissertation.

RQ 1: *What are the design dimensions of PIPs that enable interactive value creation?*

RQ 2: *How can these design dimensions be grouped to provide a useful tool for designers of PIPs?*

Step 2—From scratchboard to opening: Having identified design dimensions enabling interactive value creation for PIPs, this study addresses the lack of existing information on how to design, build, and operate PIPs. The scientific literature emphasises critical components like leadership, management, and business model in securing the sustainability and financing of PIPs (Chronéer, Ståhlbröst, & Habibipour, 2019). In practitioner-oriented literature (e.g., Doorley & Witthoft, 2012; Nestle, Glauner, & Plugmann, 2021), insights regarding how to develop innovative mindsets and design a PIP's interior and room layout can be found, but most research showcases existing PIPs. It does not teach how to build one nor how the design process must be structured to increase the chances of a PIP's sustainable implementation. Therefore, the second study explores the necessary design steps from scratchboard to opening. The following research questions were formulated and are addressed in Part IV.

RQ 3: *How can a PIP systematically be designed?*

RQ 4: *What are the challenges and turning points in the design process of a PIP?*

Step 3—Managing continuous PIP innovation: At some point during the life cycle of a PIP, when maturity has been reached, it may become necessary to innovate in order to respond to the changing needs of PIP users or market competition (Parker, Van Alstyne, & Choudary, 2016; Teece, 2017). While such innovation processes undertaken for the sake of 'self-renewal' can be lengthy and challenging to observe, the COVID-19 pandemic has provided the opportunity of studying these in fast forward. Using brick-and-mortar retail as an example, the following research questions were formulated and are addressed in Part V of this dissertation:

RQ 5: *What were strategic responses and activities of retailers in reaction to the COVID-19 crisis?*

RQ 6: *Did these strategic responses and activities lead to sustainable innovation?*

Step 4—The toolkit for designing PIPs: The preceding steps explore the design of PIPs at different stages during their life cycle. To be effective at supporting designers in creating sustainably successful PIPs, the practical implications and artifacts resulting from these empirical studies must be evaluated in terms of their usefulness and ease of use. Therefore, the following research questions were formulated and are addressed in Part IV of this dissertation.

RQ 7: *Are the developed artifacts (from Parts III–V) applicable (ease of use) and useful (perceived usefulness) for the design process of a PIP?*

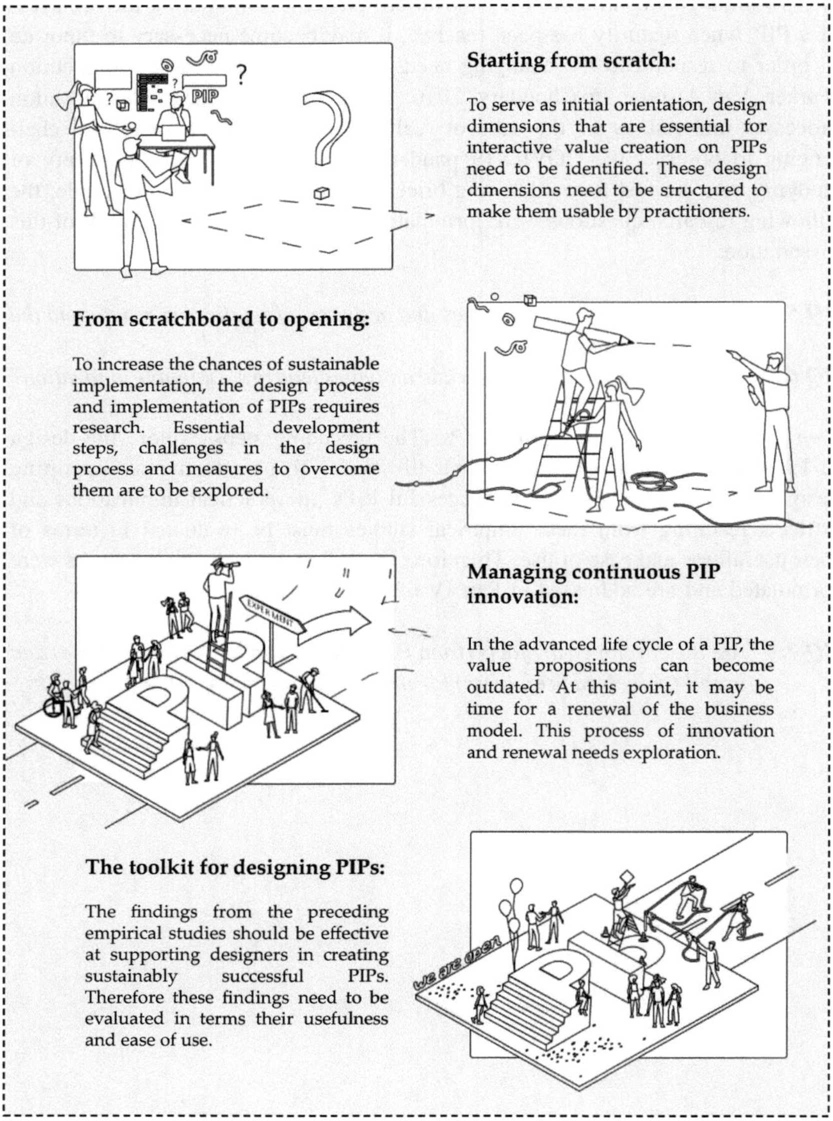

Figure 2.1 Research objectives during the life cycle of a PIP

Research Paradigm and Research Design

3

This chapter introduces the research design of this dissertation, as well as the embraced research paradigm. Research paradigms address the philosophical stance toward science. In this, a research paradigm represents the fundamental assumptions and beliefs in how the world is perceived by the researcher. They serve as thinking frameworks, guiding the behaviour and methodological choices of researchers (Wahyuni, 2012).

3.1 A Pragmatist Stance

This dissertation is inspired by knowledge gained in previous projects and the professional careers of the researchers. This makes it almost impossible to adopt a paradigm that requires the separation of body and mind when it comes to the generation of new knowledge (Cartesian dualism) (Korte, 2009). However, in addition to positivist or postpositivist (critical realist) research, qualitative research in information systems can also be executed following the paradigm of pragmatism, which is connected 'with action, intervention and constructive knowledge' (Goldkuhl, 2012, p. 136).

M. Perez Mengual, *Designing Physical Interaction Platforms*,
Markt- und Unternehmensentwicklung Markets and Organisations,
https://doi.org/10.1007/978-3-658-41920-2_3

Pragmatism as a philosophical movement has its roots in late-19th-century America, and Charles Sanders Peirce (1839–1914) is considered its founder. Other early and influential pragmatists were William James (1842–1910), John Dewey (1859–1952), Chauncey Wright (1830–1875), and George Herbert Mead (1863–1931). These pragmatists were united in their rejection of Cartesian dualism, challenging the then contemporary understanding of truth (Wetter-Edman, 2014). They were dissatisfied with the belief that all knowledge rests on indubitable foundations and that bias and prejudice can be addressed by methodical doubt (Bernstein, 2010). According to Bernstein (2010), they rejected the 'quest for certainty' and the 'spectator theory of knowledge' (p. X). Instead, they developed an alternative to the predominant Cartesianism of their time—'a self-corrective conception of human inquiry based upon an understanding of how human agents are formed by, and actively participate in shaping, normative social practices' (Bernstein, 2010, p. X).

Pragmatism extends the interaction between body and mind to include the interaction with the external world. Pragmatism, therefore, represents a practice-oriented research philosophy. From a pragmatist point of view, truth is neither discovered nor invented. Instead, truth is constructed as a by-product of processes solving real problems (Wetter-Edman, 2014). For this reason, pragmatism is a paradigm that refuses to be associated with either of the two sides of the 'paradigm war' between positivism and interpretivism (Wahyuni, 2012). Pragmatist researchers start with their research question and select their research methodology based on it, focusing on 'what works best' (Kaushik & Walsh, 2019; Wetter-Edman, 2014). They see research philosophy as a continuum between the rigid positions of positivism and interpretivism. Objectivist and subjectivist perspectives are not mutually exclusive (Wahyuni, 2012). Instead, both can be applied and combined to understand phenomena—emphasising the researcher's choice regarding what works best to address the research question. Pragmatist researchers can thus apply quantitative, qualitative, or mixed-methods research in order to analyse phenomena (Morgan, 2014). The pragmatist stance is particularly suited for constructing knowledge that is useful in action (Göran Goldkuhl, 2012a). Therefore, this stance works well in relation to the overall research questions of this dissertation, related to the design process of PIPs. In addition, literature in the field of information systems (Göran Goldkuhl, 2012a) has demonstrated that pragmatism is an appropriate paradigm for the application of co-creative methods such as action research (AR) and design research (DR). This dissertation applies AR in Part IV and DR, in the form of taxonomy development, in Part III. Furthermore, both AR and DR represent methods linked to engaged scholarship, where researchers and practitioners collaboratively act upon the research subject.

3.2 The Engaged-scholarship Approach

PIP design is a research subject that cannot be explored from a purely external perspective. Instead, practical knowledge and its application is required to construct new knowledge in the field. The engaged-scholarship approach presented by Van de Ven (2007) offers a suitable approach for this type of organisational and social research. The basic assumption is that academic and professional knowledge are related, despite being discrete domains (Mathiassen & Nielsen, 2008). Instead of following the notion that knowledge is generated through isolated experiments in lab environments and then diffused into practice, engaged scholarship takes a more interactive approach. Here, academics and practitioners interact through various activities, helping each other grow through joint learning (Mathiassen & Nielsen, 2008). Engaged scholarship is thus defined as 'a participative form of research for obtaining the different perspectives of key stakeholders (researchers, users, clients, sponsors, and practitioners) in studying complex problems' (Van de Ven, 2007, p. 9). In line with the pragmatist stance, engaged scholarship emphasises the importance of the process of inquiry, moving beyond traditional dichotomies such as rigour versus relevance and positivist versus interpretivist. Van de Ven (2018) argues that 'researchers can significantly increase the likelihood of producing knowledge that advances theory and practice by engaging others whose perspectives are relevant' (p. 37). Van de Ven (2007, 2018) indicates the following four ways in which engaged scholarship can be practised: (1) basic research with stakeholder advice; (2) collaborative research where knowledge is co-produced; (3) evaluation research, where practitioners influence how study findings are interpreted; and (4) action research, where interventions are designed to solve a specific problem. Choosing among these different approaches is based on two factors: (1) whether the purpose of a study is to examine basic questions of description, explanation, and prediction, or applied questions of design, evaluation, or action intervention, and (2) the degree to which a researcher examines the problem domain as an external observer or an internal participant' (Van de Ven, 2018, p. 38).

The empirical work of this dissertation was conducted directly in line with the engaged-scholarship approach. The expert interviews finalising the development of the PIP taxonomy in Part III relate to evaluation research (3), as experts were invited to assess the taxonomy's overall applicability and usefulness. Part IV directly applies the action research method (4), wherein a PIP design process was created and executed (as an intervention) to address the problem of a specific client in practice. The multiple-case study in Part V utilises interviews and field visits that were conducted in an active and informed style, which can be perceived as basic research with stakeholder advice (1), undertaken to describe and explain a phenomenon. Part VI again applies the action research method (4), utilizing insights and artifacts from Parts III-V in interventions during a PIP design project.

3.3 Overall Research Design

This dissertation explores *how a physical interaction platform (PIP) can be designed in a systematic and structured way.* In line with the pragmatist research paradigm (Göran Goldkuhl, 2012a; Wahyuni, 2012) and the engaged-scholarship approach (Van de Ven, 2007, 2018), this dissertation employs several research methods across three studies to address the research subject. These studies are described in detail in Parts III, IV, V and VI of this dissertation. Figure 3.1 provides an overview of the research paradigm and the overall research design of the empirical work in this dissertation.

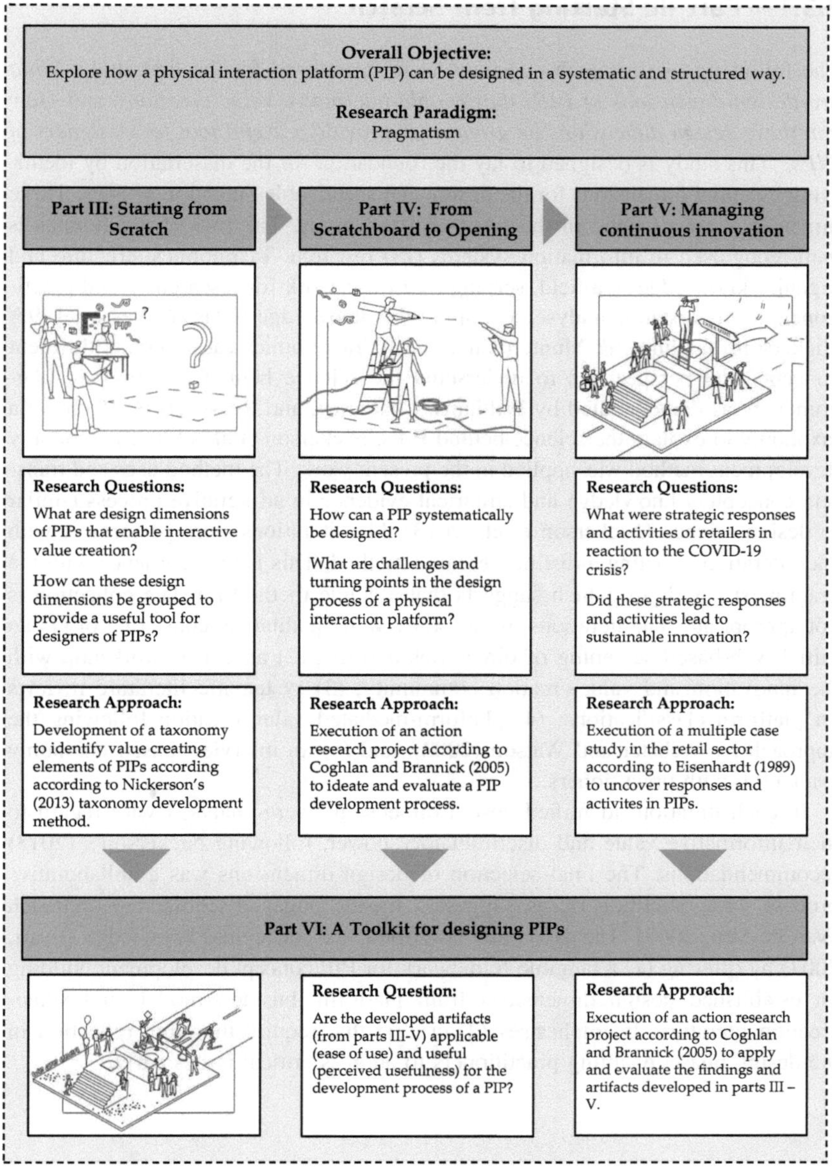

Figure 3.1 Overall research design

3.3.1 Part III: Starting from Scratch

The following two research questions were formulated for the first study: *What are design dimensions of PIPs that enable interactive value creation?* and *How can these design dimensions be grouped to provide a useful tool for designers of PIPs?* This study is designed to lay the foundation for the dissertation by identifying essential dimensions for the design and sustainable operation of PIPs. These dimensions are grouped in the form of a taxonomy. The role of taxonomies is well recognised in information systems (IS) research. Taxonomies structure and organise knowledge in a field, serving as a framework for researchers and practitioners to understand, analyse, and apply this knowledge (Glass & Vessey, 1995; Nickerson, Varshney, & Muntermann, 2013). Taxonomies can integrate different concepts and perspectives to understand the science behind an observed phenomenon, as demonstrated by Williams, Chatterjee, and Rossi (2008). To build a taxonomy to explain the science behind PIPs, Nickerson et al.'s (2013) taxonomy development method was applied in the present work. The method uses and transfers conceptual knowledge and empirical evidence in an iterative process similar to design science (Nickerson et al., 2013). Five iterations were performed, with each iteration adopting a distinct research method. This is in accordance with the pragmatist paradigm, which suggests that a single method for data collection is not appropriate. The iterations in this study were qualitative, consisting of (1) an initial web-based screening of directories of PIPs; (2) an expert workshop with the innovation and value-creation community; (3) systematic literature reviews on platform classifications; (4) platform-mediated value creation following the approach by Webster and Watson (2002); and (5) an interview-based taxonomy evaluation with practitioners.

In each iteration, identified design dimensions were analysed with regard to their informative value and discriminatory power, following Nickerson's (2013) recommendations. The final selection of design dimensions was a collaborative process with practitioners, as suggested by the engaged-scholarship approach (Van de Ven, 2007). The taxonomy contributes to conceptual knowledge (Iivari, 2007) by offering (1) a tangible framework for PIP concept development building on established design dimensions from platform, business-model, and value-creation literature. It emphasises (2) criteria that require thorough reflection in the design phase, enabling practitioners to address critical issues early.

3.3.2 Part IV: From Scratchboard to Opening

The second study was used to formulate two research questions: *How can a PIP be developed?* and *What are the challenges and turning points in the development process of a PIP?* To answer these questions, action research (AR) was carried out (Lewin, 1946). AR is an interventionist approach (Ollila & Yström, 2020), where the researchers use their knowledge to assist practitioners in solving real-world problems (Lindgren, Henfridsson, & Schultze, 2004). Through AR, it is possible to generate relevant practical insights while advancing scientific knowledge at the same time (Susman & Evered, 1978). AR was selected for several reasons: (1) AR is a science that is practice-oriented and whose implications lead to solutions for practice-relevant problems (Lindgren et al., 2004). It is thus in line with the pragmatist paradigm and the engaged-scholarship approach given its process-oriented nature. (2) AR is a proven method for use in organisations to solve organisational problems (e.g., Lindgren, Henfridsson, & Schultze, 2004). (3) More pragmatically, a powerful AR case (the 'ENIQ') was available. The AR study followed the approach of Coghlan and Brannick (2005), which has been widely adopted and provides clear guidelines on how to conduct rigorous action research. Coghlan and Brannick's (2005) AR approach is iterative, where each iteration (or AR cycle) consists of the following four phases: (1) diagnosis, (2) planning action, (3) taking action, and (4) evaluating action. Two AR cycles were conducted as part of this study—one for the concept development of the PIP and one for its implementation. During these cycles, the researchers, together with the client, formed a development team with the goal of creating a PIP. This close collaboration was maintained throughout the entire process of problem-solving and required constant feedback, reflection, and the joint implementation of action (Van de Ven, 2007). The main contribution of this study, consisting of two models, was done following abductive reasoning, combining the insights from the AR with theoretical concepts from the literature (Coghlan & Shani, 2021; Dubois & Gadde, 2002).

3.3.3 Part V: Managing Continuous Innovation

The third study was used to formulate the following research questions: *What were strategic responses and activities of retailers in reaction to the COVID-19 crisis?* and *Did these strategic responses and activities lead to sustainable innovation?* These questions relate to retail PIPs, representing PIP reconfiguration processes caused by external circumstances. To answer these questions, a multiple-case comparative research strategy was applied (Eisenhardt, 1991). Case research facilitates the understanding of dynamics that are present in single settings (Eisenhardt, 1989). Following this, case research was selected given that the COVID-19 pandemic provided a unique opportunity to study the reconfiguration of PIPs. The identification of suitable cases was done in several steps. Expert interviews and desk research led to the creation of a database with 91 possible cases. Following purposive sampling to maximise variation across cases (Suri, 2011), eight cases were selected for the multiple-case study, originating from a German metropolitan region. Data was collected over a five-month period, with two survey dates per case, employing interviews, field visits, and desk research. Thus, this case research can be described as basic research with stakeholder advice conducted according to the engaged-scholarship approach (Van de Ven, 2007). Following Yin's (2003) guidelines, each case was analysed individually to discover particularities within the cases. After that, a comparative cross-case analysis was performed to identify patterns and discover similarities and differences between the cases (Eisenhardt, 1989). Gioia et al.'s approach (Gioia, Corley, & Hamilton, 2013) was applied for data analysis, resulting in three distinct coding phases. Open coding and axial coding (Corbin & Strauss, 2008; Gioia et al., 2013) were applied to capture the essence of the data. These were linked to theoretical concepts from the literature via systematic combining (Dubois & Gadde, 2002). This made it possible to identify the response strategies and activities of PIPs regarding external circumstances.

3.3.4 Part VI: A Toolkit for Designing PIPs

The fourth study was used to formulate one research question: *Are the developed artifacts (from Parts III–V) applicable (ease of use) and useful (perceived usefulness) for the design process of a PIP?* To assess this question, the study draws on design science literature, which suggests action research is a suitable approach for evaluating artifacts (e.g., Hevner, 2007; Prat et al., 2015; Venable et al., 2016). The AR method represents a naturalistic evaluation (Venable, Pries-Heje, & Baskerville, 2012; Venable et al., 2016) characterised by real users using real artifacts to solve real problems (Sun & Kantor, 2006). Similar to the study featured in Part IV of this dissertation, this research follows the cyclical AR approach of Coghlan and Brannick (2005). The AR study took place in the context of developing a 'Future Retail Store' (FRS). The FRS is a collaborative PIP development project between the Fraunhofer IIS and two project partners aiming to advance brick-and-mortar retail. Two AR cycles were conducted over 14 months, focusing on (1) refining the FRS concept and (2) defining organisational roles for the sustainable operation of the FRS. The data-collection process during the AR project included workshop sessions, meetings, observations, and written project documentation such as meeting minutes, e-mails, presentations, and workshop protocols. Additionally, reflections between senior researchers took place bi-weekly to evaluate development progress and artifacts used. Following Walsham (2006), the evaluation of the artifacts was based on interpreting the impact of the artifacts during the AR project.

Structure of the Thesis 4

This dissertation explores *how a physical interaction platform (PIP) can be designed in a systematic and structured way.* For this purpose, this dissertation is divided into a total of six parts. As illustrated in Figure 4.1, Parts I and II lay the foundations for the empirical work presented in Parts III, IV, V, and VI. Part VII concludes this dissertation by reflecting upon the empirical findings.

Part I introduces the research subject of physical interaction platforms. Chapter 1 describes the motivation for embarking on this dissertation. Chapter 2 explains the overall research objective and introduces the part-specific research questions. Chapter 3 outlines the research paradigm and presents the overall research design. Chapter 4 describes the structure of the dissertation.

Part II introduces the key concepts used throughout the dissertation. Chapter 5 explains the objectives and structure of Part II. Chapter 6 describes spaces for physical interaction, introducing their different forms and domains and the value generated by these. Chapter 7 provides an overview of platforms—in particular, platform business models, value creation on platforms, and initial insights into the design of platforms are described. Following this, Chapter 8 deals with design theory and highlights approaches to systematic design. Chapter 9 summarises the key concepts introduced in the context of PIPs.

Part III presents the first empirical study of this dissertation—the development of a taxonomy. The study identifies elements (design dimensions) necessary for value creation and the sustainable operation of PIPs in an iterative process. Chapter 10 explains the objectives and structure of the study. Chapter 11 introduces the research approach that includes Nickerson et al.'s

Supplementary Information The online version contains supplementary material available at https://doi.org/10.1007/978-3-658-41920-2_4.

M. Perez Mengual, *Designing Physical Interaction Platforms*,
Markt- und Unternehmensentwicklung Markets and Organisations,
https://doi.org/10.1007/978-3-658-41920-2_4

(2013) taxonomy-development method. Chapter 12 details the development process by describing the data and methods used in each iteration. Chapter 13 introduces the taxonomy, followed by a description of each design dimension. Chapter 14 highlights the application of the taxonomy as a classification tool using two illustrative cases. Chapter 15 discusses the theoretical contributions and implications for practitioners. Chapter 16 provides a short summary, looks toward future research, and situates the study in the context of the entire dissertation.

Part IV presents the second empirical study of the dissertation—an action research study. The study details the process steps and organisational levels through which a PIP is designed. Chapter 17 explains the objectives and structure of the study. Chapter 18 introduces action research and illustrates the steps, including data collection and analysis, undertaken in this study. Chapter 19 details the findings of the first action research cycle (concept development). Building on this, Chapter 20 highlights the findings of the second action research cycle. Chapter 21 discusses the findings and develops two models—a process model and an organisational-level model. Furthermore, the theoretical contributions and practical implications are highlighted. Chapter 22 provides a short summary and outlook for future studies, relating the findings to the context of the dissertation.

Part V presents the third empirical study—a multiple-case study. The study took place in the German retail sector and investigated the reconfiguration processes of PIPs. Chapter 23 explains the objectives and structure of the study. Chapter 24 provides additional theoretical background regarding the reconfiguration processes and business models of PIPs. Chapter 25 details the research process, including case sampling, data collection, and analysis. Chapter 26 illustrates the findings of the multiple-case study. Chapter 27 discusses the findings, revealing theoretical contributions and practical implications and formulating design principles for sustainable PIP design. Chapter 28 provides a short summary, placing the insights in the context of this dissertation.

Part VI presents the fourth empirical study of this dissertation—an action research study. The study applies and evaluates the findings generated in Parts III–V. Chapter 29 explains the objectives and structure of the study. Chapter 30 briefly summarises the findings from Parts III–V, relating them to one another and to existing scholarly work. Chapter 31 provides background details about the study´s action research project. Following this, Chapter 32 describes the first action research cycle and its results. Chapter 33 describes the second action research cycle. Chapter 34 discusses the insights of Part VI, placing them in the context of the entire dissertation. Chapter 35 provides a brief summary and outlook for future research.

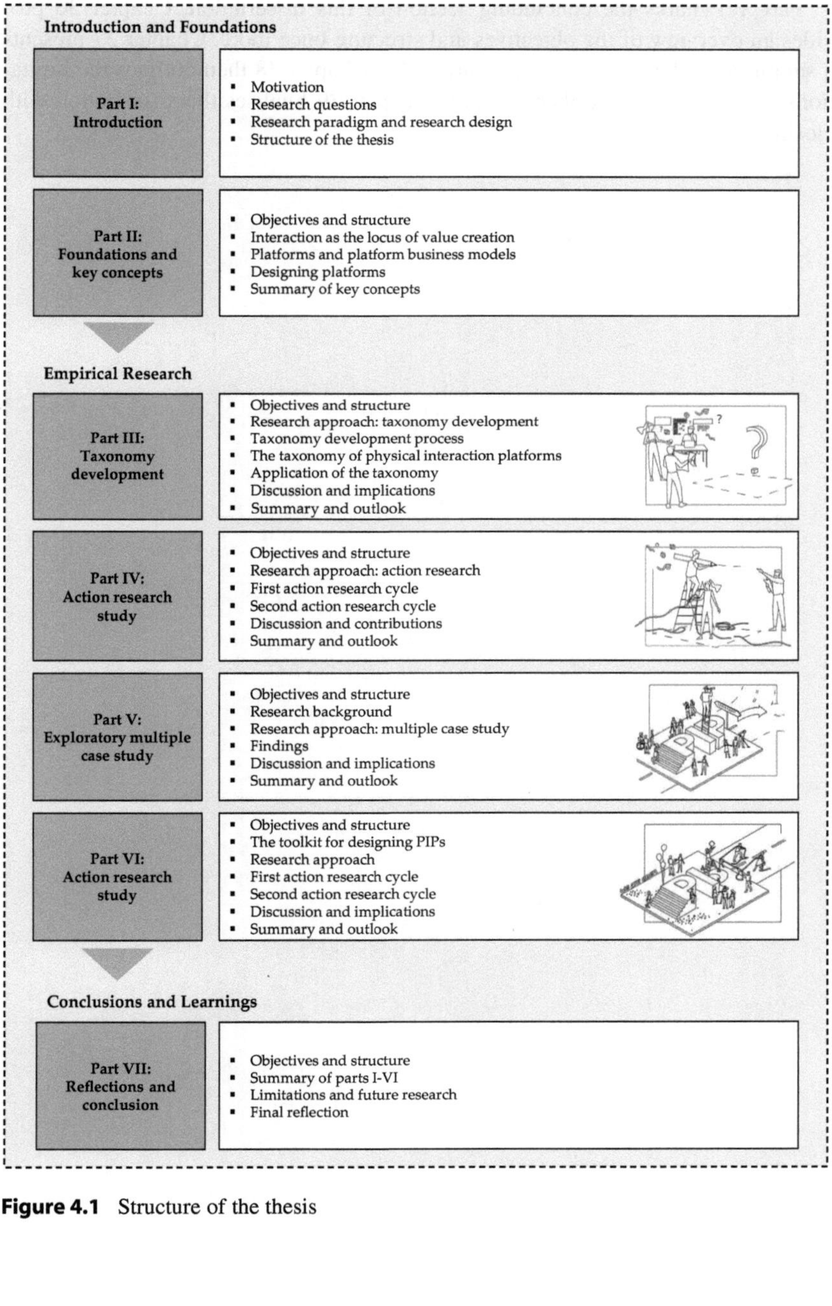

Figure 4.1 Structure of the thesis

Part VII marks the concluding section of this dissertation. Chapter 36 provides an overview of the objectives and structure once more. Chapter 37 presents a summary of the previous parts (Parts I–V). Chapter 38 then outlines the limitations and avenues for further research. Chapter 39 finalises this dissertation with closing remarks.

Part II

Theoretical Foundations: Key Concepts of This Dissertation

5 Objectives and Structure

Part II introduces the theoretical background of this dissertation. The foundations that serve as the basis for the investigation of PIPs are found in the following three distinct streams of literature: (1) service-dominant logic (SDL) and interactive value creation, (2) (platform) business models, and (3) approaches to the systematic design of platforms. SDL and interactive value creation explain what actually happens in the PIP interactions and how value is generated for the platform actors. Research on (platform) business models provides an established structure of the design dimensions and highlights what is required to operate sustainable platforms. Their introduction and description in this part is intended to support the reader in putting the following empirical studies of this dissertation into the context of current research. Moreover, this triad of theoretical foundations explains how a PIP can be designed in a systematic and structured way.

Part II is structured as follows: Chapter 6 introduces SDL and interactive value creation, explaining why interactions are at the core of value creation and should thus serve as a starting point for the design process of PIPs. Chapter 7 presents the concept of (platform) business models, highlighting elements required for the sustainable operation of PIPs. Additionally, strategies for designing and launching digital platforms are reviewed. Chapter 8 introduces design theory, which contributes to the previously introduced strategies, providing both structure and reasoning. Chapter 9 synthesises and summarises key concepts that are used throughout this dissertation. The structure of Part II is shown in Figure 5.1.

M. Perez Mengual, *Designing Physical Interaction Platforms*,
Markt- und Unternehmensentwicklung Markets and Organisations,
https://doi.org/10.1007/978-3-658-41920-2_5

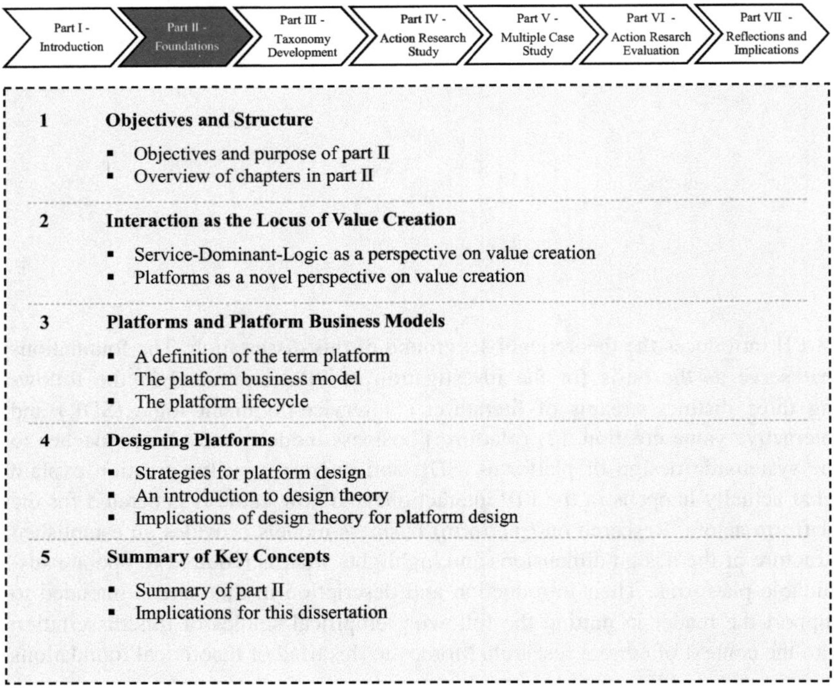

Figure 5.1 Structure of Part II

6 Interaction as the Locus of Value Creation

To explore the design of PIPs, first, it is necessary to introduce an understanding of value and value creation. This is a debated topic, and this chapter explains why interactions are the locus of value creation and, therefore, a crucial point of departure when designing PIPs. Chapter 6 introduces these theoretical perspectives, contributing to the conceptual understanding of this dissertation.

6.1 Service-Dominant-Logic as a Perspective on Value Creation

The terms value and value creation are omnipresent in business literature but often remain vague. As both are essential when examining PIPs, some elaboration of these concepts is useful. Value, value creation, and value co-creation are closely linked and are subsumed under the paradigm of value creation, forwarded and publicised by Vargo and Lusch (2004) in their seminal paper on Service-Dominant-Logic (SDL).[1]

The SDL paradigm offers a novel perspective on economic exchange. It opposes the traditional focus of value creation in value chains (e.g., manufacturing products), represented by the traditional Goods-Dominant-Logic (GDL). While GDL concentrates on transactions (of goods or services) and value-in-exchange, SDL regards the exchange of services within or via interactions as the basis of economic activity. In this paradigm, goods are only a means of transporting services. This means that a car is seen as a vehicle for mobility, while

[1] Similar ideas are presented in the paradigms of interactive value creation (Reichwald & Piller, 2009) and Service Logic (Grönroos, 2011). SDL was chosen as it has received widespread attention and is continuously advanced by the academic community.

M. Perez Mengual, *Designing Physical Interaction Platforms*,
Markt- und Unternehmensentwicklung Markets and Organisations,
https://doi.org/10.1007/978-3-658-41920-2_6

a mobile phone is a service for enabling communication. Here, the focus is on users interacting with goods, by which a service is provided and so-called value-in-use—the service beyond the good—unfolds. Thereby, SDL is focused on the interaction and resulting value (Vargo & Lusch, 2004) (not the transaction itself as in GDL).

SDL emphasises the role of the customer or user as a co-creator of value (Vargo, Maglio, & Akaka, 2008). It proposes that each actor integrates their own resources (Vargo & Lusch, 2017; Vargo et al., 2008) to create value as an interactive process between the user and resources and/or different users. This means: only by taking up a mobile phone and entering a phone number the user creates value; in this example, a pleasant conversation. This process of value co-creation is called resource integration (Vargo & Lusch, 2011) since an actor uses not only their own resources but also integrates them with the resources of the other actor(s) involved (Baron & Warnaby, 2008; Edvardsson, Kristensson, Magnusson, & Sundström, 2012). The phone per se has no benefit for the user. Only when used for communication and a pleasant conversation, can the value derived from resource integration be perceived and captured as value-in-use. The example of a pleasant conversation also highlights the concept of value-in-context, which extends to social and cultural dimensions (Chandler & Vargo, 2011; Eggert, Ulaga, Frow, & Payne, 2018).

Following the SDL approach to value creation, the customer or user perceives and defines value while using a service: 'value is always uniquely and phenomenologically determined by the beneficiary' (Vargo & Lusch, 2017, p. 47). This implies that organisations cannot create or pass on value but only offer value propositions perceived and used by customers or users (Vargo & Lusch, 2008b). Hence, from this perspective, value propositions are put forward by, for example, a mobile phone producer as an outcome of their resource integration; however, it is up to the user to create value based on the organisation's value proposition[2] or propositions (Helkkula, Kelleher, & Pihlström, 2012; Strandvik, Holmlund, & Edvardsson, 2012). The customer perceives and defines value while using a 'service' (Vargo & Lusch, 2016, 2017)—this can, in the example of a mobile phone, be positive value-in-use from a pleasant conversation or not-so-positive value when unannounced advertising calls annoy the owner of the mobile phone.

The value of any good or service stems from positive usage—i.e., the positive interaction of a user with a service. Interactions are contextualised, joint actions in

[2] This also works in conjunction with Moore's concept of value propositions (Moore, 1993). This concept is used in practice, for example in the value proposition canvas or business model canvas, to define which value co-creation offering should be enabled and offered by an organisation.

which two or more actors interact and apply or integrate their resources (knowledge, skills, resources) (Vargo & Lusch, 2008a). Such interactions are enabled by some sort of place, space, or interface. In the example of the mobile phone, the operating system and a user interface with keys to dial a number enable the interaction. In surroundings like a shop, interactions are enabled by items on display and consultation through retail staff (or reviews in an online shop). As well, a workshop between colleagues in an organisation can be regarded as a space for interaction and value co-creation. A workshop functions as a platform for interaction as it allows people to come together at the same time and place with a mission to collaborate. Whereas the mobile phone only offers an interface for 'self-service' value-creation, the latter examples involve bringing forward or contributing a space or human resources to the value co-creation, as in PIPs.

6.2 Platforms as a Novel Perspective on Value Creation

Evolving from its initial formulation in 2004, the focus of the SDL paradigm has shifted away from the 'customer' to 'multiple actors' as co-creators and determinants of value (Vargo & Lusch, 2017). SDL also incorporates mechanisms that facilitate value creation, such as institutional arrangements (interdependent congregations of institutions) and service ecosystems (networks of actors extending beyond dyadic interactions) (Vargo & Lusch, 2017). Furthermore, the paradigm now extends beyond the interactions of individuals to include many social interactions guided by both context and culture. Therefore, the facilitation of interaction—that is, bringing together the actors and resources (e.g., mediated by platforms)—takes on greater importance.

Ramaswamy and Ozcan (2018) have followed up on these mechanisms, proposing that value creation is determined by so-called platformed interactions, which focus on the interactional dimension of value creation. They define value creation as the 'enactment of interactional creation across interactive system-environments (afforded by interactive platforms), entailing agencing engagements and structuring organizations' (Ramaswamy & Ozcan, 2018, p. 200). The emphasis is on creating a platform for interaction, understood as a virtual space or physical location, leading users to engage through interfaces and guiding principles, such as rules, norms, and beliefs, enabling and constraining action (Vargo & Lusch, 2017)

Ramaswamy and Ozcan (2018) focus on the idea of platforms, indicating that by enabling and orchestrating interactions, platforms facilitate interactive value creation for all actors. Breaking this down into a model (Figure 6.1), they propose that value is created through interactions composed of artifacts, people, processes, and interfaces—the so-called APPI components. Artifacts include 'physical and digitalized things,' processes are 'digitized and more conventional processes of interaction,' persons are 'individuals in their roles as customers, employees, partners, and any other stakeholders,' and interfaces are 'physical and digitized means by which an entity comes into contact with another entity' (Ramaswamy & Ozcan, 2018, p. 198). The interaction between these components is the embodiment of value creation.

Additionally, the framework defines 'experienced outcomes,' 'resourced capabilities,' 'agencing engagements,' and 'structuring organizations' (Ramaswamy & Ozcan, 2018). These concepts suggest that value creation by platformed interactions is an ongoing, repeated process. 'Experienced outcomes' refers to the realisation of value generated. Based on this, 'structuring organizations' refers to how a governing body stabilises the relations of APPI components. 'Agencing engagements' refer to the processes by which an actor (person) enters into a relationship with other APPI components of a platform. Finally, 'resourced capabilities' refers to the resources used in the interaction. As in SDL, this concept is strongly linked to the integration of resources (cf. Vargo & Lusch, 2008b, 2017) but extends beyond the actors' resources alone.

In their model, Ramaswamy and Ozcan (2018) combine a platform perspective that focuses heavily on the orchestration of interactions, along with a value-creation perspective focused on interaction itself. Although Ramaswamy and Ozcan (2018) designed the co-creation framework to explain the interactions of interactive online platforms, they call for its application in other settings to explain the interactional creation of value. Their work provides a tangible framework to analyse and describe dimensions that enable value creation on platforms, facilitating the structured design of PIPs.

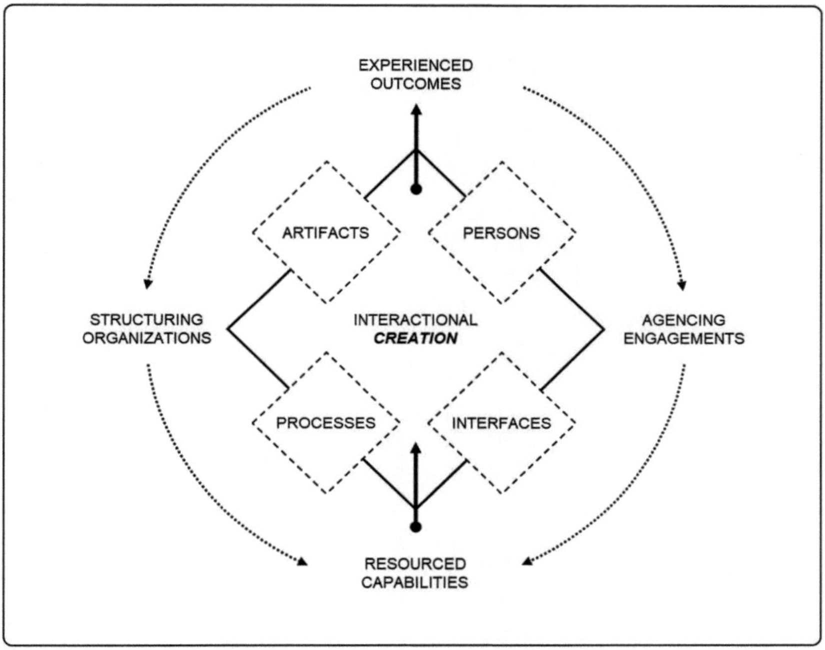

Figure 6.1 Co-Creation Framework (CCF) according to Ramaswamy & Ozcan (2018)

7 Platforms and Platform Business Models

Chapter 7 looks more deeply at the theoretical foundations regarding the concept of platforms. It begins with the introduction and definition of the term platform and elaborates this novel perspective on how value creation can be orchestrated. Building on this, platform business models and the platform life cycle are presented in more detail.

7.1 A Definition of the Term Platform

What exactly is a platform? The term platform is often used in connection with multi-sided markets, as a connecting element between players. However, there is no widely accepted definition for either the term 'platform' or 'multi-sided market' (D. S. Evans, Schmalensee, Noel, Chang, & Garcia-Swartz, 2011). Platforms are a phenomenon occurring in various industries (Evans, 2008). Today, the term platform usually refers to digital technologies that are generally perceived as minimising transaction costs or enabling interactions that could not otherwise take place (D. S. Evans & Schmalensee, 2005). When a platform connects different actors, it is called a multi-sided platform (MSP).

Nevertheless, MSPs are not a phenomenon of the digital world—they have been around for many centuries. They have simply received a boost in popularity in recent years, stimulated by digitisation and the internet. In essence, MSPs are quite simple: they connect two or more previously unlinked groups of users (D. S. Evans, 2003; Rochet & Tirole, 2003). In other words, they take on the role of an intermediary or matchmaker (D. S. Evans & Schmalensee, 2016; Gawer & Cusumano, 2014). Newspapers are an example of early platforms, linking readers and advertisers. City marketplaces and trade fairs are also examples of early platforms connecting buyers and sellers (Sanchez-Cartas & León, 2021). Today,

M. Perez Mengual, *Designing Physical Interaction Platforms*,
Markt- und Unternehmensentwicklung Markets and Organisations,
https://doi.org/10.1007/978-3-658-41920-2_7

the continuous development of information and communication technologies and global networking allows these formerly localised interactions to take place on a massive global scale (Sanchez-Cartas & León, 2021).

Nevertheless, Evans's (2003) definition has been criticised as being too broad. The mere intermediation between two or more groups of actors applies to many markets (Sanchez-Cartas & León, 2021). For this reason, the academic discourse uses another definition based on the existence of network effects—the utility for actors on side 'x' increases with the number of actors on side 'y' (McIntyre & Srinivasan, 2017; Sánchez-Cartas & León, 2018). These two definitions—(1) connecting two or more sides of actors and (2) the presence of network effects—are the unifying basis of many definitions of the term platform (cf. Anderson & Coate, 2005; Evans, 2003; Parker & Van Alstyne, 2005; Schiff, 2003).

This can be explained through the example of a physical marketplace in a city. The place brings together both buyers and sellers. The more buyers there are, the more attractive the market is for sellers, as there are more potential customers. The same is true in reverse—the more sellers there are, the greater the supply of goods and the greater the price competition; ergo, the market is more attractive to buyers. The only difference with a digital marketplace is that a physical market is limited by its spatial dimensions and cannot be scaled indefinitely.

7.2 The Platform Business Model

Current scholarly literature seeks to understand the omnipresence of MSPs, which are transforming entire industries (de Reuver, Sørensen, & Basole, 2018). This enormous research interest has been caused by the disruptive potential of platforms and their connections with organisations and markets. Today, MSPs are the most powerful business models 'due to their adaptability and ability to handle complexity, rapid scale-up, and value capture' (Abdelkafi, Raasch, Roth, & Srinivasan, 2019, p. 553). Amazon, Facebook, Airbnb, Google, and Uber are among the highest valuated companies in the world, and all are platforms (Parker et al., 2016).

These high valuations are based on the platforms transforming the driving power of our economy from supply-side economies of scale to demand-side economies of scale (Van Alstyne & Parker, 2017). Demand-side economies of scale exist when the value of a service increases with the number of users. This leads to users interacting with other users, thereby creating mutual value (Van Alstyne & Parker, 2017). The more extensive the network of platform users, the better the matchmaking between users—the network effects mentioned above (Gawer & Cusumano, 2014; McIntyre & Srinivasan, 2017).

Regarding the business model, the novelty of platform thinking is that physical assets become increasingly insignificant. Instead, the main asset of a platform lies in the network of actors, who take on the roles of providers and consumers (Van Alstyne & Parker, 2017). Platforms do not control supply chains—i.e., the means of production—as traditional, linear businesses do. Platforms create and control the means of exchange and connection. Therefore, platform business models, in essence, consist of the following two elements: (1) the network of users (the platform ecosystem) and (2) the platform core, which enables and controls the interaction between users (Boudreau & Hagiu, 2009).

Following this, running a platform is fundamentally different from running a traditional value-chain business. For example, instead of controlling production, platform operators fulfil various roles, including orchestrating the platform ecosystem, determining governance rules to balance platform control, and providing value-creation and value-appropriation mechanisms that lead actors to engage with the platform (Gawer & Cusumano, 2014; Ghazawneh & Henfridsson, 2013; Mukhopadhyay & Bouwman, 2019; Parker et al., 2016; Tiwana, 2014).

Once again, using the example of platforms like Amazon, Airbnb, and Uber, another characteristic is apparent. These platforms basically follow the idea of SDL (Vargo & Lusch, 2017), introduced in the previous chapter. They focus on the value that is created in the interaction with the platform (Ramaswamy & Ozcan, 2018). Trying to create a positive experience for the user goes beyond simply enabling a transaction. Amazon, for example, is not simply a marketplace—it tries to offer customers the best possible experience in terms of ordering, delivery, and dealing with complaints. Thus, the interaction with the platform itself is engaging and generates value.

7.3 The Platform Lifecycle

A central point in the academic discourse on platforms is market competition. When is the right time to enter a market? Is it possible to compete against a market leader? How can a platform maintain its position? These questions lead to a larger question—what is the typical life cycle of a platform?

The literature offers relatively little on the life cycle of platforms itself. However, similar approaches can be found in the literature on business ecosystems, put forward by Moore (1993). He proposes four evolutionary stages of a business ecosystem—birth, expansion, leadership, and self-renewal (Moore, 1993). Since their initial formulation, these four stages have been adopted by Teece (2017) in a perspective on the platform life cycle. Notably, a significant number of platforms do not make it through all four stages (Yoffie, Gawer, & Cusumano, 2019).

The birth stage typically begins with an entrepreneur identifying a business opportunity. The next step is to design a business model, including value propositions, value creation, and value-capturing mechanisms (Teece, 2017). This may require some experimentation, as the most profitable constellations may not be readily apparent. The first tasks in readying the platform for operation are identifying lead customers, establishing relationships with suppliers (Moore, 1993), and initiating interactions on the platform. Additionally, Parker et al. (2016) highlight three key factors crucial to the birth phase as follows: maintaining liquidity, optimising matching quality between the users of the platform, and building trust with users to facilitate engagement with the platform.

The expansion stage is dedicated to scaling the platform's ecosystem of users, aiming to achieve maximum market coverage (Moore, 1993). In this phase, it is important that the ecosystem reaches a critical mass of users so that network effects can occur (Parker & Van Alstyne, 2005). At this point, it is vital to start balancing the two or more sides of the market, ensuring that interactions generate enough value for all users to warrant their engagement (Parker et al., 2016).

The leadership stage starts once a platform has maturity, both regarding its core that mediates interactions as well as a sufficiently large ecosystem of users. The aim of this stage is primarily to further strengthen the market position and maintain strong bargaining power (Moore, 1993). This stage is, therefore, more concerned with strategizing than the functional development of the platform. For example, actions by rival platforms must be countered, and possible market niches must be identified (Teece, 2017).

Once the maturity of a platform has been reached, research suggests focusing on self-renewal by incrementally innovating the platform's offerings (Tiwana, 2014). To remain vibrant, a platform must adapt to the needs of its users while simultaneously reacting to a competitive environment (Parker et al., 2016; Teece, 2017). The search for opportunities for innovation must begin early (Teece, 2017). Innovations can consist of supplementing the missing core functionalities of the platform or adding new functionalities to the platform (Parker et al., 2016). Failure to innovate turns the initial advantage of not controlling physical assets into a disadvantage. Competitors can quickly fill market niches or, in the worst case, promise new interactions that are better aligned with users' needs (Thomas, Le Masson, Weil, & Legrand, 2021).

The last stage in particular, self-renewal, can be aptly explained using the example of the super-platform Amazon. Amazon was founded in 1994 as an e-commerce marketplace. After the market position was secured, further complementary modules were developed. In 2006, data centres and cloud services were built; today, Amazon Web Services is the most profitable part of the company (Teece, 2017).

Designing Platforms

8

Chapter 8 focuses on the theoretical foundations of PIP design. Following Tura, Kutvonen, and Ritala (2018) and Dell'Era, Altuna, Magistretti, and Verganti (2017), platforms can be perceived not only as intermediaries in multi-sided markets but also as designed entities. To highlight this aspect of platforms, this chapter introduces systematic approaches and strategies to platform design. Following this, an introduction to design theory is given, which explains the reasoning of the design processes. In combining both foundations, the implications of design theory for the systematic and structured design of platforms are highlighted.

8.1 Strategies for Platform Design

As introduced previously, current research on platforms relates to their functionality and economic impact. In terms of recommendations for the design process of platforms, mostly practitioner-oriented literature or 'playbooks' are available (e.g., Evans & Schmalensee, 2016; Memon, 2021; Parker et al., 2016; Reillier & Reillier, 2017). This is because value creation in platform-based ecosystems depends on the participation and involvement of many stakeholders (Ramaswamy & Ozcan, 2018). While studying the embodiment of this value creation is possible (e.g., through case studies), researching the general design of enabling conditions is a more complicated matter. Platform-mediated value creation depends significantly on the ability of a platform to stimulate the engagement of stakeholders (McIntyre & Srinivasan, 2017). To facilitate this engagement in the first place, a platform requires ex-ante design (Tura et al., 2018). Tura et al. (2018) identify the following four core general design categories that guide platform design choices: platform architecture, value-creation logic, governance, and

M. Perez Mengual, *Designing Physical Interaction Platforms*,
Markt- und Unternehmensentwicklung Markets and Organisations,
https://doi.org/10.1007/978-3-658-41920-2_8

platform competition. These four dimensions must be designed before a platform can be launched and are reflected in the structure of the 'playbooks' mentioned earlier.

Drafting the platform architecture typically begins with designing the core interaction that will take place on the platform (Parker et al., 2016). The core interaction is a product of the value unit, the participants, and the matching mechanisms (Parker et al., 2016) and defines the main purpose of the platform (Tura et al., 2018). The value unit defines what is exchanged (e.g., products, services, or information) by the platform participants (Parker et al., 2016). The matching mechanism determines how the market sides, i.e., the participants, are connected (Reillier & Reillier, 2017).

The value-creation logic details the core interaction by defining the actor roles, revenue model, and value propositions for each of the market sides (Reillier & Reillier, 2017). The actor roles comprise the participants on the platform, while the revenue model determines the cost of participation for the different actor roles (Parker et al., 2016). The value propositions answer the question of why the actors should engage with the platform. Ideally, the value propositions of the platform are created by combining producer and consumer problems (Memon, 2021). Another critical element of the value-creation logic is considering how network effects can be created, thus drafting how the platform can grow and scale up (Reillier & Reillier, 2017; Van Alstyne & Parker, 2017).

The governance of a platform is shaped by the owner (who owns the platform) and the provider (who manages the platform). These two actors establish and enforce the ecosystem rules (Cusumano, Gawer, & Yoffie, 2019), determining who is allowed access to the platform. A high degree of openness gives actors increased freedom to create value but may also hinder the ability of the owner and provider to regulate the platform. Governance includes the rules that structure the interaction on the platform, i.e., norms and laws defining what is allowed within the platform's ecosystem (Parker et al., 2016). Rules are important in maintaining balance on a platform, encouraging positive interactions while mitigating negative ones (Reillier & Reillier, 2017). In this, rules are required to achieve high levels of actor engagement with the platform, which ideally attracts more participants (network effects).

Platform competition includes aspects that are relevant beyond the concept phase—that is, launching and scaling the platform, as well as securing its position against competitors (Tura et al., 2018). Parker et al. (2016) list eight strategies that have been proven to launch platforms successfully. For example, 'piggybacking' is a strategy wherein a new platform uses the customer base of an existing platform (e.g., PayPal using the eBay auction platform to scale its network of users). Evans and Schmalensee (2016) discuss additional strategies focused on achieving a critical mass of participants. These strategies aim at attracting platform participants from all platform sides to solve the 'chicken and egg' problem, a phenomenon in which the platform is only attractive once one side has been populated (e.g., Amazon is only attractive for merchants if there are enough consumers, and vice versa). In addition, the literature discusses how platforms can enter new markets and establish their market position. Typically, it is difficult to enter markets where there is already a dominant platform—this is also described as a 'winner takes it all' market (Cusumano et al., 2019). It is therefore advised that a platform starts in a niche market and designs a unique competitive position (Cusumano et al., 2019; Tura et al., 2018). Additionally, platforms need to consider how they want to deal with innovation and further development, which is related to the self-renewal of a platform, as mentioned earlier (Moore, 1993; Teece, 2017). An important approach here is modularisation—i.e., adding additional components to the platform without jeopardising the core business—which is often done by inviting third-party participants onto the platform (Parker et al., 2016; Thomas, Le Masson, Weil, & Legrand, 2021).

8.2 An Introduction to Design Theory

The strategies presented in the previous section are derived from successful cases in the market. These playbooks all use examples of successful platforms (e.g., Amazon, Google, Uber, PayPal) to illustrate 'how a platform could work.' However, the aspects of structured design and the logic of reasoning within a design process are missing. To address these gaps, an introduction into design theory is provided here, which acts as the overall theoretical lens of this dissertation.

As the forefather of design theory, Herbert Simon argues in his book *The Sciences of the Artificial* that a science of design is needed that is a 'tough, analytic, partly formalizable, partly empirical, teachable doctrine' (Simon, 1996, p. 113) In particular, it is important how knowledge about design can be formalised, i.e., captured and communicated (Gregor & Jones, 2007). Gregor (2006) has shown how design can be perceived as one of the five classes of theory relevant to IS research as follows: (1) theory for analysis and description; (2) theory for explanation; (3) theory for prediction; (4) theory for prescription (explanation and prediction); and (5) theory for design and action. Theory for design and action is distinctive, as it focuses on 'how to do things.' It provides descriptions of how develop 'artifacts' (Gregor, 2006; Gregor & Jones, 2007). The range of the term 'artifacts' is subject to debate. In IS research, the term 'artifact' is often used to describe technological products or managerial interventions (Gregor & Jones, 2007), though in its broader sense, it can be used to describe something that is artificially constructed by humans, such as a PIP (Richard Baskerville & Pries-Heje, 2010). This makes design theory distinct from other theories in the natural sciences (e.g., research in physical or social domains), which aim at understanding reality (Richard Baskerville & Pries-Heje, 2010). Instead, design theory tries to serve und answer to human purposes (March & Smith, 1995): 'Rather than producing general theoretical knowledge, design scientists produce and apply knowledge of tasks or situations in order to create effective artifacts' (p. 253).

Importantly, however, there is no consensus among scholars about the definitive use of the term 'design theory,' with some using it synonymously with the term 'design science' (Gregor & Jones, 2007). While some scholars recognise design as comprising a theory (e.g., Walls, Widmeyer, & El Sawy, 1992), others (e.g., Hevner, 2007; March & Smith, 1995) perceive it more as a research activity, using the term 'design science' instead of 'design theory.' Terminology use thus depends on individual perspectives. While purely development-focused approaches can certainly be seen as research activities, other approaches include additional perspectives, such as the process of reasoning in design, as in C–K theory (Hatchuel & Weil, 2003; Le Glatin, Le Masson, & Weil, 2017). This terminology debate highlights an important understanding of design as a theory—it can be understood as a dualist construct. Design theory includes both the design of artifacts (thus outcome-oriented) and design as a process (Richard Baskerville & Pries-Heje, 2010).

Design theory has evolved beyond its pure problem-solving focus, which was emphasised in its beginning (Simon, 1996). Although this focus remains paradigmatic in the field, it does not capture the essence of designing (Reich, 2013). The theoretical part of design concerns the reasoning in design—that is, the 'systematic exploration of the object of study whichever lens we choose to look at from' (Reich, 2013, p. 218). Design theory is not about solving a problem—it is about solving a problem in the best possible way.

8.3 Implications of Design Theory for Platform Design

But what is 'the best possible way'? Simon (1997) proposed that decision-making when solving a problem should be based on a 'satisficing' principle. This principle introduces subjectivity as follows: 'rules of thumb, heuristics or ad hoc moves as basic decision-making processes' (Hatchuel, 2002, p. 261). Whether the decisions made lead to satisfaction is defined within the decision process (Hatchuel,

2001). When designers work on a problem, they discuss possible alternatives, goals, hurdles, and procedures. The goal of this problem-solving process is to identify alternatives that can be evaluated in terms of their satisfaction (You & Hands, 2019). In this context, it is understood that 'it is possible to determine a desired state of affairs, which enables a designer to solve a problem by continually translating between the state and process descriptions of the same complex reality' (You & Hands, 2019, p. 1347). From this perspective, the success of a project is not based on a technology or market but on how well a project and design process is carried out (Cooper, 1990). The academic literature on design is extensive, as are the design processes proposed therein (cf. Gericke & Blessing, 2012). In the following, aspects relevant to the systematic and structured design of platforms are highlighted.

To effectively approach the design process, the decomposition of a problem—i.e., a design task—into smaller sub-problems is essential (Bender & Gericke, 2021). Subsequently, a solution can be sought for each sub-problem. The sum of the sub-solutions may be the solution for the initially formulated problem or the design task (Bender & Gericke, 2021).

Platform design involves the structured exploration of alternatives (Le Masson, Weil, & Hatchuel, 2009). Design is most successful when alternative solutions to a problem are developed and evaluated regarding their feasibility. The challenge here is to find a balance in the creation process. Too many alternatives, i.e., an excessive expansion of the search space, leads to the unnecessary expenditure of time. The creation must follow a defined strategy, reasonably reducing the number of alternatives at an early stage (Fricke, 1996).

A frequent challenge in the design process is to overcome fixation (Agogue & Cassotti, 2013). The so-called fixation effect occurs when the first solution or alternative identified strongly influences the subsequent exploration of further solutions (Jansson & Smith, 1991). Contemporary design literature (e.g., on C–K theory) introduces practical methodologies used to overcome the fixation effect (Hatchuel, Le Masson, & Weil, 2011; Le Masson, Weil, & Hatchuel, 2017).

Designing a platform is not a sequential process; rather, it is an iterative process and must be understood as a co-evolution of problems and their solutions (Wynn, Eckert, & Clarkson, 2007). This process should be constantly observed and design steps should be tracked. It may be that at a later time, previously acquired knowledge, e.g., developed alternatives, will be of use again (Le Masson et al., 2017).

Summary of Key Concepts 9

Part II introduced the theoretical concepts of service-dominant logic, platforms and platform business models, and systematic approaches to platform design. Each of these three concepts holds valuable insights concerning the systematic and structured design of sustainably successful PIPs (Figure 9.1).

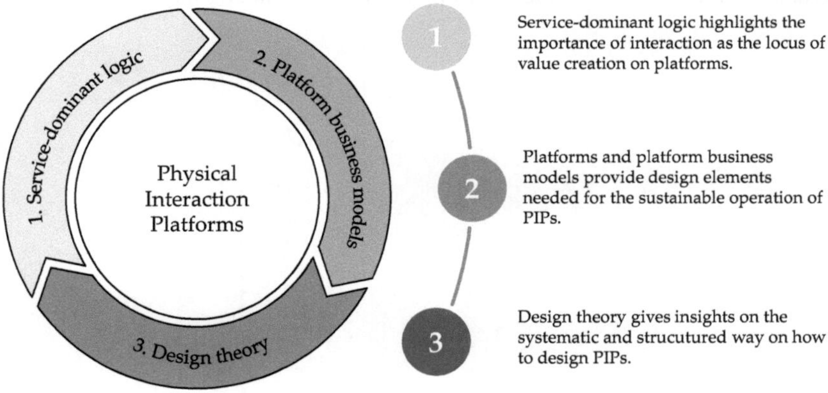

Figure 9.1 Key concepts of this dissertation

SDL shows the importance of interactions for value creation. Value is created in interactions, which is why they should be a central point of departure for the systematic and structured design of PIPs. Furthermore, SDL shows that successful platforms go beyond the mere facilitation of transactions. Platforms create value not only through intermediating between two or more actors but also

M. Perez Mengual, *Designing Physical Interaction Platforms*, Markt- und Unternehmensentwicklung Markets and Organisations, https://doi.org/10.1007/978-3-658-41920-2_9

through interacting with the platform itself. The chapter on platforms and platform business models reveals the basic design elements and mechanisms needed for a sustainable platform. The chapter also shows that different phases in the life cycle of a platform require different actions and strategies. The chapter on platform design provides an overview of current practical guidelines on platform design. In addition, design theory introduces a foundation of what constitutes a structured and systematic design process.

These theoretical foundations are the basis for the empirical studies presented in the following parts of this dissertation. The studies are organised around the life cycle of a platform. In Part III, the basic elements of PIPs are identified, which serve as a starting point for designers seeking to conceptualise and build a PIP. Part IV describes the design process of a PIP, from conceptualisation to launch, highlighting challenges and turning points. Part V takes a closer look at how to manage continuous innovation once a PIP has reached maturity. Part VI combines the findings from Parts III to IV into a toolkit for designing PIPs, evaluating their ease of use and usefulness. Finally, Part VII summarises and synthesises the overall findings and implications, concluding the dissertation.

Part III

Starting from Scratch: A Taxonomy to Identify Design Elements of PIPs

Objectives and Structure 10

This dissertation seeks to explore *how a physical interaction platform (PIP) can be designed in a systematic and structured way.* Part III supports this objective by gathering and structuring theoretical and practical knowledge about the design dimensions that constitute PIPs. As mentioned above, for scholars seeking to understand and practitioners seeking to design such spaces, two challenges arise. First, due to the heterogeneous nature of interaction spaces, it has become increasingly challenging to navigate through the various names, concepts, and operationalisations of PIPs (Bogers et al., 2017; Enkel et al., 2020). Second, for practitioners seeking to build such places, it remains unclear what dimensions are essential for the design and sustainable operation of PIPs. Most research has focused on specific aspects of these interaction spaces—e.g., the collaboration that takes place there (Greve, Martinez, Jonas, Neely, & Möslein, 2016) or how collaborative innovation is organised (Ollila & Yström, 2016). However, little is known about the design process required to build a PIP from scratch. As platform design processes have been described as structured explorations of alternatives (Le Masson, Weil, & Hatchuel, 2009), a tangible framework for the initial conceptualisation of physical interaction platforms is needed.

To achieve this, Part III seeks to contribute by developing a taxonomy for the conceptualisation of PIPs. Taxonomies structure and organise knowledge in

---

Part III of this dissertation builds upon and extends a conference contribution, which was presented and discussed at the 15th Research Colloquium on Innovation & Value Creation in Nuremberg, Germany (Perez Mengual, 2020). Further, an earlier version of this study was presented and discussed at Annual R&D Management Conference 2021 in Glasgow, Scotland (Perez Mengual, Danzinger & Roth., 2021). An adapted version of this study is currently under review in the 2nd round of an international management journal (Perez Mengual, Danzinger & Roth., 2022).

M. Perez Mengual, *Designing Physical Interaction Platforms*, Markt- und Unternehmensentwicklung Markets and Organisations, https://doi.org/10.1007/978-3-658-41920-2_10

various fields, enabling researchers and practitioners to understand, analyse, and apply this knowledge (Nickerson et al., 2013). Part III identifies design dimensions and characteristics of PIPs that can be used to distinguish and develop different types of PIPs. Meanwhile, this section seeks to answer the following research questions:

RQ 1: *What are the design dimensions of PIPs that enable interactive value creation?*

RQ 2: *How can these design dimensions be grouped to provide a useful tool for designers of PIPs?*

Part III is structured as follows. Chapter 12 describes the research method used to develop the taxonomy—Nickerson et al.'s taxonomy development method (Nickerson et al., 2013). This method consists of several iterative steps, which are described in detail. Chapter 13 presents the results in the form of a taxonomy. The taxonomy´s categories and the corresponding design characteristics are described in detail. Chapter 14 highlights the application and usefulness of the taxonomy using two illustrative examples. Chapter 15 discusses the results and points out the implications for both theory as well as practitioners. Chapter 16 summarises the results of Part III and puts them in the context of the entire dissertation. The structure of Part III is shown in Figure 10.1.

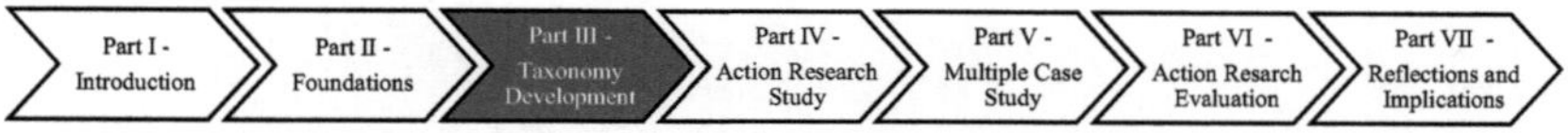

1 Objectives and Structure

- Objectives and purpose of part III
- Overview of chapters in part III

2 Research Approach: Taxonomy Development

- The iterative apporach towards developing taxonomies
- Evaluation and ending conditions for taxonomy development

3 Taxonomy Development Process

- Description of five iterative development steps
- Review of ending conditions

4 The Taxonomy of Physical Interaction Platforms

- The PIP taxonomy containing 18 dimensions
- Detailed descriptions of these dimensions

5 Application of the PIP Taxonomy

- Illustrative case: Open Innovation Lab
- Illustrative case: Co-Working Space

6 Discussion and Implications

- Theoretical and practical contributions
- Implications for building PIPs

7 Summary and Outlook

- Summary of findings and limitations of the research
- Implications for this dissertation

Figure 10.1 Structure of Part III

Research Approach: Taxonomy Development

11

Due to their increasing popularity, PIPs have received widespread scholarly attention. Research has explored how PIPs can facilitate collaborative innovation (Ollila & Ystrӧm, 2016; Peschl & Fundneider, 2014) and how they are used for the development, testing, and commercialisation of innovations (Steen & van Bueren, 2017). Several existing typologies have sought to describe the nature of PIPs, either based on the actors that drive innovation (Leminen et al., 2012), the type of PIP ownership, and actor engagement (e.g., temporary or continuous) (Roth et al., 2014) or based on their purpose (e.g., explorative or exploitative) (Dell'Era & Landoni, 2014). However, information on how to develop, build, and operate PIPs is scarce. Chronéer et al. (2019) emphasise key components like leadership, management, and business models to secure sustainability and financing for PIPs. Greve et al. (2016) have described critical factors for facilitating co-creation, such as customer engagement, relationship management, and design layout.

To account for these various theoretical and practical aspects when designing PIPs, a tool that provides structure and aggregated knowledge for the design process is required. Taxonomies can help structure the complex knowledge of research fields to explain similarities and differences between objects of interest (Nickerson et al., 2013). A taxonomy is a uniform model by which objects can be classified using defined criteria, categories, or classes. Originally, the term taxonomy was used in scientific disciplines to describe a type of hierarchical classification (e.g., the Linnaean taxonomy for the classification of organisms, cf. Buck & Hull, 1966). In IS research, emphasis is put less on the hierarchical nature of classifications and instead on their ability to explain complex phenomena concisely. They serve as basic mechanisms for organising and structuring knowledge that can be used to understand complex phenomena (Wand, Monarchi, Parsons, & Woo, 1995).

M. Perez Mengual, *Designing Physical Interaction Platforms*,
Markt- und Unternehmensentwicklung Markets and Organisations,
https://doi.org/10.1007/978-3-658-41920-2_11

In IS research, taxonomies are often used to classify new phenomena and thereby make them tangible. Examples of taxonomies in our context include the classifications of Living Labs by Leminen (2013) and Roth et al. (2014), which deal with operator models for Living Labs, each at a different level of abstraction. Two different approaches can be applied to develop taxonomies (Bailey, 1994; Nickerson et al., 2013). Empirically derived taxonomies use statistical approaches and instruments to examine a large number of cases, thereby identifying common features. By using cluster analysis, feature sets are formed, which results in a so-called numerical taxonomy (Bailey, 1994). Deductive taxonomies, on the other hand, are theory based and conceptual. Modern approaches to taxonomy development combine both approaches and can be found in the methods of Bailey (1994) and Nickerson (2013). While Bailey (1994) proposes a combination of different quantitative and qualitative methods for taxonomy development, Nickerson et al. (2013) presents an iterative approach that is strongly inspired by design science research (Hevner, 2007). The taxonomy as an artifact is defined by its purpose and should be built according to its intended use. While Bailey's (1994) paper provides an overview of good practice for taxonomy building, Nickerson's (2013) offers a precisely outlined method, including recommendations for goal setting and specified ending conditions that indicate when the taxonomy-building process is complete.

Part III seeks to contribute by providing a tool in the form of a taxonomy that brings the design dimensions of PIPs into a logical order. This taxonomy provides a structure for analysis and guidance for the development of PIPs. With researchers and practitioners as users in mind, the resulting artifact should be easy in its application and complexity. The taxonomy development method of Nickerson et al. (2013) results from a comprehensive review of 73 papers and their individual approaches to developing taxonomies. As a synthesis of these approaches, Nickerson et al.'s (2013) method is an iterative process that allows researchers to develop taxonomies, both conceptually (based on theoretical knowledge) and empirically (based on observations).

The method is rigorous, clearly describing the development steps as well as the ending conditions that terminate the taxonomy development process. It has been applied in several contexts (Hunke, Engel, Schüritz, & Ebel, 2019; Remane, Nickerson, Hanelt, Tesch, & Kolbe, 2016), proving its robustness and usefulness for taxonomy development. It consists of the following three phases: (1) preliminary instructions, where the meta-characteristic and ending conditions are defined; (2) the development process, consisting of several iterations; and (3) the evaluation, which checks if the ending conditions are met, and if they are, causes the development process to terminate (Figure 11.1).

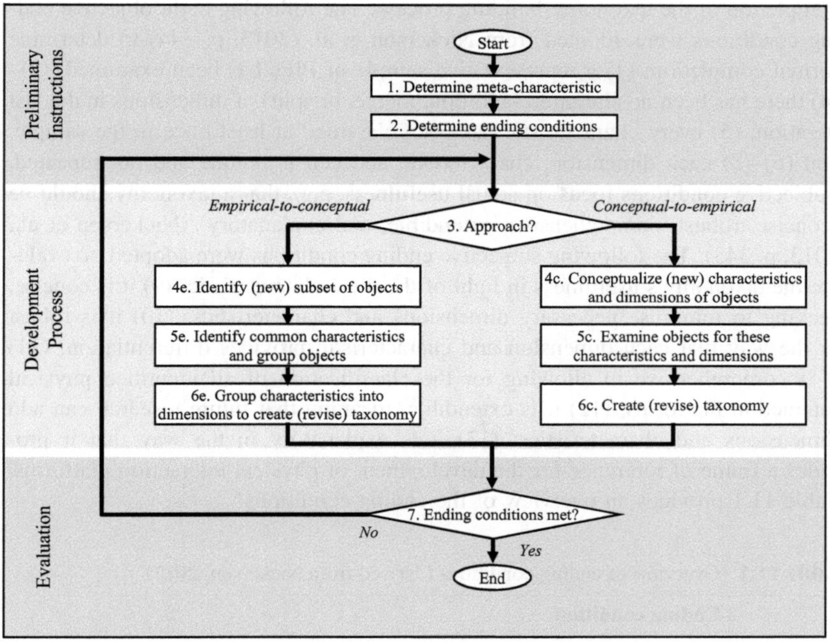

Figure 11.1 Taxonomy development method (adapted from Nickerson, 2013)

11.1 Preliminary Instructions

The method formulates two preliminary instructions to be followed before starting the taxonomy development process. First, researchers need to define a meta-characteristic that describes the taxonomy's intended purpose, which shapes the development process (Nickerson et al., 2013). Each dimension and characteristic selected must follow in logical consequence for the expected use of the taxonomy (Nickerson et al., 2013). The primary purpose of this taxonomy of physical interaction platforms is (1) to provide the basis for a morphological analysis of existing PIPs and (2) to serve as a starting point for practitioners seeking to design value-creating PIPs. The meta-characteristic is defined as 'relevant for the design and description of value creation on physical interaction platforms.' Furthermore, Nickerson et al. (2013) formulate ending conditions that determine the completion of the taxonomy-building process. The following eight objective ending conditions were adopted from Nickerson et al. (2013, p. 344) to determine formal completion: (1) a representative sample of PIPs has been examined, (2)–(4) there has been no alteration (addition, merge, or split) of dimensions in the last iteration, (5) every characteristic has been classified at least once in the sample, and (6)–(8) each dimension, characteristic and cell is unique and not repeated. Subjective conditions focus on actual usefulness, e.g., that a taxonomy should be 'concise, robust, comprehensive, extendible, and explanatory' (Nickerson et al., 2013, p. 343). The following subjective ending conditions were adopted, to evaluate the taxonomy's usefulness in light of the meta-characteristic: (9) it is concise, seeking to minimise necessary dimensions and characteristics, (10) it is robust in the way that each dimension and characteristic provides differentiation, (11) it is comprehensive in allowing for the classification of all identified physical interaction platforms, (12) it is extendible, meaning that future research can add dimensions and characteristics, (13) it is explanatory in the way that it provides a frame of reference for the development of physical interaction platforms. Table 11.1 provides an overview of the ending conditions.

Table 11.1 Overview of ending conditions (derived from Nickerson, 2013)

	Ending condition
Objective	(1) All objects or a representative sample of objects have been examined
	(2) No object was merged with a similar object or split into multiple objects
	(3) At least one object is classified for every characteristic of every dimension
	(4) No new dimensions or characteristics were added in the last iteration
	(5) No dimensions or characteristics were merged or split in the last iteration
	(6) Every dimension is unique and not repeated
	(7) Every characteristic is unique within its dimension
	(8) Each cell (combination of characteristics) is unique and is not repeated
Subjective	(9) Concise
	(10) Robust
	(11) Comprehensive
	(12) Extendible
	(13) Explanatory

11.2 Taxonomy Development Process

After completing the preliminary instructions, building the taxonomy includes two independent approaches—conceptual-to-empirical and empirical-to-conceptual—each consisting of three steps (Nickerson et al., 2013). The conceptual-to-empirical approach represents the deductive iteration. Researchers begin with the conceptualisation of dimensions and characteristics, building upon experience and existing knowledge. Little guidance is provided by Nickerson's (2013) method, suggesting that researchers should rely on their knowledge of the field and the corresponding scientific methodology to validate whether characteristics or dimensions need to be added, refined, or deleted. As a result of this iteration, either a taxonomy is created (if ending conditions are met) or revised (if ending conditions are not met). Alternatively, the empirical-to-conceptual approach represents the inductive iteration. This allows researchers to use real-world observations for taxonomy development. In this approach, a sample of objects is identified, and common characteristics among these objects are identified and grouped into dimensions to create or revise the taxonomy, depending on the ending conditions. Again, this approach provides considerable freedom to researchers in terms of sampling and data collection. Nickerson (2013) suggests that 'objects should be the ones with which the researchers are most familiar or that are most easily accessible. The subset could be a random sample, a systematic sample, a convenience sample, or some other type of sample' (p. 345). The development of the PIP taxonomy, iterated using both the empirical-to-conceptual as well as the conceptual-to-empirical approaches, creates a profound classification that is based on current literature and existing knowledge as well as observations of real-world objects. The development of the PIP taxonomy was conducted in five iterations, as shown in Table 11.2 below: (1) screening of PIPs, (2) academic workshop, systematic literature reviews of (3) platform classifications and (4) platform-mediated value creation and (5) a taxonomy evaluation by practitioners. Each iteration added or modified the design dimensions and characteristics of the PIP taxonomy.

Table 11.2 Iterations in the taxonomy building process

No.	Iteration	Iteration type	Description
1	Initial screening	Conceptual	First screening of PIPs; review of related literature.
2	Academic workshop	Empirical	Presentation and discussion of the first iteration of the PIP taxonomy in an academic workshop.
3	Systematic literature review (1)	Conceptual	Systematic review of the extant platform literature (taxonomies and classifications) to provide thorough structure, dimensions and characteristics.
4	Systematic literature review (2)	Conceptual	Second systematic search of literature to fill a logical gap in the taxonomy regarding interaction and value creation on platforms.
5 a–e	Interview-based evaluation	Empirical	Conduction of interviews with operators and designers of existing PIPs to evaluate and advance the taxonomy.

11.3 Evaluation Approach

Nickerson's method (2013) relies on predetermined ending conditions that indicate when taxonomy development is complete. While objective ending conditions can be simply checked by a team of researchers, subjective ending conditions are prone to ambiguous interpretations. As the method does not provide any guidelines on subjective ending conditions, other researchers have come up with their own evaluation approaches, mainly consisting of the repeated application of the taxonomy (Chasin, von Hoffen, Cramer, & Matzner, 2018), the use of the taxonomy to determine archetypes (Blaschke, Haki, Aier, & Winter, 2019; Remane, Nickerson, Hanelt, Tesch, & Kolbe, 2016), or classification by independent reviewers (Hunke, Engel, Schüritz, & Ebel, 2019). In contrast, the PIP taxonomy should go beyond its use as a classification instrument—it should also serve as a starting point for the design of physical interaction platforms. Therefore, case-based interviews with designers, practitioners, and managers of physical interaction platforms were conducted to evaluate the taxonomy's applicability for its intended use (i.e., the meta-characteristic). The next chapter provides a comprehensive description of the iterations and the dimensions/characteristics that were added or revised.

Taxonomy Development Process 12

This section summarises the results of the PIP taxonomies' development steps. A comprehensive description of each iteration is provided, including insights generated during the process as well as dimensions and characteristics added in each instantiation of the taxonomy. Table 12.3 provides a structured overview of dimensions added or modified during each step of this iterative process.

12.1 Iteration 1: Conceptual to Empirical

In the first iteration the conceptual-to-empirical approach was used. At this stage, little guidance exists on how to identify relevant dimensions. According to Nickerson et al. (2013), researchers should use their knowledge of 'existing foundations, experience, and judgment to deduce what they think will be relevant dimensions' (p. 346). Following this approach, an initial open screening of PIPs, as well as a review on related literature, was conducted. Lists and directories of Living Labs, co-working spaces, (corporate) innovation hubs, accelerators and incubators, maker spaces, fab labs, and innovative retail concepts were screened to get more familiar with the various types of PIPs (see Table 12.1 for an overview of screened directories). This screening was followed by a review of the related literature: research on innovation spaces (Fritzsche, Jonas, Roth, & Möslein, 2020; Greve et al., 2016; Mortara & Parisot, 2018; Roth et al., 2014), spaces for collaboration (R. B. Bouncken & Reuschl, 2018; Capdevila, 2015, 2019) and marketplaces (Alexander & Blazquez Cano, 2020; Warnaby & Shi,

Supplementary Information The online version contains supplementary material available at https://doi.org/10.1007/978-3-658-41920-2_12.

M. Perez Mengual, *Designing Physical Interaction Platforms*,
Markt- und Unternehmensentwicklung Markets and Organisations,
https://doi.org/10.1007/978-3-658-41920-2_12

2019), as well as frameworks and taxonomies for (digital) platforms (e.g. Van Alstyne & Parker, 2017) and their business models (e.g. Täuscher & Laudien, 2018).

Table 12.1 Sources for initial PIP screening

Search term	Search results
Living Lab	European Network of Living Labs (openlivinglabs.eu); InnoLab-Project (innolab-livinglabs.de)
Co-working spaces	Co-working space listing (coworkingresources.org); co-working space worldwide map (coworker.com); co-working space reservation service (deskbookers.com)
Incubator	Comprehensive list of start-up incubators and accelerators (incubatorlist.com); Search engine for start-up incubators (eu-startups.com)
Corporate Innovation Labs	Global directory of corporate R&D and innovation labs (fanaticalfuturist.com); List of 85 corporate innovation labs (cbinsights.com)
Makerspace	List of 300 makerspaces (maker-faire.de); list of US makerspaces (makerdirectory.com)
Hackerspace	Comprehensive list of all active hackerspaces worldwide (hackerspaces.org);
FabLab	Comprehensive list all of FabLabs worldwide (fablabs.io);
Retail concept	List of new retail concept stores worldwide (insider-trends.com)

Following this, the first version of the taxonomy was conceptualised, incorporating design dimensions from existing scholarly knowledge. The taxonomy used an overarching business model structure (Gassmann, Frankenberger, & Csik, 2013), following similar work describing (digital) platform-based value creation (Lis & Otto, 2021; Perscheid, 2020; Rix et al., 2020; Weking et al., 2020). In total, fifteen dimensions were identified from the PIP screening and the literature, comprising the first iteration of the PIP taxonomy: *engagement, position, location, surface area, appearance, ecosystem dimension, customer type, access, provider, value orientation, core activity, value type, revenue source, revenue streams,* and *performance indicator*. Due to its conceptual nature, the taxonomy did not meet several ending conditions.

12.2 Iteration 2: Empirical to Conceptual

This first conceptualisation of the taxonomy (shown in Figure 12.1) was presented at a workshop during an academic conference in November 2020. Nine academics from the fields of innovation and value creation participated in the workshop, discussing the content and structure of the taxonomy.

	Dimension	Characteristics				
Physical Attributes	Engagement	Temporary	Permanent			
	Position	Stationary	Mobile			
	Location	Rural	Outer-City	Inner-City		
	Surface Area	Small	Medium	Large		
	Appearance	Basic	Premium			
Value Creation	Ecosystem Dimension	Local	Regional	National	International	
	Customer Type	Private	Business	Public		
	Access	Open	Indirect	Closed Space		
	Provider	Company	Intermediary	Public Organisation	Alliance	
Value Delivery	Value Orientation	Societal	Social	Environmental	Commercial	Research
	Core Activity	Transaction	Production	Innovation	Matchmaking	Service Delivery
	Key Value Proposition	Financial Value	Emotional Value	Social Value	Informational Value	Environmental Value
Value Capture	Revenue Source	Buyer	Seller	Third Party		
	Revenue Streams	Commissions	Subscriptions	Sales	Sponsorship	Public / Private Funding
	Performance Indicator	Qualitative	Quantitative	Mixed		

Figure 12.1 First conceptualisation of the taxonomy

No new dimensions were added, modified, or deleted in the second iteration. Instead, the workshop served as an interim evaluation of the taxonomy's orientation, and it provided valuable insights for improvement: (1) the overall approach of the taxonomy was evaluated positively regarding its comprehensibility; (2) the taxonomy's abstraction level was perceived as too high, lacking 'hands-on aid' for designers; and (3) delving more deeply into the literature on digital platforms and their business model designs was suggested to provide a more actionable structure for the taxonomy's design dimensions.

12.3 Iteration 3: Conceptual to Empirical

Following the workshop feedback, the conceptual-to-empirical approach was used in conducting a systematic literature review (SLR) on existing platform taxonomies (vom Brocke et al., 2009). As a methodological approach, an SLR allows the researcher to examine a large number of academic publications rather than concentrating on individual studies, which often have a specific focus area (Petticrew & Roberts, 2005). Additionally, SLRs are particularly suited for discovering publications on little-explored issues (Fink, 2020). This SLR follows the guidelines set out by Webster and Watson (2002): (1) identify articles through searching scientific databases (for both journal and conference articles); (2) move backward, examining the citations in the identified articles, and (3) forward, examining articles that cite the identified articles.

To identify relevant literature, the Elsevier Scopus database was searched. The search string was developed in an iterative process (vom Brocke et al., 2009). Based on relevant keywords from the first two iterations, search terms were entered experimentally into the Scopus database, independently and in various combinations, thereby testing their usefulness. By explicitly excluding (e.g., 'cloud') or including (e.g., 'business') keywords, it was possible to achieve significantly more precise results. The final search string consisted of the following combination of Boolean search queries (Karimi, Pohl, Scholer, Cavedon, & Zobel, 2010):

TITLE(platform) AND ABS(taxono* OR typolo* OR ontolo* OR classific* OR morpho*) AND ALL(business) AND NOT(cloud).

The search was carried out in the winter of 2020 over the course of four weeks and revealed 149 articles that were subject to further screening for relevancy. After title screening, 40 articles remained for abstract screening, leaving 11 articles for full reading and detailed content analysis. Forward and backward searching added 3 more articles, leading to a total of 14 articles included in the final selection (see Annex B in the electronic supplementary material) (Figure 12.2).

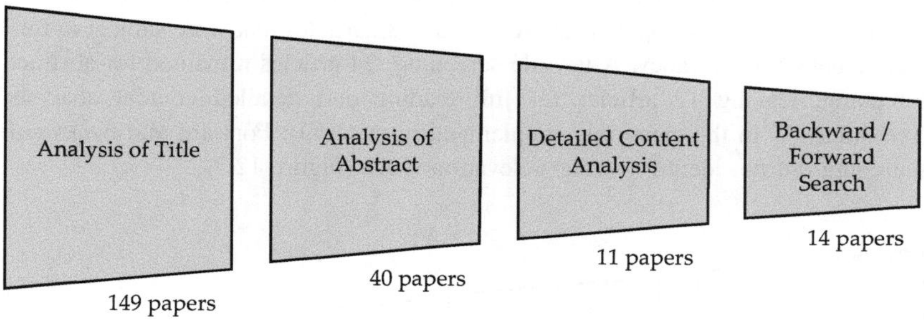

Figure 12.2 Research funnel of the 1st systematic literature review

The final selection of articles included platform taxonomies from the fields of crowdwork (Howcroft & Bergvall-Kåreborn, 2019), collaborative innovation (Aryan, Bertling, & Liedtke, 2021), sharing economy (Chasin et al., 2018), payment (Diniz, Siqueira, & van Heck, 2019), e-commerce (Holland & Gutiérrez-Leefmans, 2018), mobility (Stehlin, Hodson, & McMeekin, 2020), smart city (Walravens, 2014), and platform envelopment (Hermes, Kaufmann-Ludwig, Schreieck, Weking, & Böhm, 2020), as well as more general business model taxonomies (Gatautis, 2017; Kim & Min, 2019; Rix et al., 2020; Staykova & Damsgaard, 2015; Täuscher & Laudien, 2018). To structure our findings from the articles, we applied a classic content analysis strategy. Using the content analysis software MAXQDA, the articles were coded to identify relevant dimensions and corresponding characteristics. The identified dimensions were then checked regarding their transferability to physical interaction platforms.

12.4 Iteration 4: Conceptual to Empirical

The third iteration of the PIP taxonomy highlighted a critical weak point. Existing taxonomies and frameworks are very well suited to classifying platforms, but they do not explain the value creation that takes place on the platforms. However, precisely this aspect is essential in order to offer assistance for practitioners seeking to design PIPs. Therefore, a second systematic literature search on the value-creation mechanisms of platforms was conducted. The search focused on existing literature reviews on this topic. The search string was developed in the same iterative manner as in the third iteration (vom Brocke et al., 2009), consisting of the following Boolean search terms:

TITLE-ABS(value creation AND platforms) AND ABS(literature review).

The search in the Scopus database revealed 82 articles that were subject to further screens for relevancy. After title screening, 24 articles remained for abstract screening, leaving 12 articles for full reading and detailed content analysis (see Annex C in the electronic supplementary material). Forward and backward searching did not identify further relevant articles (Figure 12.3).

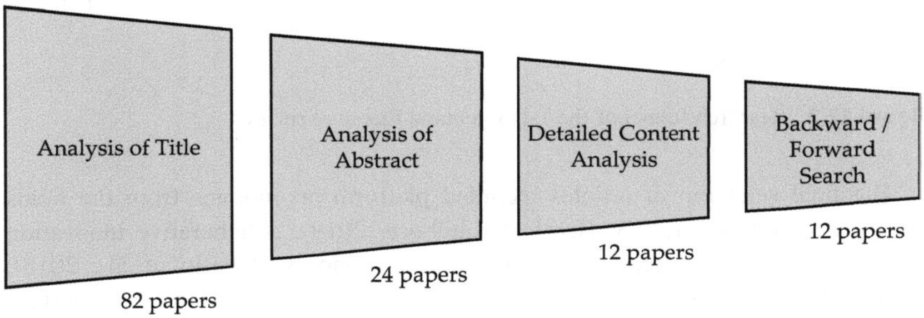

Figure 12.3 Research funnel of the 2nd systematic literature review

The final selection included articles outlining the current state of research on value (co-)creation (Buhalis, Andreu, & Gnoth, 2020; Tudose, Agafitei, & Avasilcai, 2020; Zhang, Lu, Torres, & Cobanoglu, 2020), value creation in ecosystems (Arreola González, Pfaff, & Krcmar, 2019; de Oliveira & Cortimiglia, 2017; Gomes, Facin, Salerno, & Ikenami, 2018; Rietveld & Schilling, 2020), service-dominant logic (Dam, Le Dinh, & Menvielle, 2020), the governance mechanisms of platforms (Alves, Oliveira, & Jansen, 2018; Mukhopadhyay & Bouwman, 2019), and platform business models (To et al., 2018; You et al., 2020). Various dimensions and characteristics and additional findings from these articles were coded using MAXQDA.

12.5 Iteration 5: Empirical to Conceptual (Evaluation with Experts)

The third and fourth iterations provided additional information and structure to address issues identified in the interim evaluation (the expert workshop) and provided a sound conceptual basis for the PIP taxonomy. The fifth iteration followed an empirical-to-conceptual approach, taking the form of expert interviews. Expert interviews are an efficient way of gathering data about a given phenomenon. Experts can serve as 'crystallization points' with high levels of practical knowledge (Bogner, Littig, & Menz, 2009). Therefore, this method was considered appropriate to further develop the taxonomy and to evaluate its usefulness.

A purposive sample (Nickerson et al., 2013) of PIPs was created. To avoid contextual bias, the PIPs were selected according to the characteristics of physical size (small to large) and orientation (innovation, co-working, operation) in order to ensure a heterogeneous sample (Suri, 2011). Interview partners were selected based on their experience in operating and setting up the respective PIP. All interviewees held diverse but high-ranking positions, as shown in Table 12.2. The interviews took place in February and March 2021. They were conducted in German, either face-to-face or via a video-conferencing tool.

Table 12.2 Overview of interview partners

Iteration No.	PIP Type	Interview Partner
5a	Open Innovation Lab	Managing Director
5b	Open Innovation Lab	Scientific Advisor
5c	Innovation Hub	Senior Manager Innovation
5d	Co-Working Space	Managing Director
5e	Start-Up Incubator	Head of Education

The interviews were conducted in a qualitative, open-ended format. The interview partners were presented with the taxonomy and asked to perform a number of tasks as follows: 1) classify their PIP using the taxonomy, (2) add missing dimensions and characteristics, (3) identify dimensions and characteristics ambiguous to them and (4) discuss and contribute actively when certain dimensions and characteristics are missing or ambiguous. The experts were thus invited to contribute their knowledge in a collective and cooperative process of knowledge construction (Meuser & Nagel, 2009). The interviews were recorded, and notes were taken. After each interview, the taxonomy was adjusted according to the expert feedback. Therefore, each interview is a separate iteration of the taxonomy. Table 12.3 provides an overview of the dimensions added or modified for each separate iteration.

Table 12.3 Overview of dimensions added or modified during the iterative process

Dimension	Iterations								
	1	2	3	4	5. Iteration—Interviews				
					5a	5b	5c	5d	5e
Engagement	•	•	•	•	•	•	•	•	•
Position	•	•	•	•	•	•	•	•	•
Accessibility	•		•	•	•	•	•	•	•
Customer Type	•	•	S						
Actor Segments			•	•	R	•	•	•	•
Industry Focus			•	•	R	R	•	•	•
Location	•	•							
Surface Area	•	•							
Appearance	•	•							
Platform Role			•	•	•	•	•	•	•
Core Activity	•	•	•	•	•	•	•	•	•
Value Orientation	•	•							
Key Value Proposition	•	•	S						
Monetary Incentives			•	•	•	•	•	•	•
Non-Monetary Incentives			•	•	•	•	•	•	•
Ecosystem Dimension	•	•		•	•	•	•	•	•
Platform Sides				•	•	•	•	•	•
Coordination Mechanism				•					
Launch Strategy					•	•			
Provider	•	•			•	•			
Owner				•	•	•	•	•	•
Decision Rights				•	•	•	•		
IP Control				•	•	•	•	•	•
Content Control					•	•	•	•	•
Pricing Policy			•	•	•	•	S	•	•
Profit Orientation							•	•	•

(continued)

Table 12.3 (continued)

Dimension	Iterations								
	1	2	3	4	5. Iteration—Interviews				
					5a	5b	5c	5d	5e
Revenue Orientation			R	•					
Revenue Mechanism	•	•	R	•	•	•	•	•	•
Revenue Source	•	•							
Key Performance Indicator	•	•	•	•	•	•	•	•	•
Dimension contained in iteration			•						
Dimension renamed in iteration			R						
Dimension split in iteration			S						

12.6 Completion of the Iterative Development Process

After each iteration, the taxonomy was reviewed concerning the predefined ending conditions. After the last iteration (5e), all ending conditions were satisfied, completing the taxonomy building process. Table 12.4 highlights the ending conditions adopted from Nickerson (2013, p. 344) and their status after each iteration.

Table 12.4 Status of ending conditions after each iteration

Ending Condition	1	2	3	4	5 a	5 b	5 c	5 d	5 e
(1) All objects or a representative sample of objects have been examined									✓
(2) No object was merged with a similar object or split into multiple objects								✓	✓
(3) At least one object is classified for every characteristic of every dimension							✓	✓	✓
(4) No new dimensions or characteristics were added in the last iteration								✓	✓
(5) No dimensions or characteristics were merged or split in the last iteration							✓	✓	✓

(continued)

Table 12.4 (continued)

Ending Condition	**1**	**2**	**3**	**4**	**5 a**	**5 b**	**5 c**	**5 d**	**5 e**
(6) Every dimension is unique and not repeated								✓	✓
(7) Every characteristic is unique within its dimension	✓	✓	✓	✓	✓	✓	✓	✓	✓
(8) Each cell (combination of characteristics) is unique and is not repeated	✓	✓	✓	✓	✓	✓	✓	✓	✓
(9) Concise				✓	✓	✓	✓	✓	✓
(10) Robust								✓	✓
(11) Comprehensive					✓	✓	✓	✓	✓
(12) Extendible	✓	✓	✓	✓	✓	✓	✓	✓	✓
(13) Explanatory			✓	✓	✓	✓	✓	✓	✓

13 The Taxonomy of Physical Interaction Platforms

After analysis and evaluation, the resulting taxonomy includes 18 core dimensions, each with a subset of characteristics describing PIPs (Figure 13.1). To provide better structure, the dimensions are grouped into the following categories: *physical architecture, customers, key value propositions, value creation,* and *revenue logic.* In line with the principle of parsimony (Bailey, 1994), some dimensions (marked with *) allow for the selection of multiple characteristics to reduce the taxonomy´s overall complexity.

13.1 Physical Architecture

One significant difference compared to digital platforms is that PIPs have physical properties that are difficult to change. While digital platforms can theoretically be scaled indefinitely, the physical properties of PIPs have important influence on whether the intended actor segments can be reached in terms of time and geographical location (Aryan et al., 2021).

13.1.1 Engagement

Engagement describes whether the PIP takes place in an event-oriented manner or whether it is set for the long term and designed for continuity (Roth et al., 2014). A fundamental distinction is made between temporary and continuous engagements—e.g., between a pop-up laboratory and an institutionalised innovation space.

M. Perez Mengual, *Designing Physical Interaction Platforms*,
Markt- und Unternehmensentwicklung Markets and Organisations,
https://doi.org/10.1007/978-3-658-41920-2_13

13.1.2 Position

Position describes the mobility of a PIP. A mobile PIP often has the character of a campaign, moving purposefully to places where relevant actors are located (e.g., the BMW Guggenheim Lab). Stationary PIPs are infrastructures geared towards continuity (e.g., corporate innovation labs).

13.1.3 Accessibility to the public

Accessibility to the public describes the extent to which PIPs are open to the respective customer groups (Rix et al., 2020). An open PIP allows uncontrolled access (e.g., to an open innovation lab), whereas a closed PIP is not accessible to the public (e.g., a corporate innovation lab). A PIP with controlled accessibility uses specific selection mechanisms such as memberships, invitations, or events.

13.2 Platform Actors

13.2.1 Actor Segments

The actor segments dimension describes possible actors the PIP connects as participants, including business-to-business (B2B), business-to-consumers (B2C) or consumers-to-consumers (Rix et al., 2020; Täuscher & Laudien, 2018). A notable phenomenon that can be noted in this context, often occurring in spaces with open access, is the so-called 'consumerized B2B,' where businesses appear in the form of private persons not immediately displaying their business affiliation or intent.

13.2.2 Industry Focus

Industry focus specifies whether the PIP enables vertical or horizontal integration (Täuscher & Laudien, 2018), where the former means the PIP focuses on a specific industry or group of customers with specialised requirements or needs (e.g. the IKEA Space 10[1], an innovation lab focusing solely on the future of living), while the latter occurs when the PIP meets the demands of several industries or a large group of customers (Li et al., 2006).

[1] Space 10 is a research and design lab in Copenhagen supported by IKEA. The lab follows a collaborative approach, regularly hosting exhibitions and events and inviting people to come and share their thoughts with the designers of the lab.

	Dimension	Characteristics					
Physical Architecture	*Engagement*	Temporary	Continuous				
Physical Architecture	*Position*	Stationary	Mobile				
Physical Architecture	*Accessibility to public*	Open	Controlled	Closed			
Platform Actors	*Actor segments**	B2B	B2C	C2C			
Platform Actors	*Industry focus*	Vertical	Horizontal				
Key Value Propositions	*Platform role**	Market creation	Operation	Co-creation			
Key Value Propositions	*Core activity**	Transaction	Innovation	Matchmaking / networking	Co-working	Service provision	
Key Value Propositions	*Monetary incentives**	Cost reduction	Additional sales	Performance increase	Decreased time-to-market	No incentive	
Key Value Propositions	*Non-monetary incentives**	Access	User experience	Social exchange	Visibility	Information/ scouting	
		Testing/quality control	Organisational transformation	Inspiration	No incentive		
Value Creation – Ecosystem	*Ecosystem dimension*	Local	Regional	National	International		
Value Creation – Ecosystem	*Platform sides*	One-sided	Two-sided	Multi-sided			
Value Creation – Governance	*Owner*	Single organisation	Multi-organisation	Community			
Value Creation – Governance	*IP control*	Proprietary	Open access				
Value Creation – Governance	*Content-control*	Responsible for content	Partially responsible for content	Not responsible for content			
Revenue Logic	*Profit orientation*	Non-profit	For-profit				
Revenue Logic	*Pricing policy*	Symmetric	Asymmetric	No pricing			
Revenue Logic	*Revenue mechanism**	Transaction fee	Subscriptions	Direct selling	Project-based	Third-party funding	
Revenue Logic	*Key performance indicator**	Revenue	Number of interactions	Productivity increase	Media coverage	Ecosystem growth	PIP utilisation

Figure 13.1 The taxonomy of physical interaction platforms

13.3 Key Value Propositions

The category of key value propositions contains descriptions of the benefits offered to the platform participants and what kind of value is generated (Gassmann et al., 2013). Value propositions are essential to facilitating interaction and gaining traction. Without properly designed offerings as well as monetary and non-monetary incentives, a PIP will have difficulties attracting platform actors (Mukhopadhyay & Bouwman, 2019).

13.3.1 Platform Role

A key difference lies in the role that the PIP fulfils—market, operation, or co-creation (Hermes et al., 2020; Konietzko, Bocken, & Hultink, 2019). Market PIPs orchestrate economic interactions between the platform actors as a central asset for creating value (Chasin et al., 2018; Van Alstyne & Parker, 2017). Operation PIPs act as a connecting element between platform actors to facilitate the joint provision of products or services (e.g. the Y Combinator[2] providing the necessary development infrastructure to start-up companies). Finally, co-creation PIPs serve as enablers of open innovation, empowerment and citizen and community participation (Konietzko et al., 2019). They typically enable the exchange of knowledge and information and provide means for feedback, creation, innovation, learning, and networking (You et al., 2020).

13.3.2 Core Activity

Core activity comprises the interaction that takes place between the platform actors. This interaction may focus on product transactions (e.g., in stationary retail), joint innovation activities, matchmaking or networking between platform actors, providing office spaces, or providing services mediated by the PIP (e.g., equipment for maker spaces) (Holland & Gutiérrez-Leefmans, 2018).

[2] Y Combinator is a US-based start-up incubator headquartered in California, supporting companies during their start-up phase with funding, consultancy and business contacts.

13.3.3 Monetary Incentives (to Platform Actors)

It can be distinguished between monetary incentives and non-monetary incentives. Monetary incentives focus on utilitarian value by providing advantages in price or cost as well as increasing efficiency or performance (Gatautis, 2017; Täuscher & Laudien, 2018). Additionally, PIPs can offer benefits in terms of additional sales, essentially functioning as a sales channel. For open innovation labs, decreased time-to-market can serve as an incentive due to co-creation activities building target audiences (O'Hern & Rindfleisch, 2010).

13.3.4 Non-monetary Incentives (to Platform Actors)

Non-monetary incentives focus on emotional or social value (Gatautis, 2017; Täuscher & Laudien, 2018). They serve as an important motivational factor for participation in PIPs. For businesses, PIPs can offer access to a certain target group (e.g., for recruiting purposes) or act as a tool for organisational transformation (e.g., by offering a testbed for the application of innovation toolsets). PIPs can also provide visibility (e.g., for start-ups or in terms of employer branding) or serve as testbeds for user tests and quality control. For people seeking inspiration, social exchange, information, or simply interested in an entertaining user experience, PIPs serve as focal points.

13.4 Value creation

For platforms, value creation takes place non-linearly in interactions orchestrated by the platform (Ramaswamy & Ozcan, 2018). Central aspects of value creation include the platform ecosystem with potential actors and platform governance, i.e., rules that shape the interactions taking place (Parker et al., 2016). Governance clarifies who may participate, how value is created and divided, and how conflict is resolved (Parker et al., 2016).

13.4.1 Platform Ecosystem: Ecosystem Dimension

In the context of PIPs, we can classify the geographic dimension of the ecosystem, ranging from local to international (Rix et al., 2020; Täuscher & Laudien,

2018). This applies to both stationary and mobile PIPs. In the case of stationary PIPs, this refers to the catchment area of the recurring participating actors, while in the case of mobile PIPs, this relates to the radius of action. In the PIP taxonomy, the largest geographic dimension includes the smaller ones (e.g., a regionally operating PIP includes actors from the local vicinity).

13.4.2 Platform Ecosystem: Platform Sides

Platforms always facilitate interaction between two or more different actors. Platform sides refers to how many different groups the platform addresses. A distinction can be made between one-sided, two-sided, and multi-sided platforms. One-sided means only one group is addressed, as apparent in communities where the PIP links different community members to each other (e.g. in the case of the Noisebridge[3] hackerspace). While a clear distinction as to where to set boundaries between groups may not always be evident, in the present work, one-sided platforms mean that the target group is addressed by the same value proposition. Two-sided means that the platform facilitates interaction between two different groups of actors, such as between a private person and a corporation. In this case, separate value propositions are needed for the platform actors—e.g., in marketplaces, where one actor (seller) has a large audience to sell to and the other actor profits from the supplier-price competition. Multi-sided means that the interaction takes place between three or more different actors—e.g., between private persons, corporations, research organisations, and governmental agencies.

13.4.3 Governance: Owner

The owner dimension of a taxonomy details whose property the platform is, and the owner role determines who has decision rights, is responsible for the PIP's development, and ensures the PIP's functionality (Gatautis, 2017; Parker et al., 2016). The owner role can be occupied by a single organisation, a federation of multiple organisations, or a community of people. This means that decision rights are located within one platform actor, shared among a defined group of platform

[3] Noisebridge is an anarchist hackerspace community in San Francisco. It is a registered non-profit corporation and run entirely by volunteers.

actors, or held equally among all platform actors. The owner role and corresponding decision rights are essential to the control of the platform's ecosystem (Mukhopadhyay & Bouwman, 2019; Parker et al., 2016).

13.4.4 Governance: Intellectual Property Control

Intellectual property (IP) control specifies the handling of IP that is generated during interactions on the PIP. IP control can take on the form of proprietary IP or open access. Proprietary means that the IP is the sole property of certain actors, and the platform makes efforts (in the form of contracts, access restrictions, etc.) to protect these rights. Open access means that the content of interactions and the resulting IP is shared by all platform actors. For closed/corporate PIPs, IP control is usually less of an issue, with IP belonging to the platform owner—the corporation. In the context of hackerspaces, for example, where computer code is shared among users or incubators hosting events such as hackathons, IP rights require definition.

13.4.5 Governance: Content Control

Content control refers to the degree to which the platform owner is responsible for what is happening during the interactions taking place in the PIP (Walravens, 2014). Content control has a strong influence on how the PIP acts towards the platform actors. On the extreme side, content control could rely on communities managing themselves with the risk of unwanted behaviour, or it could take the form of an enforcing authority relying on strict rules, possibly deterring platform actors. Thus, content control is about balancing the norms and rules of a PIP (Diniz et al., 2019; Mukhopadhyay & Bouwman, 2019; Parker et al., 2016)

13.5 Revenue Logic

The revenue logic category contains all dimensions of monetisation and the measurement of the success of a PIP. It describes how the PIP transforms value delivered to the platform actors into revenue. However, especially in the context of third-party-funded PIPs, performance is often not measured in terms of revenue but in terms of other performance indicators, as illustrated below.

13.5.1 Profit Orientation

Profit orientation can be divided into non-profit and profit-oriented (W. You et al., 2020), which strongly impacts the business structure (e.g. limited liability company, partnership, corporation) and associated benefits (e.g. tax exemption) the PIP can adopt. On the downside, a society or association may only act according to its statutes, and any revenue generated must be reinvested, thereby severely impacting the organisation's adaptability.

13.5.2 Pricing Policy

Pricing policy distinguishes three categories of pricing—symmetric, asymmetric, and no pricing. Symmetric means that revenue is taken from all participating platform actors (e.g., in a co-working space, all co-workers pay their share). Asymmetric means that revenue is only taken from one participating platform actor, or at least not distributed equally among the platform actors. The pricing dimension provides information about how difficult it is for a platform to acquire stakeholders. With symmetrical pricing, the market is in equilibrium; with asymmetrical pricing, a platform is subsidised on one side (Jullien & Pavan, 2019; Kaiser & Wright, 2006). There are also platforms that do not have a pricing policy. In this case, funding is subsidised by third parties.

13.5.3 Revenue Mechanism

The revenue mechanism deals with the way revenue is generated. It can be distinguished between transaction fees, subscriptions, retail sales, project-based revenue, and third-party funding (Chasin et al., 2018; Täuscher & Laudien, 2018). Transaction fees entail that a set percentage of each transaction or interaction is kept by the platform owner. Subscriptions comprise any type of regular income generated by the platform through membership fees. Direct selling is associated with any transaction that involves the sale of products or services over the counter. Project-based revenue is generated through the execution of projects (i.e., an innovation project). Third-party funding summarises any revenue generated from additional sources (e.g., sponsorship or governmental funding).

13.5.4 Key Performance Indicator

In the context of physical interaction platforms, which can take a variety of different forms, such as living labs, makerspaces, or corporate innovation hubs, revenue is not always the key performance indicator (KPI) to measure the platform's success. Additional KPIs include the number of interactions, productivity increases, media coverage, ecosystem growth, and PIP utilisation. The number of interactions is strongly associated with network effects, measuring how many actors are using the platform. Productivity increases include any kind of performance improvement that occurs through the use of the platform (i.e., increased innovation output). Media coverage refers to the amount of attention the PIP receives in the media, while ecosystem growth refers to new entrants/actors into the platform's ecosystem. The KPI of PIP utilisation is often used in the context of corporate platforms or co-working spaces and refers to the amount of occupancy or how often the PIP is used by the platform actors.

Application of the PIP Taxonomy 14

To illustrate the usefulness of the taxonomy in describing PIPs, this chapter illustrates the application of the taxonomy. Two examples were chosen to show that the taxonomy works for several manifestations of PIPs—JOSEPHS as an open innovation (OI) lab and WeWork as a co-working space.

14.1 Illustrative Case: Open Innovation Lab

JOSEPHS was founded in 2014 in Nuremberg, Germany. It is an open innovation lab where products and services are developed co-creatively. JOSEPHS acts as an innovation platform and mediates between companies and individuals. Product and service innovations are exhibited by companies in an area of 400 m^2. Individuals are invited to discover them, try them out, and contribute their own ideas in order to advance product and service innovations and bring them to market maturity (Figure 14.1).

M. Perez Mengual, *Designing Physical Interaction Platforms*,
Markt- und Unternehmensentwicklung Markets and Organisations,
https://doi.org/10.1007/978-3-658-41920-2_14

14.1.1 Classification of Physical Architecture of the JOSEPHS OI Lab

The JOSEPHS OI lab was designed for permanent use and is located at a stationary site in the centre of Nuremberg. It is open daily during regular hours, comparable to those of retail stores. Visitors can patronise JOSEPHS at any time during these hours and without an appointment. Accessibility is therefore classified as open.

14.1.2 Classification of Platform Actors of the JOSEPHS OI Lab

JOSEPHS mediates between companies and private individuals. The actor segments are, therefore, primarily classified as B2C. This refers to the interaction taking place within JOSEPHS. Of course, each platform that appears as a standalone entity requires some functionalities that are B2B—e.g., acquisition activities and services such as training and workshop facilitation. However, in the case of the JOSEPHS, these serve as support for B2C interaction. The industry focus is classified as horizontal, as companies from different industries are addressed. Furthermore, the products and services on display change every three months to offer variety to visitors.

	Dimension	Characteristics					
Physical Architecture	*Engagement*	Temporary	**Continuous**				
Physical Architecture	*Position*	**Stationary**	Mobile				
Physical Architecture	*Accessibility to public*	**Open**	Controlled	Closed			
Platform Actors	*Actor segments**	B2B	**B2C**	C2C			
Platform Actors	*Industry focus*	Vertical	**Horizontal**				
Key Value Propositions	*Platform role**	Market creation	Operation	**Co-creation**			
Key Value Propositions	*Core activity**	Transaction	**Innovation**	**Matchmaking/ networking**	**Co-working**	**Service provision**	
Key Value Propositions	*Monetary incentives**	Cost reduction	Additional sales	Performance increase	**Decreased time-to-market**	**No incentive**	
Key Value Propositions	*Non-monetary incentives**	**Access**	User experience	Social exchange	**Visibility**	Information/ Scouting	
Key Value Propositions	*Non-monetary incentives**	**Testing/quality control**	**Organisational transformation**	**Inspiration**	No incentive		
Value Creation – Ecosystem	*Ecosystem dimension*	Local	**Regional**	National	International		
Value Creation – Ecosystem	*Platform sides*	One-sided	**Two-sided**	Multi-sided			
Value Creation – Governance	*Owner*	**Single organisation**	Multi-Organisation	Community			
Value Creation – Governance	*IP control*	Proprietary	**Open access**				
Value Creation – Governance	*Content-control*	Responsible for content	**Partially responsible for content**	Not responsible for content			
Revenue Logic	*Profit orientation*	**Non-profit**	For-profit				
Revenue Logic	*Pricing policy*	Symmetric	**Asymmetric**	No pricing			
Revenue Logic	*Revenue mechanism**	Transaction fee	Subscriptions	Direct selling	**Project-based**	**Third-party funding**	
Revenue Logic	*Key performance indicator**	**Revenue**	**Number of interactions**	Productivity increase	**Media coverage**	Ecosystem growth	**PIP utilisation**

Figure 14.1 Classification of the JOSEPHS OI Lab

14.1.3 Classification of Key Value Propositions of the JOSEPHS OI Lab

The role of the JOSEPHS platform can be classified as co-creation. Its purpose lies in the facilitation of joint innovation activities. Regarding the monetary incentives, the participating companies profit from a decreased time-to-market for their products and services. In terms of non-monetary incentives, JOSEPHS provides access to knowledge from a large pool of visitors, increases visibility for each company, and serves as a testbed for the company's products and services. Furthermore, companies use JOSEPHS to teach their employees agile and innovative development approaches, thereby driving organisational transformation. Consumers/visitors of JOSEPHS have no financial incentive for participation. They participate mainly because they are looking for inspiration and exciting, novel products and services.

14.1.4 Classification of Value Creation of the JOSEPHS OI Lab

The ecosystem of JOSEPHS is classified as regional. The participating actors are recruited from a larger peripheral area around the physical location. The platform mediates between companies and consumers and can therefore be classified as two-sided. JOSEPHS is operated by one company (single-organisation owner) with centralised decision rights. As it is an OI laboratory, there is no direct IP control. All ideas generated there can be used by the participating stakeholders in the spirit of open access. The organisation that operates JOSEPHS is not directly responsible for the content exhibited there, but it selects the participating companies and enforces rules (i.e., no political content). Therefore, the level of content control is classified as partial responsibility.

14.1.5 Classification of Revenue Logic of the JOSEPHS OI Lab

JOSEPHS is part of a non-profit organisation and is therefore not permitted to have a purely profit-oriented orientation. Pricing is asymmetrical: companies pay for their presence on site and for the generated data. For visitors, JOSEPHS is free of charge. The main revenue mechanisms are paid projects (each company's presence is a project) and third-party funding from the federal government. The success of JOSEPHS is measured with several KPIs. Revenue stands for itself but also indicates the overall attractiveness of the OI lab concept for companies. Other important KPIs relate to the quality of interactions taking place, i.e., the number of interactions, media coverage, and utilisation of JOSEPHS (e.g., through events).

14.2 Illustrative Case: Co-working Space

Founded in 2010 in New York City, WeWork is a commercial company that provides flexible, shared workspaces and services for entrepreneurs and businesses. With 800 locations in more than 100 cities, WeWork brokers available office space between landlords and users. WeWork operates the digital brokerage platform and serves as the on-site contact, as well as taking care of the interior design of the office and shared spaces. Each of the 800 co-working spaces operates according to the same principle; for the following example, any WeWork co-working space in, say, Berlin, London, or Tel Aviv can be imagined (Figure 14.2).

14.2.1 Classification of Physical Architecture of a WeWork Co-working Space

WeWork's co-working spaces are designed for permanent use and are located at stationary sites. To gain access to a WeWork space, a membership is needed. Access to the space is therefore controlled.

14.2.2 Classification of Platform Actors of a WeWork Co-working Space

WeWork mediates office space between real estate providers and entrepreneurs or companies and can therefore be classified as B2B. The industry focus is horizontal, as WeWork is aimed at anyone who needs a flexible workplace, regardless of industry affiliation.

Layer	Dimension	Characteristics				
Physical Architecture	*Engagement*	Temporary	**Continuous**			
Physical Architecture	*Position*	**Stationary**	Mobile			
Physical Architecture	*Accessibility to public*	Open	**Controlled**	Closed		
Platform Actors	*Actor segments**	**B2B**	B2C	C2C		
Platform Actors	*Industry focus*	Vertical	**Horizontal**			
Key Value Propositions	*Platform role**	Market creation	**Operation**	Co-creation		
Key Value Propositions	*Core activity**	Transaction	Innovation	Matchmaking/ networking	**Co-working**	Service provision
Key Value Propositions	*Monetary incentives**	**Cost reduction**	Additional sales	Performance increase	Decreased time-to-market	No incentive
Key Value Propositions	*Non-monetary incentives**	**Access**	**User experience**	Social exchange	Visibility	Information / Scouting
Key Value Propositions	*Non-monetary incentives**	Testing/quality control	Organisational transformation	Inspiration	No incentive	
Value Creation – Ecosystem	*Ecosystem dimension*	**Local**	Regional	National	International	
Value Creation – Ecosystem	*Platform sides*	One-sided	**Two-sided**	Multi-sided		
Value Creation – Governance	*Owner*	**Single organisation**	Multi-Organisation	Community		
Value Creation – Governance	*IP control*	**Proprietary**	Open access			
Value Creation – Governance	*Content-control*	Responsible for content	**Partially responsible for content**	Not responsible for content		
Revenue Logic	*Profit orientation*	Non-profit	**For-profit**			
Revenue Logic	*Pricing policy*	Symmetric	**Asymmetric**	No pricing		
Revenue Logic	*Revenue mechanism**	Transaction fee	**Subscriptions**	Direct selling	Project-based	Third-party funding
Revenue Logic	*Key performance indicator**	**Revenue**	Number of interactions	Productivity increase	Media coverage	Ecosystem growth	**PIP utilisation**

Figure 14.2 Classification of a WeWork co-working-space

14.2.3 Classification of Key Value Propositions of a WeWork Co-working Space

The role of the WeWork platform can be considered 'operation' since its purpose is only the provision of workspace. Likewise, the core activity lies in the provision of workspace and related utilities. The provided benefit consists of the monetary incentive of cost reduction, as well as the non-monetary incentives of access to workspace and good user experience through booking systems and all-inclusive packages in terms of utilities.

14.2.4 Classification of Value Creation of a WeWork Co-working Space

The ecosystem of a WeWork co-working space is classified as local, meaning that the catchment area of the actors is usually spatially limited to a given city. The platform mediates between property owners and users and can therefore be classified as two-sided. However, the platform is operated by one company (single-organisation owner) with centralised decision rights. IP created on the platform remains owned by the actors (e.g., entrepreneurs and companies) and is not shared within these spaces, therefore classified as proprietary. WeWork is partly responsible for the content of the interactions using the platform, in the sense that the work of the actors is not controlled, but rules are enforced (e.g., no use of office space for retail, medical, or non-business purposes).

14.2.5 Classification of Revenue Logic of a WeWork Co-working Space

WeWork is a listed company and has a clear for-profit orientation. The pricing is asymmetrical. Only the tenants (entrepreneurs and companies) pay for the use of the WeWork platform. The landlords are attracted to the platform by other incentives such as low effort. In order to use WeWork, a flexible membership must be subscribed to, which is scaled according to the respective requirements. The revenue mechanism can therefore be classified as a subscription. WeWork is less concerned with the quality of the interactions taking place, instead focusing on increasing revenue, which is achieved by maximising utilisation.

Discussion and Implications 15

This chapter discusses the theoretical contributions and practical implications of the PIP taxonomy. Practitioners and designers of PIPs can benefit from the taxonomy as a basis for applying morphological analysis and the systematic exploration of ideas and concepts (Geum, Jeon, & Lee, 2016; Le Masson et al., 2009). The taxonomy functions as a tool for creativity and analysis, leading to the right questions being asked and thereby paving the way for sustainable and prosperous PIPs. However, it is acknowledged that building and operating a vibrant PIP goes beyond choosing design characteristics—a focus on organisational fit, employees and the community is also needed.

A classification instrument for physical interaction platforms: The taxonomy provides a tool for scholars to classify different types of PIPs. Contrary to other classifications (Gryszkiewicz, Lykourentzou, & Toivonen, 2016; McCrory, Schäpke, Holmén, & Holmberg, 2020), the developed taxonomy does not label PIPs (e.g. 'living lab' or 'innovation hub'). Instead, it allows a classification based on design characteristics, more accurately describing what is happening in the PIP. It is hoped that this approach will assist in sorting through the different conceptualisations, definitions and operationalisations of innovation spaces (Bogers et al., 2017) and will thus contribute to advancing the understanding of these different places and spaces for collaborative innovation.

PIP design is business model design: Contemporary research focuses strongly on 'what' happens in PIPs. This research contributes to an area underrepresented in the literature: 'how' PIPs can be designed (Westerlund et al., 2018). Derived from the literature on platform business models, the developed taxonomy emphasises the value creation mechanisms of PIPs. It is suggested that designing PIPs should be understood as a business model development process (Van Alstyne & Parker, 2017) that involves designing value propositions for PIP actors, designing

M. Perez Mengual, *Designing Physical Interaction Platforms*, Markt- und Unternehmensentwicklung Markets and Organisations, https://doi.org/10.1007/978-3-658-41920-2_15

the value creation mechanism and ensuring long-term operation by designing a revenue model.

A starting point for PIP concept development: Building on established design dimensions from the well-known business model and value creation literature, the taxonomy offers a simple and tangible approach to PIP design. It can be used to run through different scenarios, comparing them to each other in terms of organisational requirements and available resources. In this respect, the taxonomy is strongly influenced by the theoretical contributions of Ramaswamy and Ozcan (2018), as value creation results from a constellation of physical artifacts, internal processes and people. Having a clear idea of interactions and target groups at an early stage is essential, as the scalability of network effects is highly dependent on the geographical location. The selection of a suitable property should therefore correspond to the PIP concept. Conversely, if a property is already available, the taxonomy can help to develop a concept appropriate to the location. The taxonomy development process also showed that many design dimensions of online platforms can be transferred to physical platforms but must be interpreted differently. For example, the incentives and value propositions of PIPs are often far more diverse and tactile than those of digital platforms, which tend to be more specialised in their value proposition.

Development of long-term operating PIPs: One observed phenomenon is that innovation spaces are often created and quickly disappear again (Berengian, 2017; Osorio et al., 2019). This applies both to the corporate context as well as to innovation spaces in the research landscape. Through the business model structure, the taxonomy reveals design dimensions necessary for creating sustainable and permanently successful PIPs. The taxonomy should lead designers towards asking the right questions: What is the actual value proposition of the PIP? How do we get the stakeholders on board, so that network effects emerge? How do we secure long-term financing beyond the launch? What kind of success do we report to our stakeholders? The taxonomy integrates research from several disciplines involving value creation, performance (Osorio et al., 2019), ecosystems, and governance (Alves et al., 2018; de Oliveira & Cortimiglia, 2017; Mukhopadhyay & Bouwman, 2019; Peschl & Fundneider, 2014), extending them to important aspects of business administration that are necessary for the sustained operation of the PIP. With the taxonomy as a basis, such dimensions can be considered at an early stage, leading overall to sustainable, long-term engagement.

Advancement of existing PIPs: In addition to its function as a tool in concept development, the taxonomy can also be used for the further development of existing PIPs. Classifying one's own PIP can highlight potential inconsistencies between dimensions. Especially for dimensions that allow multiple selections, the taxonomy can support further development. What would it be like if an innovation lab (core activity: innovation) also sold developed products (core activity: transaction)?

Implications for PIP operation: The taxonomy also provides guidance for the operational management of the PIP. In particular, issues such as accessibility, IP control, and content control require the establishment of internal processes and rules that ensure the functioning of the PIP. Accessibility plays a role in defining opening hours and has an impact on staff capacity and efforts. Early clarification of how to deal with IP arising in the PIP is essential, especially in the case of a PIP with multiple owners. The creation of appropriate frameworks has a decisive influence on trust in the interactions and, thus, on the effectiveness of the PIP. Content control has effects on both external and internal actors. This example is particularly familiar in large, opinion-forming tech companies. Is Facebook a media company and thus responsible for its content, or is it really just a platform for third-party content? This question also applies to PIPs and influences, among other things, the external appearance as an unaffiliated site or as an intermediary for other actors. With regard to internal stakeholders, content control determines how conflicts are resolved. Does the owner intervene and clarify the situation in the event of undesirable behaviour or breaches of rules? Is there an ombudsperson who mediates between conflicting parties? Or are conflicts discussed by the entire community? Each of these variants has a strong influence on the atmosphere and ecosystem of a PIP.

Meeting organisational requirements: The taxonomy refers exclusively to designable dimensions related to value creation on PIPs. We recognise that this is only the starting point for a development process and that this development process must begin with an assessment of an organisation's orientation and employees. Developing a PIP without organisational fit will not work—it requires alignment with an organisation's strategy, processes and, most importantly, employees and community.

Expectation management of policymakers: Insights gained from this research hold implications for policymakers, who frequently provide funding for PIP development projects. As with digital platforms, it is vital to understand a PIP as an innovation, i.e. something new to the organisation building it. PIPs offer new interactions and functionalities to the actors using them, requiring behavioural changes from the actors operating, as well as from the actors using the PIP.

Thus, creating a PIP goes beyond simply creating a physical space. Configuring its value-creating elements and allowing the formation of a PIP's actor ecosystem is time-intensive. Therefore, necessary changes to the original design should be encouraged and understood as an evolution of the PIP. This disruptiveness, time- and resource-intensity and the need for continuous (re-)configuration should be considered when planning and funding future PIP development projects.

16 Summary and Outlook

Building on Nickerson et al.'s (2013) method, the present research developed a taxonomy for physical interaction platforms such as innovation labs, co-working spaces, makerspaces, and incubators. A total of five iterations were conducted, three of which were conceptual in nature based on a screening of the empirical field and systematic literature reviews, and two iterations were conducted on an empirical basis in the form of an expert workshop and expert interviews with operators of PIPs. The taxonomy brings together insights from current research on innovation spaces with insights from business model and value (co-) creation research. It consists of a total of 18 dimensions summarised in the following five groups: physical architecture (engagement, position, accessibility), platform actors (actor segments, industry focus), key value propositions (platform role, core activity, monetary incentives, non-monetary incentives), value creation (ecosystem dimension, platforms sides, owner, IP control, content control), and revenue logic (profit orientation, pricing, revenue mechanism, KPI). The taxonomy was evaluated with regard to its reliability and discriminatory power. Moreover, it fulfils the defined meta-characteristic by describing dimensions and characteristics that are important for explaining PIP value creation, thereby serving as a design framework for practitioners and designers seeking to conceptualise PIPs. It allows replication and application to a large number of cases and is extendible to further design characteristics (Nickerson et al., 2013).

The taxonomy contributes to the theory of innovation spaces as it provides a structure for the classification and accordingly aligned discussion of PIPs. The taxonomy also highlights the criticality of the business model as part of PIP design. Beyond physical layout, PIP designers must develop value propositions for the PIP actors, the value creation mechanism and a revenue model. It will be a worthwhile topic for future research to explore in-depth the role of a PIP's business model and to gain a better overview of business models applied in PIPs.

M. Perez Mengual, *Designing Physical Interaction Platforms*,
Markt- und Unternehmensentwicklung Markets and Organisations,
https://doi.org/10.1007/978-3-658-41920-2_16

Yet, there are limitations to this research. As described by Nickerson (2013), a taxonomy is never really exhaustive and perfect—rather, it is based on intended audience and usefulness. In addition, a qualitative approach in the form of expert interviews was deliberately chosen for the evaluation. Despite a selection of heterogeneous PIPs with different orientations, the list remains limited. It cannot be ruled out that an increase in the number of cases would reveal additional characteristics. However, to emphasise the plasticity of the taxonomy, researchers are strongly encouraged to adapt it according to their own purposes and research findings (as suggested by Nickerson et al., 2013).

The insights generated during the taxonomy development process have implications for the remainder of this dissertation. The PIP taxonomy illustrates design dimensions necessary for PIP value creation. This implies that systematic and structured PIP design within these dimensions is possible, leading to the following research questions: *How can a PIP systematically be designed?* (RQ 3) and *What are the challenges and turning points in the design process of a PIP?* (RQ 4). These questions are investigated in Part IV of this dissertation, which explores the design process of a PIP from conceptualisation to opening.

Part IV

From Scratchboard to Opening: An Action Research Study to Explore the Design Process of PIPs

Objectives and Structure 17

This dissertation seeks to explore *how a physical interaction platform (PIP) can be designed in a systematic and structured way.* Part IV supports this objective by exploring the design process of a PIP, from first conceptualisation to final implementation. Part III explored which design dimensions and characteristics comprise a PIP. However, a process is needed that leads to the identification and selection of these individual characteristics. Furthermore, there is more to design processes than purely combining design characteristics. Part IV examines the dynamics and challenges of PIP design processes. To shed light on this issue, a 17-month action research study was conducted, consisting of two cycles of the following AR phases: diagnosing, planning action, taking action, and evaluating action (Coghlan & Brannick, 2005). The study took place at the EUREF Campus in Berlin, accompanying the design process of a PIP from early conceptualisation to implementation. This section of the dissertation seeks to answer the following research questions:

RQ 3: *How can a PIP systematically be designed?*
RQ 4: *What are the challenges and turning points in the design process of a PIP?*

Part IV is structured as follows. Chapter 18 introduces the action research methodology (Brannick & Coghlan, 2007) and describes the study´s particular AR project in detail. Following this, Chapters 19 and 20 describe both AR cycles and their respective results. Chapter 21 highlights and discusses the effects of the

---

Part IV of this dissertation builds upon and extends a conference contribution, which was presented and discussed at the 16th Research Colloquium on Innovation & Value Creation in Leipzig (replaced to Nuremberg), Germany (Perez Mengual, 2021).

M. Perez Mengual, *Designing Physical Interaction Platforms*, Markt- und Unternehmensentwicklung Markets and Organisations, https://doi.org/10.1007/978-3-658-41920-2_17

interventions in both AR cycles and proposes a systematic process as well as an organisational model for designing PIPs. Chapter 22 points out the implications for both theory as well as practitioners. In addition, it summarises the results of Part IV and puts them in the context of this dissertation. The structure of Part IV is shown in Figure 17.1.

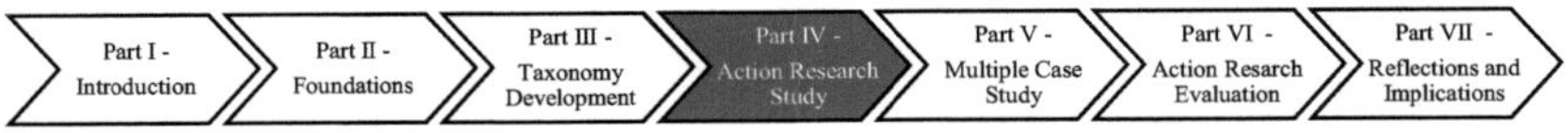

1 Objectives and Structure

- Objectives and purpose of part IV
- Overview of chapters in part IV

2 Research Approach: Action Research

- Action research case and context
- Data collection and analysis

3 First Action Research Cycle

- Description of first AR cycle: concept development
- Findings of first AR cycle

4 Second Action Research Cycle

- Description of second AR cycle: implementation
- Findings of second AR cycle

5 Discussion and Contributions

- Discussion of findings
- Structured approach for building PIPs
- Organisational model for building PIPs

6 Summary and Outlook

- Summary of findings and limitations of the research
- Implications for this dissertation

Figure 17.1 Structure of Part IV

18 Research Approach: Action Research

Given the intention to research how a physical interaction platform can be built, action research was chosen as the mode of inquiry. Action research was originally developed by Kurt Lewin as a contrast to experimental social psychology to establish a science that is practice-oriented and whose implications lead to solutions of practice-relevant problems (Lewin, 1946). The methodology developed by Lewin has been adopted by management researchers for use in organisations to solve organisational problems (e.g., Lindgren, Henfridsson, & Schultze, 2004). AR as a scientific method allows for the development and testing of practical interventions using organisations as a 'real-world laboratory.' By observing the actual change resulting from the intervention, both theoretical and practical knowledge can be created (Lindgren et al., 2004). With AR, it is possible to generate relevant practical insights while simultaneously advancing scientific knowledge (Susman & Evered, 1978). AR also fulfils another purpose—the researcher influences the outcome, i.e., the developed solution (Susman & Evered, 1978). Instead of just studying a real-world problem, action researchers use their knowledge to assist practitioners in solving real-world problems (Lindgren et al., 2004). Accordingly, AR is particularly suited to investigating developmental processes in organisations, like the development of a PIP. Moreover, AR serves as an umbrella term for several interventionist approaches (Baskerville & Wood-Harper, 1998; Huang, 2010; Ollila & Yström, 2020). The present research follows the approach of Coghlan and Brannick (2005), as it is widely adopted and provides clear guidelines on how to conduct rigorous action research. According to Coghlan and Brannick (2005), action research is iterative, consisting of cycles. Each cycle involves four different stages as follows:

M. Perez Mengual, *Designing Physical Interaction Platforms*,
Markt- und Unternehmensentwicklung Markets and Organisations,
https://doi.org/10.1007/978-3-658-41920-2_18

- **Diagnosis stage:** The first phase begins with an assessment of the situation as it is. Researchers and practitioners identify issues and challenges. Theoretical foundations of possible actions are articulated.
- **Planning action stage:** Based on the analysis that took place in the diagnosis phase (i.e., the context and the goal of the project), the intervention in the form of articulated actions is planned.
- **Taking-action stage:** In the taking-action phase, previously planned actions or interventions are implemented.
- **Evaluating-action stage***:* In the evaluating phase, the results of the actions are examined to determine whether the intervention was correctly implemented and what effect it had. This stage also determines what will happen in the next action research cycle.

Implementing AR cycles requires close collaboration between researchers and practitioners (the organisation) throughout the entire research project. AR demands that the researcher becomes completely immersed in the organisation being researched (Avison, Davison, & Malaurent, 2018). The more active the role of the researcher and the closer the cooperation between researcher and practitioners, the greater the understanding and learning effects are for all actors involved.

18.1 The Case Context: The European Energy Forum (EUREF)

This research takes place within the context of the European Energy Forum–Campus (EUREF), a 'living lab of the *Energiewende*.' It is located in the Tempelhof–Schöneberg district, southeast of the city centre of Berlin. The 5.5-hectare campus is located on the site of a former gasworks and combines modern architecture with protected cultural heritage brick-and-mortar buildings. The entire campus pursues the idea of a model urban quarter. On the one hand, the quarter stands as a model for a climate-neutral, resource-saving intelligent city of tomorrow (EUREF, 2021). The EUREF campus offers a modern energy infrastructure, including a smart grid, charging stations, autonomous and electric vehicles, wind turbines, biogas plants, and photovoltaic systems (Engels et al., 2019). On the other hand, the EUREF campus serves as a real-world laboratory where technologies related to climate protection and sustainability can be researched and tested. For this, the campus hosts more than 5,000 researchers, engineers, and employees from 150 companies, (research) institutions, and start-ups. These actors all work cooperatively on topics related to the *Energiewende* (EUREF, 2021).

18.2 The Case: Fraunhofer ENIQ

As a major actor in research on the *Energiewende*, the Fraunhofer society seeks to contribute to the EUREF campus ecosystem by establishing a location on site. This action research focuses on the development of this location—the Fraunhofer ENIQ (an acronym for energy intelligence). At the beginning of this research in August 2019, a building where the PIP was to be set up existed as a shell. A first definition of goals and the first concept drafts indicated that an innovation laboratory and technology showroom for topics related to research on climate and energy was to be created. Beyond that, the ENIQ was intended to bundle the interests of the various Fraunhofer institutes into a joint external presence. In this way, a unified and targeted approach to relevant actors from industry and politics was to be achieved, with the aim of knowledge and technology transfer from within the Fraunhofer society. Additionally, ENIQ was intended to serve as a forum for exchange among researchers. The development process of the ENIQ (conceptualisation and implementation) took place as a 19-month (August 2019–February 2021) collaborative project between the Fraunhofer IIS and the Fraunhofer CINES cluster with the associated Fraunhofer institutes. During this period, the entire development process, from initial concept development to implementation and (soft) opening, was executed. In this, the ENIQ represents a powerful example (Siggelkow, 2007) of the design process of PIPs, which has not yet been addressed in the literature. Although this research is based on a single project, generalising from this does not necessarily pose a problem (Gioia et al., 2013). Given the comprehensive project scope, the results from this action research project can be applied in structuring future PIP design processes (Halkier, 2011; Huang, 2010).

18.3 Research Process

Following Coghlan and Brannick (2005), two action research cycles were conducted over 19 months. The first AR cycle was completed in 11 months (August 2019–June 2020) to develop a concept and business model for the PIP (see Table 18.1 for an overview of the AR phases). During this cycle, theoretical knowledge was translated into interventions and implemented in the participating organisation together with the development[1] team. The evaluation of these interventions was positive but revealed some challenges concerning the implementation of the developed concept.

Table 18.1 Overview of 1st action research cycle: Concept development

1st Action Research Cycle: Concept Development		
Diagnosing	August 2019	Examination of provided information material, initial discussions with the client, assessment of the initial situation and the location
Planning Action	September 2019	Design of a structured PIP development process, creation of material to support the process (e.g., workshop material, interview guidelines)
Taking Action	October 2019–June 2020	Implementation of the PIP development process, data collection via interviews, workshops and meeting notes, intermediate evaluations
Evaluating Action	June 2020	Evaluation of the concept development process, analysis and presentation of the results, consideration of subsequent steps

With an understanding of these challenges, a second AR cycle was initiated (July 2020–February 2021). The focus of the interventions in the second AR cycle was on, e.g., the definition of workflows, team building, interior design, procurement processes, and internal and external communication (see Table 18.2 for an overview of the AR phases). The evaluation of the second AR cycle highlighted challenges arising during implementation as well as approaches that have made it possible to overcome these challenges.

[1] In principle, the terms 'design' and 'development' can be used synonymously. In the context of this study however, the term 'development team' is used to emphasise the implementing character. The term 'design process', on the other hand, refers more to keeping the big picture of the PIP in mind.

Table 18.2 Overview of 2nd action research cycle: Implementation

2nd Action Research Cycle: Implementation		
Diagnosing	June 2020	Diagnosis is made by the evaluation of the first AR cycle
Planning Action	July 2020	Planning of the activities necessary for the implementation of the concept
Taking Action	July 2020–January 2021	Execution of the planned activities, monitoring of numerous operationalisation activities, data collection via meeting notes
Evaluating Action	February 2021	Evaluation of both the development and the implementation results

18.4 Data Collection

The action research began with reviewing existing material to become familiar with the task and challenges and to get an idea of the PIP's target industry (climate and energy). This included desk research on the surroundings of the PIP (e.g., geo-location, public transport availability, pedestrian frequency, etc.), a review of project-related documents (lease agreement, concept drafts, etc.), and interviews with the members of the development team. During the AR project, the researchers were deeply involved in the development of the PIP and took on the roles of companion, orchestrator, and coordinator. In total, 59 meetings and exchanges took place between members of the development team and the embedded researcher during the project (see Table 18.3). The data material consisted of meeting minutes, e-mails, transcripts of stakeholder interviews, calculations and cost structures for the PIP, press coverage and press releases, as well as written project documentation (e.g., various versions of result presentations).

In the next sections, the results of this project are described. As two AR cycles for concept development and implementation were carried out, the results are described separately. The first section describes the results of the concept development, while the second section describes the results of the implementation.

Table 18.3 Overview of meetings with researcher participation

Meeting Type	Timespan	Meeting Purpose	Meeting Duration	People involved
Milestone Meetings (12 Meetings)	October 2019 to January 2021	Large coordination workshops, presentations for executives, and project meetings in which the further course of the project was decided. External actors were often included in these meetings, such as members of the organisation and decision-makers.	4–8 hours	3–5 persons from the project team (depending on topic and capacity) + researchers
Jour Fixe (14 Meetings)	April 2020 to July 2020	Coordination and status updates during the final steps of the first AR cycle. The jour fixes were replaced by sprint meetings in the second AR cycle.	60–90 minutes	2 persons from the project team + researchers
Sprint Meetings (8 Meetings)	September 2020 to January 2021	Planning, executing and evaluating work steps during the second AR cycle.	2–3 hours	3–4 persons from the project team (depending on topic and capacity) + researchers
Bilateral Exchange (25 Exchanges)	March 2020 to November 2020	Advice, coordination, and collaborative work between members of the project team and the researchers.	30–60 minutes	1 person from the project team + researchers

19 First Action Research Cycle: Concept Development

The first AR cycle started in August 2019. The research team was commissioned to structure and participate in the concept development process of the ENIQ.

19.1 Diagnosis Phase

The diagnosis phase of the concept development cycle marks the start of the overall project. Here, this phase was concentrated on collecting information about the 'as is' situation (as depicted in Table 19.1) to gain an understanding of the project's current state of development. This information was essential to specify the briefing and get an understanding of the overall goal of the project, as well as current and future challenges. To map the current state as effectively as possible, interviews with the persons responsible for the design process were conducted. Furthermore, a document analysis was carried out, including the following documents: floor plan, existing lease agreement, position papers of the clients, and a rough outline of the PIP to be developed. The 'starting situation' was as follows:

M. Perez Mengual, *Designing Physical Interaction Platforms*, Markt- und Unternehmensentwicklung Markets and Organisations, https://doi.org/10.1007/978-3-658-41920-2_19

Table 19.1 Starting Situation of PIP Development

Dimension	Description
PIP Facilities	Exhibition and event space with a 1.200 m^2 area; at the time the project started (August 2019), the building was in a shell condition; expected completion of the building in summer 2020.
PIP Timeframe	Long-term lease agreement (10 years); expected start of operations, Summer 2020.
PIP Environment	EUREF–Campus, Berlin Tempelhof-Schöneberg; cluster site with many other companies (corporations, start-ups, research institutions, and universities); good transport links, but not in a central location nor well frequented by visitors.
PIP Idea	Addressing various actors (e.g., from politics, business, society, and research), informing them about current research on the topics of climate and energy, and stimulate dialogue.
PIP Development Team	The PIP development team consists of 5 persons from different institutes of the Fraunhofer society. The capacity and involvement of these persons in the design process varies due to other commitments.
PIP Funding	The PIP receives starting capital from the German Fraunhofer society. Additional funding is expected from the PIP having a business model and governmental subsidies.

From there, the following two challenges were identified: (1) the need for a structured design process to advance the initial idea into a working concept, and (2) to support that process, the need for additional data to feed the process and validate assumptions (e.g., regarding actor requirements, attractiveness of the location, etc.).

19.2 Planning-action Phase

Together with the development team, a process was outlined to create a data-supported and consistent concept (see Figure 19.1). The researcher's existing project experience with the establishment and operation of an open innovation lab (the JOSEPHS OI Lab), as well as knowledge from the literature on how to set up platforms and interaction spaces, was drawn upon (e.g., Doorley & Witthoft, 2012; Parker et al., 2016). The resulting PIP design process was based on the design thinking approach, i.e., the division into problem and solution space (Meinel & Leifer, 2011). The process was structured in the following five steps:

1. **Designing core interactions:** The first step was designed to identify relevant actors for the PIP and conceptualise how these actors should interact with each other. These defined 'core interactions' serve as a starting point for the PIP design process (Parker et al., 2016). The core interactions should also consider possible restraints (e.g., location of the PIP, accessibility, etc.).
2. **Identifying and validating stakeholder requirements:** This step validates assumptions regarding the identified core interactions so that decisions in the PIP design process are grounded in empirical data. In addition, further requirements of platform actors are identified.
3. **Consolidating stakeholder requirements:** This step brings together relevant stakeholders for two reasons—(1) to discuss and prioritise core interactions, refine the requirements, and manage expectations; and (2) to inform platform actors about the PIP's existence, thereby gradually activating the PIP's ecosystem.
4. **Exploring design elements:** Based on the results of Step 3, mechanisms and design elements of comparable PIPs (e.g., innovation labs and comparable concepts) are identified and analysed concerning their transferability to the PIP.
5. **Finalising the concept:** All findings from the previous steps are consolidated into a final concept. This concept consists of the PIP's business model as well as mechanisms and design options supporting that business model.

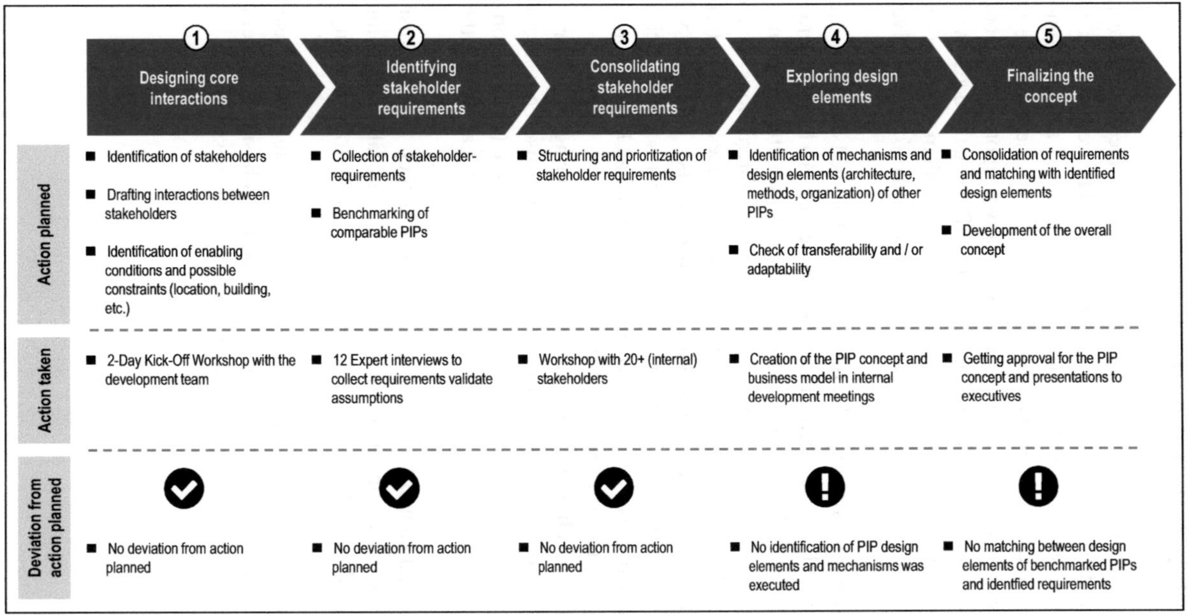

Figure 19.1 Overview of the PIP´s development process and execution

19.3 Taking-action Phase

In this phase, the outlined process was implemented. All steps were jointly carried out by the development team and the researchers. The researchers took on an advisory role to maintain a holistic perspective (Ollila & Yström, 2020) but were also actively involved in the operational work, e.g., by facilitating workshops and conducting interviews. The following section provides a detailed explanation of how the planned actions were executed.

1. **Designing core interactions:** The process began with a two-day workshop (5 development team members, 2 researchers). The workshop was held on-site and included a tour of the building and surrounding area. The agenda included (1) a collection of goals for the PIP, (2) the creation of a stakeholder map, (3) the prioritisation of stakeholders based on their importance to PIP development, and (4) the creation of corresponding stakeholder personas. Based on this, (5) initial core interactions between the personas were outlined and ranked according to the value they would generate through the PIP.
2. **Identifying and validating stakeholder requirements:** Based on the stakeholder personas, 12 representatives were identified and interviewed. The interviews resulted in significant refinement of the PIP's core stakeholders, i.e., who generates the most value from using the PIP. Additionally, PIP benchmarking was conducted. Comparable PIP concepts were examined to identify best practices regarding their value propositions, i.e., what established PIPs offer their stakeholders. The results were discussed in a workshop with the development team, resulting in a selection of core interactions facilitated by the PIP.
3. **Consolidating stakeholder requirements:** This step was implemented as a workshop with a large number of stakeholders (20 +). The two most promising core interactions of the PIP were discussed. The workshop was successful in managing expectations, informing stakeholders, and validating interim results of the design process.
4. **Fine-tuning instead of exploring design elements:** Following the stakeholder workshop, the development team intensified collaboration to design the PIP concept in detail. Here, the originally outlined approach was deviated from. The original idea of identifying and transferring mechanisms from other PIPs (such as architecture, methods, and organisation) turned out to be impractical at this point. Instead, the development team proceeded with the refinement of the ENIQ concept by analysing existing data and making design decisions.

The resulting concept was a multi-layer platform with core interactions centred around (1) technology sales, (2) science communication, and (3) internal science management.

5. **Presenting instead of finalising the concept:** Originally, the concept was to be developed by matching existing PIP mechanisms with the requirements of stakeholders. At this point, the carried-out approach deviated. The last phase of concept development was dedicated to coordination within the organisation (e.g., presentations to executives, activating the ecosystem, etc.) to obtain final feedback and approval.

19.4 Evaluating-action Phase

The actions of the PIP design process are evaluated in this phase. In the evaluation, both the development team and the researchers were involved in discussing what occurred during the process, reflecting on positive and negative aspects. Overall, the outlined PIP design process was successful in developing a consistent concept, which was presented to executives of the organisation and formally approved. The evaluation of the PIP design process was centred around the following three aspects: the structure of the process, managing the process, and the impact of the outcomes.

The discussion of the structure of the PIP design process relates to the content of the process steps. In this case, (1) the kick-off workshop focused on stakeholders and core interactions, and the stakeholder interviews were rated as largely positive. Both activities were highly useful for structuring the development and gaining knowledge. (2) The stakeholder workshop fulfilled its function in terms of expectation management, the validation of previous project results, and the initial activation of an ecosystem. However, new content and insights (except for the validation) were not generated. (3) The identification of mechanisms of other PIPs, i.e., the benchmarking of architecture, methods, organisation, etc., brought only limited benefits. The results of the benchmark have been used in the development process for illustration, inspiration ('What kind of PIP concepts exist on the market?'), and delimitation ('What should our PIP *not* be like?'). However, the matching of elicited requirements with existing design options, i.e., in a modular way, was not done.

Managing the PIP design process refers to the way the process is perceived from an emotional and social perspective. Two findings are worth highlighting here. (4) Initiating the design of a PIP involves risk and uncertainty. The structure and data-driven nature of the process provided comfort and is confidence-inspiring for the development team, as design decisions can be made based on empirical data. (5) The PIP design process appears to be exciting but is demanding. This poses two challenges: first, attrition of design team members occurs, especially if multiple organisations (or organisational units) are involved and/or team members are working in hybrid roles. Second, new stakeholders gain interest in the project. Although they can act as a new resource, they might challenge the consensus among the development team, jeopardising the existing state of work. Therefore, the degree to which the design process is opened requires careful consideration.

The outcome of the design process was a PIP with a platform business model. This represented a (business-model) innovation for the governing organisation, requiring a certain degree of organisational transformation. Many existing administrative processes were based on the requirement that assets (such as a PIP) are assigned to an organisational unit. However, due to the novelty of the PIP concept, there were difficulties in identifying a distinct ('owning') organisational unit. Thus, following the concept phase, there were challenges in the PIP–organisation interface, leading to the following question: How can a PIP and an administrative organisation fit together?

Second Action Research Cycle: Implementation

20

The second AR cycle started in June 2020. The research team was commissioned to support the operationalisation and implementation of the developed concept.

20.1 Diagnosis Phase

Following the concept development, the project team embarked on a second AR cycle to facilitate the implementation of the concept. In discussion with the development team, it became apparent that the PIP design process led to a good result, but there was a subsequent lack of structure and guidance regarding how to implement the concept in practice. There were challenges regarding the ownership of the PIP in the organisation, the clarification of responsibilities, and moving from conceptual work to hands-on implementation.

20.1.1 Ownership of the PIP

The PIP touched on the competencies and responsibilities of different organisational units without being assigned to one. As a result, the PIP was not properly allocated within the organisation. For the implementation, this resulted in planning difficulties, as depending on allocation, cost structures, budgets, key partners, and processes necessary for the implementation of the PIP would be subject to change. Additionally, essential members of the development team were working in hybrid roles, i.e., they were partly responsible for the design of the PIP and partly for other tasks, resulting in reduced capacity concerning the concept implementation.

M. Perez Mengual, *Designing Physical Interaction Platforms*,
Markt- und Unternehmensentwicklung Markets and Organisations,
https://doi.org/10.1007/978-3-658-41920-2_20

20.1.2 Implementation

There was a clear picture of how the PIP would look and how the concept would work in practice, but individual components had not yet been detailed. For example, the exact aesthetic of the interior was not specified, including questions like 'What type of chairs will we order?' Additionally, the concept indicated that interaction artifacts in the PIP should consist of, e.g., technology demonstrators. However, which demonstrators, by whom exactly, and when they should be set up was not defined. While there was an existing core team, the internal processes regarding collaboration, collaboration tools, and team roles were not defined. This all had to be clarified under severe time pressure, as administrative processes (e.g., procurement and recruitment) had to be initiated.

20.2 Planning-action Phase

According to the diagnosis, interventions were planned in the two areas of 'ownership of the PIP' and 'implementation.' On the one hand, there was a need for clarification regarding how the PIP could fit into the organisation to ensure its long-term existence. On the other hand, the PIP was required to be in operational status quickly. For this reason, the interventions in this AR cycle are described separately—one focused on the ownership and governance within the organisation and the other on the start of operations—although they ran in parallel.

20.2.1 Ownership of the PIP

As the PIP's ownership within the organisation had not been clarified, two actions were indicated. First, discussions had to be initiated with relevant actors, answering questions such as 'How will the PIP be anchored in the organisation?', 'Who can fulfil a supporting role?', 'Can we enable cooperation between interested organisational units?', and 'Who is responsible for the operation and supporting processes (procurement, acceptance building, etc.)?' Second, supporting these discussions, the definition and articulation of value propositions for the owner role of the PIP was required (Parker et al., 2016), answering the question of why an organisational unit should adopt ownership of a given PIP.

20.2.2 Implementation

Referring to the APPI framework (Ramaswamy & Ozcan, 2018), there were difficulties in animating the developed PIP concept into real-world artifacts, people, processes, and interfaces. In an iterative process, the APPI framework was translated for the context of PIPs. Together with the development team, several steps to initiate the PIP's operation were outlined.

Artifacts incorporate everything that is physically present in the PIP to ensure its functionality and to establish interactions between the various actors. In the context of this project, this relates to the design of the interior and finding ways to initiate and support interactions.

People refers to both personnel capacities as well as to the ecosystem of actors that interact with each other in the PIP. Actions associated with the people component aim to (1) build up human resources and (2) activate partners and customers.

Processes include all digitised or analogue processes needed to build and operate the PIP. This starts with internal processes needed to coordinate the development team and enable effective communication. Business processes such as invoicing and accounting are needed for management. Lastly, a PIP also requires processes that initiate the interactions between the various platform actors.

Interfaces include all means through which an actor comes into contact with other actors. In the context of a physical PIP, this dimension is translated to 'touchpoints' that enable actors to interact with the platform and other platform actors. In the context of PIPs, this refers to, e.g., the creation of a scheduled program of events.

20.3 Taking-action Phase

The implementation of the interventions, both in terms of ownership of the PIP within the organisation and the start of operations, took place in parallel. This section describes how the intervention was carried out and where deviations or additional actions were necessary.

20.3.1 Ownership of the PIP

In an iterative process, value propositions for PIP ownership were designed. At the same time, possible owners within the organisation were actively engaged.

However, it became apparent that none of the identified options for placing the PIP's ownership within established structures of the organisation was suitable. The PIP's business model combines components that fall into different areas of responsibility, e.g., while one unit of the organisation is responsible for the communication of research activities, another unit is responsible for the sale of developed technology. No unit expressed interest in operating the PIP, as they were concerned about moving beyond their area of responsibility. Structures responsible for cross-unit cooperation were either too small or were still in the process of being established. The PIP concept, however, received strong support and endorsement, resulting in the establishment of the PIP as a new unit.

20.3.2 Implementation

To start the operation of the PIP, APPI components were designed on the following two levels: (1) infrastructure and components that enable the team to operate the PIP ('the backend') and (2) components that enable interaction between the platform actors, i.e. visitors of the PIP ('the frontend'). Table 20.1 provides an overview of the designed APPI components.

Artifacts: The PIP's interior was designed to match the demands of the platform actors (i.e., by offering exhibition space and meeting/workshop rooms). Supporting their function, proper lighting, as well as IT infrastructure, was established. For the operation of the PIP, artifacts that stimulate interaction between platform actors were compiled. These artifacts (e.g., technology demonstrators, prototypes, visualisations of research results) were collected from the associated institutes for display in the PIP, serving the purpose of mediating the interactions between visitors of the PIP and the institutes.

People: To initiate the PIP´s operation, additional personnel capacity had to be created while simultaneously activating the ecosystem of stakeholders. Most importantly, a full-time operations manager was recruited to coordinate the collection of exhibits, start the procurement processes, and coordinate the development of the interior. Another full-time position was filled to design and coordinate outreach to external and internal stakeholders. Additional support for the team was achieved through part-time student workers and the commissioning of third-party organisations (e.g., agencies).

Processes: A variety of different processes was designed. To coordinate the large number of work steps necessary to build the infrastructure, the development team borrowed from agile methodology. Weekly sprint meetings were introduced to form the basis of team collaboration. Additionally, operation processes related

Table 20.1 Overview of designed APPI Components

	Team Interaction and Infrastructure ('Backend')	Visitor Interaction ('Frontend')
Artifacts	• Room layout (e.g., meeting and workshop rooms, exhibition space) • Interior design (e.g., furniture) • Lighting concept • Technical infrastructure (e.g., internet, IT devices)	• Technology demonstrators • Prototypes • Exhibition items (e.g., interactive computers, visualisations)
People	• Full-time operations manager • Full-time sales manager • Part-time student workers • Definition of responsibility areas for the various roles • Activating the network of enabling actors (e.g., associated Fraunhofer-institutes)	–
Processes	• Agile methods (e.g., sprints) • Operation processes (e.g., planning hours of PIP operation, internal communication, curating artifacts in the exhibition) • Business processes (e.g., procurement, accounting, distribution of revenue)	• Platform onboarding processes (acquisition strategy and marketing) • Communication concept (website, press material, newsletters)
Interfaces	• Agile tools (e.g., Kanban boards) • IT equipment (e.g., for livestreaming)	• Event program • Mechanisms for capturing feedback (e.g., on technology demonstrators)

to, e.g., efficient internal communication and curating the exhibition of interaction artifacts were designed. Business processes included designing the flows of financial resources, e.g., how membership fees are collected or how income generated by the PIP is divided between platform actors. To facilitate the engagement of actors with the PIP, onboarding mechanisms were created in the form of an acquisition strategy and marketing. To support this and to engage onboarded actors, a communication concept was developed and implemented.

Interfaces: Two types of interfaces were designed: internal communication interfaces and touchpoints that enable actors to interact with each other within the same PIP. Internal communication interfaces include tools (such as a Kanban board) that enable the development team to coordinate operations (e.g., by tracking progress and creating a backlog of the tasks). An event program was developed to facilitate and orchestrate interaction among platform actors. The program consisted of a portfolio with different types of events and a roadmap for the first year of operation. Even before the official opening, prototyping of digital events was begun in order to gain experience and optimise workflows.

20.4 Evaluating-action Phase

The implementation phase was completed successfully, as the PIP was operational. Using the APPI framework as a basis for designing value-creating PIPs has been successful. In contrast to the concept-development AR cycle, the implementation was perceived as much more challenging for several reasons, including the three aspects outlined below.

First, the strictly sequential approach, i.e., starting with concept development (AR cycle 1) followed by implementation (AR cycle 2) resulted in a 'chasm'—uncertainty regarding how to begin the implementation of the concept. Using methods borrowed from agile methodology, such as Kanban boards and sprint meetings, helped in initiating the implementation and building momentum. In future PIP design processes, this connection between developing concepts in theory and testing them from an earlier stage in the design process should be emphasised. For example, developing a program of events should quickly be followed by prototyping these events. This potentially leads to benefits, such as activating the ecosystem, enhancing value propositions, and fine-tuning internal processes. As well, building the infrastructure necessary for supporting value-creating interactions in the PIP must be started at an early stage. Procurement processes and implementing interior design and lighting concepts are essential in PIP development and cause severe delays if not begun early.

Second, during the transition from the concept development to the implementation phase, the roles of the development team members had to move from a creative, theoretical role to an implementation role. This process was experienced as difficult for two reasons. First, members of the development team were working in hybrid roles, thereby reducing their capacity to handle the number of tasks associated with the implementation. Second, the lack of a coordinating function was experienced. The hiring of an operation manager and the adoption of agile methodology helped to overcome these challenges in this case. For future PIP design processes, it is suggested to clarify roles and their respective responsibilities at an earlier point, ideally at the beginning of the concept-development phase, to enable a seamless transition to implementation.

Third, organisational structures, processes, and requirements necessary for the launch of the PIP had to be established first. As the owner of the PIP in the organisation was not clarified, the design included difficulties in terms of administrative processes, e.g., procurement and approval processes. Overcoming these challenges required solution-oriented creativity and significant coordination with the organisation. Learning from that, in future PIP design processes, the clarification of ownership, contact persons, and budgets should take place at the beginning of the concept-development phase.

21 Discussion and Contributions

This research demonstrates how a PIP can be systematically designed and implemented. In this section, key insights from this research are discussed. Building on that, both a model and a revised process to structure the design of future PIPs are proposed.

21.1 Discussion: Crossing the Chasm in Building PIPs

In the ENIQ project, applying a design-thinking approach (Meinel & Leifer, 2011), combined with the CCF framework of Ramaswamy and Ozcan (2018) and insights from Parker et al. (2016), has worked well for structuring the design process. In particular, designing core interactions between platform actors is a sound point of departure for the PIP design process, especially when complemented by methods from design thinking, such as constant validation (e.g., by interviews or prototyping). Building on scholarly work which defines a PIP's central characteristic to be the ability to facilitate engagement among people and technologies (Bessant, 2020; Osorio et al., 2019) and create value through interaction (Peschl & Fundneider, 2014), this study demonstrates how a PIP can be built based on the requirements of the (intended) platform actors. However, existing research on PIP design seems to have neglected three elements that were critical in this AR study: (1) the assumption that design the design process starts without preconditions (cf. Memon, 2021; Parker et al., 2016), (2) translating theoretical contributions from the literature into practical implications for PIP concept development (cf. Greve et al., 2016), and (3) the aspect of the PIPs' organisational implementation. These three elements can be discussed in more depth as follows:

M. Perez Mengual, *Designing Physical Interaction Platforms*,
Markt- und Unternehmensentwicklung Markets and Organisations,
https://doi.org/10.1007/978-3-658-41920-2_21

(1) PIP design is bound to preconditions: In contrast to digital platforms, PIPs are bound to the physical realm. This can provide noteworthy freedom in designing, as interactions are not limited to the digital space, but also sets constraints, e.g., in terms of accessibility. This is a significant difference compared to structured design processes of digital platforms (Evans & Schmalensee, 2016; Memon, 2021; Parker et al., 2016), where the location obviously plays no role. Le Masson et al.'s (2009) statement that platform design is a structured exploration of alternatives is even more true in the case of PIPs. The location may limit core interactions or make it necessary to weigh the pros and cons of one location against another. This research contributes by bringing the design of core interactions into the context of the physical location of PIPs. Questions such as 'Can this interaction be represented in the space?' or 'Do we have the right location for such interactions?' should be the central point of departure for a design process.

(2) PIP design starts with defining organisational requirements: This AR study indicates that starting PIP design by simply focusing on the core interactions between producer and consumer, as suggested by Parker et al. (2016), has its drawbacks. This approach may seem obvious, as much research relates to facilitating interaction and collaborative innovation, where these two groups of actors are essential (Greve et al., 2016; Ollila & Yström, 2016). However, setting up the ENIQ following a user-centric development approach has led to a situation where a PIP concept was developed to fit the requirements of producers and consumers. However, the organisational framework (owner and provider) serving as the facilitating condition for the PIP was overlooked during development. Starting the PIP design process with the definition of core interactions assumes that the roles of owner and provider are already defined. In the case of ENIQ, these roles were, to a degree, still in limbo. Therefore, in contrast to prominent platform design 'playbooks' (e.g., Evans & Schmalensee, 2016; Memon, 2021; Parker et al., 2016; Reillier & Reillier, 2017), this study emphasises clarifying the roles and interests of owner and provider of the PIP first. This is for four reasons:

First, the owner role has a decisive influence on the PIP's governance rules and value-appropriation mechanisms (e.g., Tiwana, 2014). Any constraints here could influence the core interactions between consumers and producers. Second, clear ownership of the PIP is required for administrative reasons. A PIP has the potential to change the way an organisation works. In the case of ENIQ, this refers to acquisition and marketing processes, which are concentrated within the PIP. Internal interfaces, communication channels, and partners need to be defined, and existing processes require reconfiguration so that the PIP can contribute to value creation. Third, unlike digital platforms, PIPs are not focused on maximum scalability, rapid growth, and market control (Evans & Schmalensee, 2016; Reillier & Reillier, 2017). The incentives and returns of investment for the providers (i.e., the operating team) of a PIP like ENIQ are manifold, going beyond profitability but reaching into aspects like brand building, community exchange and matchmaking for public funding opportunities. Therefore, value propositions need to be designed specifically for the providers. Fourth, forming and motivating a dedicated design team is essential. In the case of ENIQ, the organisational implementation of the PIP posed a major challenge. This had less to do with describing the functions of actors involved, e.g., in terms of coordination or participation (cf. Leminen, 2013), but more with 'soft' challenges such as team dynamics and identifying the right counterparts in the 'owning' organisation. In retrospect, several aspects had to be addressed—the composition of the team, task distribution within the team, expectation management of the team members, and dealing with attrition and reduced capacities during the design process. How should the team deal with new people required to replenish the team? A shared understanding of the PIP´s current development status needs to be developed without questioning decisions already made. Lastly, if the development team transitions to operation mode, roles may change from conceptual work to daily business. It is strongly emphasised to follow an agile approach when developing, implementing, and testing the PIP concept in the final stages to ease this transition and to cross the chasm between the concept-development phase and the start of implementation.

(3) Translating insights from the literature into practical implications is difficult: Due to the nature of PIPs as physical spaces, most research is, to date, case-based, identifying single aspects that are important for the operation of a PIP. For example, Chronéer, Ståhlbröst, and Habibipour (2019) highlight key PIP components, such as leadership, management, and business models. Yet, insights gained from literature often remain abstract, providing little detail as to how key components are implemented in practice. This presents a dilemma, as research aims to explain what happens in PIPs around the world, but decoding it into practical implications can be challenging. The recognition that a PIP needs a business model to operate sustainably (Chronéer et al., 2019) is essential. Likewise, the critical factors for facilitating collaborative innovation, such as atmosphere and customer engagement (Greve et al., 2016), are important in understanding what happens in a PIP.

However, in the ENIQ case, it was challenging to determine at which point these insights should be applied in the design process. The academic literature does not refer to specific, designable elements or APPI components but rather to aggregate dimensions. This abstract knowledge alone, without tangible guidelines and inspiration, was of only limited use in the ENIQ design process. In the more practitioner-oriented literature, e.g., from the field of innovation, it can be observed that the transition from knowledge ('thinking') to implementing ('doing') is receiving increasing attention (cf. Stickdorn, Hormess, Lawrence, & Schneider, 2017). For PIP development, it can be similarly argued—to use insights from existing research on PIPs in design processes, a lean framework would be meaningful that allows for the identification of when and where to apply which insights (similar to the work of Memon (2021) on digital platforms).

21.2 Contribution: A Structured Approach for Building PIPs

This research study contributes two approaches to address the issues discussed above—the PIP composition model and the PIP design process. Combining the insights from the two AR cycles with Ramaswamy and Ozcan's (2018) CCF framework and Parker et al.'s (2016) platform strategies, a model for the PIP's organisational composition is proposed (Figure 21.1). This model suggests that a PIP needs to be built on three levels—operation, team, and infrastructure—each of which is constituted of individual APPI components. The operation level describes the visible interaction between platform actors—the consumer and producer (Parker et al., 2016). The team level refers to the provider role, which operates the PIP. The infrastructure level refers to the owner role and the physical infrastructure of the PIP. The model helps situate existing research (e.g., regarding interior design, role distribution, etc.), making it usable for a PIP design process.

Operation level: This level describes the core interactions that take place between PIP platform actors (consumers and producers; the 'frontend' of the PIP). Through the assemblage of artifacts (e.g., technology demonstrators), people (actors interacting on the platform), processes (operational processes), and interfaces (touchpoints that bring together actors and enable interaction), the PIP creates value for both the owner and the other platform actors (consumers and producers). Most elements designed in the concept-development phase (AR cycle 1) concern this level. It has to be noted that the interactions and value creation taking place on the operation level may require a transformation of the 'owning' organisation, as the PIP itself is an innovation. For example, in the context of the ENIQ, the pure existence of the PIP had an impact on collaboration and communication within the network of associated Fraunhofer institutes.

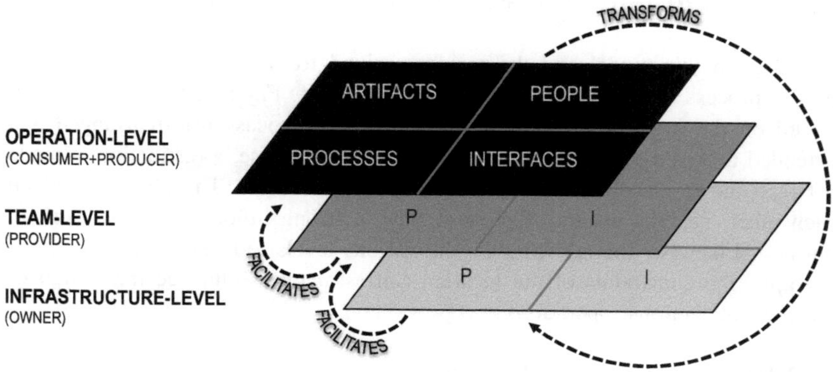

Figure 21.1 PIP composition model

Team level: The value creation that takes place on the operation level is enabled and orchestrated by a team (provider) that makes the operation of the PIP possible in the first place. Likewise, the different components (APPI) also need to be designed on the team level. This AR project demonstrates that forming a functioning team requires the definition of roles, responsibilities, and the creation of necessary resources (people). How the team members communicate and interact with each other and work in a coordinated way to operate the PIP must be designed (processes). Lastly, this team also requires equipment and the corresponding IT resources (artifacts), as well as tools and workflows (interfaces), to enable effective teamwork. The team is essential for creating a lively and engaging atmosphere in a PIP, setting the stage so that a space can come to 'life.'

Infrastructure level: This level represents the basis for the entire PIP, both in terms of physical existence and integration in the 'owning' organisation. Artifacts on the infrastructure level refer to the physical space. This means the building of the PIP, room configuration, and atmospheric interior design. Processes refer to underlying processes, e.g., business processes such as the distribution of revenue and cost structures. People and interfaces refer to internal communication, contact persons, and the hierarchical integration of the PIP into the structures of the organisation. The components of the infrastructure level are thus essential for the structured design and operation of a PIP. They create enabling conditions or constraints for both the team and core interactions of the PIP.

21.3 Contribution: A Revised Process for Building PIPs

Building on this model and the insights gained from the AR cycles, the PIP design process introduced in the first AR cycle (cf. Figure 19.1) was adapted. Based on the evaluations of both AR cycles, the process was rearranged and extended to seven phases (cf. Figure 21.2). In each phase, a distinction is made between the levels of operation, team, and infrastructure. The phases build on each other, i.e., the results of phase 1 have a strong influence on the work in phase 2. Likewise, the activities on the various levels influence each other. For example, the constraints of the location (infrastructure) influence the design of the core interactions (operation).

1. **Define preconditions:** PIP design starts with defining preconditions—principles that guide the design process. On the team level, the roles within the development team need clarification to ensure a smooth design process and subsequent implementation. On the infrastructure level, an assessment of the location is needed concerning characteristics (constraints and enabling conditions) that influence the interactions taking place there, such as visitor frequency. In addition, the roles of the PIP owner and provider, administrative processes and responsibilities, as well as the project budget require definition.
2. **Draft core interactions:** At the operation level, the goals to be achieved by the PIP are clarified in detail. Relevant actors are identified and prioritised in terms of their importance for the goals. Based on this, initial core interactions between actors are outlined and ranked according to the value they will generate through the PIP. At the infrastructure level, value propositions must be created for the owner and provider so that a sustainable operation can be ensured.
3. **Identify actor requirements:** This phase serves to validate the outlined core interactions. Assumptions made about actor requirements in previous phases are validated and enhanced with empirical material. Additionally, value propositions drafted for the owner and provider roles are validated.
4. **Draft PIP concept:** Based on validated actor requirements, a first concept of the PIP is drafted. This requires the prioritisation of actor requirements and focus on one central core interaction. The core interaction is the main source of value generated by the PIP. Therefrom, a concept can be created, including the planning of personnel capacities and roles for the PIP operation, an outlined PIP business model (e.g., Business Model Canvas for core interactions), and an initial design of the physical PIP layout (e.g., room layout, interior design, technical infrastructure).

5. **Validate PIP concept:** In this step, the drafted concept is communicated and presented to internal actors. Value propositions drafted for the owner and provider roles, now explicit in the concept, are again validated. The aim is to obtain a commitment for the operation of the PIP, both from owners and providers. This commitment includes releasing budgets and approval to proceed to implementation.
6. **Finalise PIP concept:** Based on the approved, drafted concept, the individual APPI components are developed in detail. At the operation level, this step includes, e.g., the collection of exhibition items, the creation of a PIP onboarding strategy, and a communication concept. At the team level, operation processes, such as the operation hours of the PIP, are determined. Additional personnel resources are hired, and an agile methodology to transition to implementation is introduced. At the infrastructure level, the necessary business processes are set up and initiated. The finalisation of the PIP concept runs parallel to implementation.
7. **Implement and launch:** The last phase concerns the implementation of the final PIP concept. At the operational level, this includes prototyping activities to test the function of the PIP. This can take place, for example, in the context of a soft launch. Following the soft launch, the PIP is officially opened, and relevant actors (consumers and producers) are onboarded to the PIP. At the team and infrastructure levels, the transition from development to operation mode takes place.

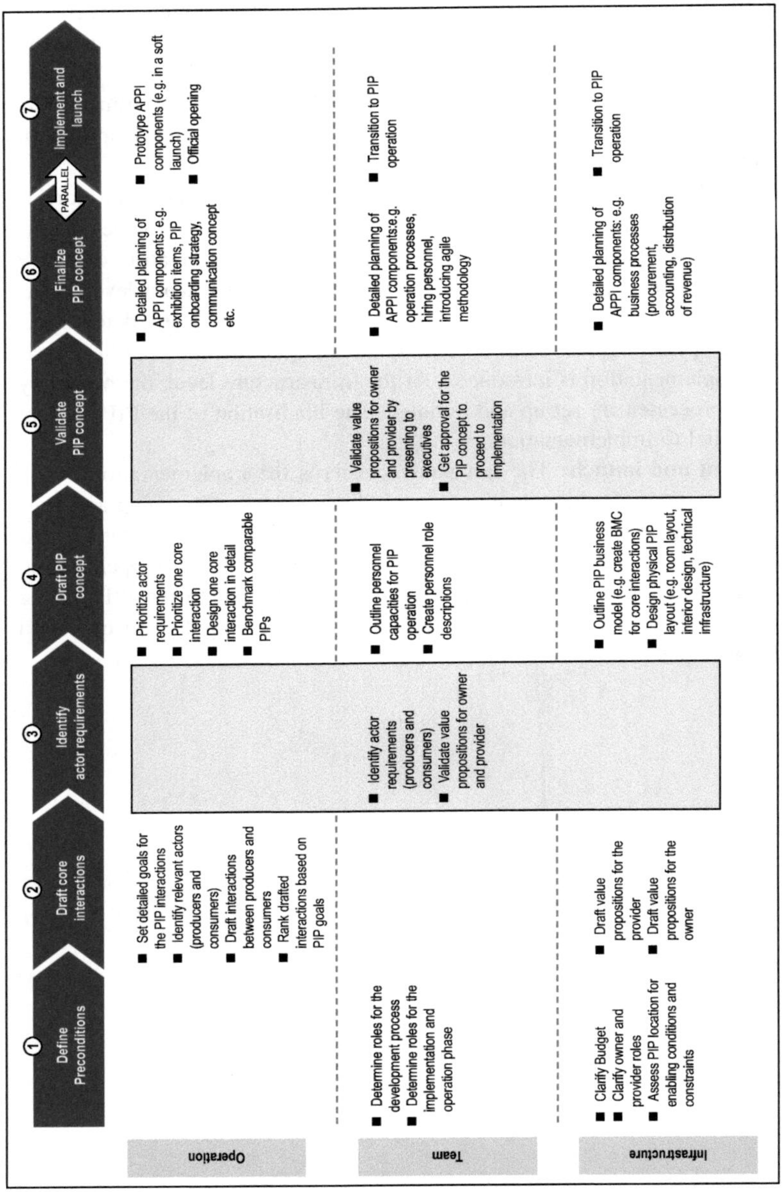

Figure 21.2 Revised PIP design process

Summary and Outlook 22

This research aims to explore how physical interaction platforms (PIPs) can be built, concerning concept development and the following implementation. The findings are based on a 19-month action research project. Insights from the literature on PIPs, value creation, and the strategic development of (digital) platforms were translated into interventions.

The findings of this action research show that PIPs are designed on three levels—operation, team, and infrastructure. The operation level describes the visible interaction between platform actors. This level is facilitated by an operating team (team level) and the organisational and physical infrastructure (infrastructure level). To enable sustainable PIP operation, all three levels need to be actively designed and integrated. This study thus uncovered the importance of interlinking and aligning internal processes and components. This enables the value creation that takes place in PIPs in the first place, as they create, initiate, or accelerate interactions. These components and processes go beyond the business model—they are mechanisms that are needed to effectively run the business model. Following this project and as a practical implication, a seven-stage process is proposed that describes the design of a PIP on the three identified levels, ranging from the definition of preconditions to the implementation and launch of the PIP. The seven-stage design process provides all steps necessary for creating a value-creating PIP. All three levels need to be aligned with one another to ensure the frictionless operation of a PIP

There are limitations to this research. This research builds on the results from a single AR project. Although the ENIQ project is a powerful example, the scope for generalisation remains limited. Nevertheless, it highlights that PIP design is a complex endeavour. In particular, future research is encouraged to explore team processes as well as the organisational implementation of PIPs.

M. Perez Mengual, *Designing Physical Interaction Platforms*,
Markt- und Unternehmensentwicklung Markets and Organisations,
https://doi.org/10.1007/978-3-658-41920-2_22

The insights generated during this AR project have implications for the remainder of this dissertation. PIP design is a complex process that must account for several organisational factors beyond the core interaction. This has implications for the use of the taxonomy developed in Part III. While the taxonomy can be used to generate early-stage concepts through combinatory design, this AR shows that designing and implementing a PIP takes more than combining design characteristics. Instead, PIP design is a dynamic process that must consider human and organisational factors, relying on agile methodology, flexibility, and prototyping. Eventually, a PIP may require changes to its original concept to suit changing requirements of participating actors (consumers, producers, providers and/or owners). This leads to the question of how this continuous innovation of a PIP can be managed during ongoing operations. Part V explores this aspect of PIP design in the wake of the COVID-19 crisis, which provides a unique opportunity to study the innovation and reconfiguration processes of retail PIPs.

Part V

Managing Continuous Innovation: A Multiple-Case Study to Explore the Sustainable Innovation of PIPs

Objectives and Structure

23

This dissertation seeks to explore *how a physical interaction platform (PIP) can be designed in a systematic and structured way.* Parts III and IV explored the design of a PIP in the early phases of its life cycle. Part V supports this objective by exploring the continuous innovation of a PIP. This can become necessary due to external circumstances or during maturity and declining phases of the lifecycle of a PIP. Part V presents a study that researches this self-renewal in the context of the COVID-19 pandemic. This crisis has posed major challenges for PIPs worldwide, caused by the lack of customer interaction necessitated by hygiene restrictions. Looking at retail PIPs, especially small and medium-sized, which were the focus of retail innovation before the COVID-19 pandemic began, this study aims to examine two main aspects. First, to set a foundation of deeper crisis-driven innovation, this study seeks to explore how exactly retail PIPs reacted to the COVID-19 crisis. The second aspect concerns the sustainability of innovative solutions, following Winston Churchill's well-cited statement, 'Never let a good crisis go to waste.' As crises can be understood as a kind of laboratory to stimulate novel thinking (Bessant, Rush, & Trifilova, 2015), a look is taken at the outcome of the laboratory experiments, i.e., the developed solutions and their sustainability after the 'lab phase' (peak of crisis). Are the developed innovations used beyond crises, similar to the concept of reverse innovation (Govindarajan & Euchner, 2012)? The following research questions were formulated accordingly:

Part V of this dissertation builds upon and extends a conference contribution, which was presented and discussed at the 31st Annual ISPIM Innovation Conference 2020 in Berlin, Germany (Perez Mengual, Danzinger & Roth., 2020).

M. Perez Mengual, *Designing Physical Interaction Platforms*,
Markt- und Unternehmensentwicklung Markets and Organisations,
https://doi.org/10.1007/978-3-658-41920-2_23

RQ 5: *What were strategic responses and activities of retailers in reaction to the COVID-19 crisis?*

RQ 6: *Did these strategic responses and activities lead to sustainable innovation?*

Part V is structured as follows. Chapter 24 presents the state of the art in literature from the fields of crisis response strategy, business models, and business model innovation. Chapter 25 introduces the multiple-case study approach (Eisenhardt, 1989) with data from eight detailed cases in the German retail sector. Chapter 26 presents the findings from both within-case and cross-case analyses. Chapter 27 discusses the research findings, i.e., the reactions of retailers towards the COVID-19 crisis and whether any of the reactions have led to sustainable innovation. Chapter 28 highlights the theoretical and managerial implications and places the results of Part V in the context of the entire dissertation. The structure of Part V is shown in Figure 23.1.

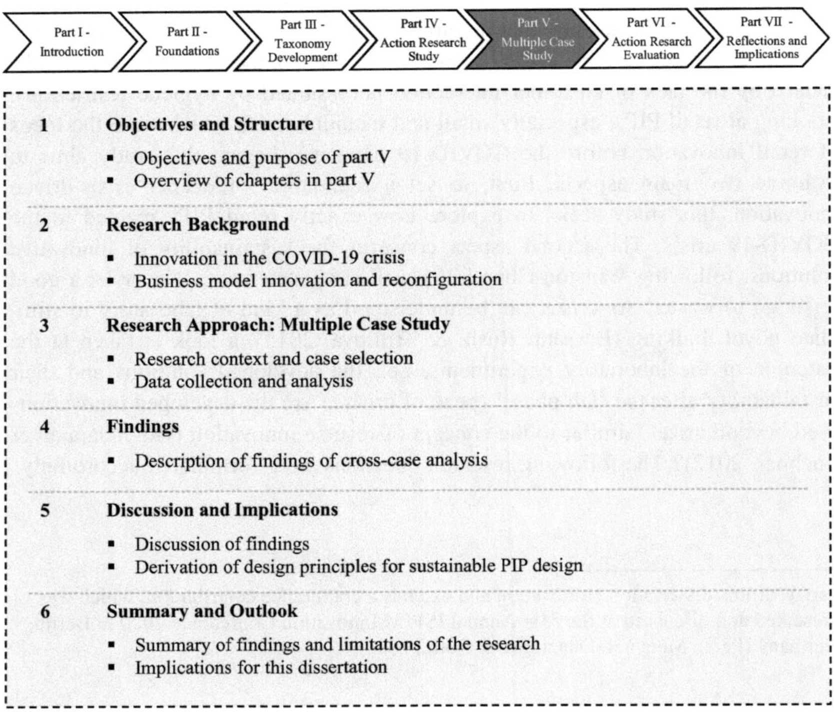

Figure 23.1 Structure of Part V

Research Background

24

This chapter provides additional theoretical background information necessary to explore the self-renewal of retail PIPs. It introduces the innovation challenges facing brick-and-mortar retail, including the impacts of the COVID-19 crisis. Furthermore, strategic responses in dealing with crises are described. Following this, the 'innovation' response, which is similar to self-renewal (cf. Teece, 2017; Wenzel, Stanske, & Lieberman, 2021), is enriched with business model literature.

24.1 The Effect of the COVID-19 Crisis on Retail

Brick-and-mortar retail is one of the industries that has been most affected by the COVID-19 pandemic. Even before the crisis, digitisation, new customer shopping behaviour, and competition from online retail posed major challenges. The traditional retail business models are generating increasingly less recognisable value compared to e-commerce. Calls for retail to reinvent itself have been made for several years (Agarwal, Breschi, & Devillard-Hoellinger, 2017; Reinartz, 2019). Except for a handful of innovative concepts, few new approaches have been seen in practice. This situation intensified dramatically in the wake of the COVID-19 pandemic in 2020 and 2021 (Fairlie, 2020). For retailers, lockdowns, operational restrictions, and hygiene guidelines have severely hampered customer interaction. Small and medium-sized retailers were particularly vulnerable to the impact of the pandemic due to limited resources and money reserves (Josephson, Schrank, & Marshall, 2017). As a result, their existing business models (BMs) were challenged as a whole (Ritter & Pedersen, 2020). But crises can also drive the entrepreneurial vision and lead to the creation of radically different solutions (Bessant et al., 2015). Whereas previous business and innovation research drew insights from humanitarian crises (cf. Bessant et al., 2015; Betts & Bloom,

M. Perez Mengual, *Designing Physical Interaction Platforms*,
Markt- und Unternehmensentwicklung Markets and Organisations,
https://doi.org/10.1007/978-3-658-41920-2_24

2014), the COVID-19 pandemic can be considered a similar shock leading to a resource-constrained scenario of forced innovation (cf. Dahlke et al., 2021; Netz, Reinmoeller, & Axelson, 2022). In the context of crises, we may thus find particularly advanced and radical innovation since existing solutions cannot be of use. Moreover, the restrictions of a crisis leave the actors little choice but to pursue a new approach (Bessant et al., 2015).

24.2 Approaches for Tackling Crises

As this study explores the reactions and responses of retail to the COVID-19 crisis, the theoretical foundation starts with an introduction to the literature on general approaches for tackling crises, including Wenzel, Stanske, and Lieberman (2021), who distinguish between four different strategic responses as to how companies can react to crises: (1) retrenchment, (2) persevering, (3) exit, and (4) innovation.

1-Retrenchment describes how companies react to a crisis by reducing costs, assets, product diversity, and overhead (Robbins & Pearce, 1993). This strategy results in a reduction of a company's overall business activities. On the positive side, retrenchment can stabilise a company's performance since it focuses on certain core activities, reduces complexity, and creates transparency for business processes. This strategy may be regarded as necessary as an immediate (short-term) response to a crisis. If this reaction to a crisis is prolonged, though, it can lead to the loss of valuable resources, capabilities, and culture (Wenzel et al., 2021).

2-Persevering is a strategy revolving around maintaining the status quo of a company's operations and mitigating the impact of a crisis. This strategy can be successful because it avoids frequent directional changes (Stieglitz, Knudsen, & Becker, 2016). In particular, diversified and international firms often implement persevering as a strategy to cope with crises (Li & Tallman, 2011). It is also often associated with the presence of slack resources. For this reason, it is regarded as a medium-term strategy, as resources will eventually be exhausted. There is also the risk that, when following a perseverance strategy, strategic renewal is missed; this can jeopardise the long-term survival of a company (Wenzel et al., 2021)

3-Exit refers to the discontinuation of an organisation's business activities. Research shows that this strategy can be applied for two reasons. First, if all other strategies and measures and therefore the business as a whole have failed, an exit is unavoidable. Second, an exit can also occur early and voluntarily if there is no prospect of the crisis improving or viable coping mechanisms (Wenzel, Cornelissen, Koch, Hartmann, & Rauch, 2020). Nevertheless, an exit strategy does not necessarily have a negative connotation, as it can form the basis for strategic renewal (Ren, Hu, & Cui, 2019). Previously tied-up resources are released and can be used for new ventures.

4-Innovating as a strategic response means that companies explicitly see a crisis as an opportunity for strategic renewal. This response can be understood as a long-term strategy and the most forward-looking reaction. It entails exploring new alternatives, expanding business activities into new sectors, and reflecting on new ways of doing business (Wenzel et al., 2021). Strong corporate governance, high decision power, and slack resources are key to this strategy for tackling crises. However, unless managers can improvise or exploit the exchangeability of their resources, strategic renewal may require the additional financial resources (Kim & Bettis, 2014).

24.3 Innovation and the COVID-19 Crisis

Innovating is a promising but challenging approach. To gain further insight here, the literature on innovation in past crises is examined. Although the COVID-19 pandemic is likely a unique crisis in terms of business and innovation research, innovative organisational behaviour is comparable to past crises, such as the financial crisis of 2008 or humanitarian crises resulting from natural disasters (Ebersberger & Kuckertz, 2021). Research shows that crises usually have a negative effect on innovation, as companies reduce their spending and innovation activities (Filippetti & Archibugi, 2011). Similar expectations were raised for the COVID-19 crisis (Dachs & Peters, 2020). At the same time, crises offer opportunities for new market entrants and can spur innovation activities of already innovative companies (Bessant et al., 2015). Through more explorative innovation strategies, companies can cope better with a given crisis (Archibugi, Filippetti, & Frenz, 2012). In addition, innovation can drive business success after a crisis and contribute to business recovery in the aftermath of the crisis (Hausman & Johnston, 2014). The COVID-19 crisis shows its specific nature here. The business of many organisations, especially those relying on physical interactions like culture, tourism, and retail, was put on hold. At the same time, many resources remained untouched, leading to potential business model innovation by means of resource reconfiguration, as observed, e.g., in the hospitality industry. For example, within a short period of time restaurants had switched to pick-up and delivery services

(Breier et al., 2021). Cooking classes, book readings, and concerts were moved to the virtual world via livestreaming (Vandenberg, Berghman, & Schaap, 2021).

24.4 Business Model Innovation

This reconfiguration of existing resources in response to the COVID-19 crisis represents a change in companies' business models. For example, a concert that is livestreamed fundamentally changes the experience for the customer and requires different skills and resources from the host. According to Gassmann, Frankenberger, and Csik (2013), a business model consists of the following: elements a) value proposition, b) value chain, c) customer segments and d) revenue model.

These elements can be configured to shape the value-creation and value-capturing mechanisms (Gassmann, Frankenberger, & Sauer, 2016). The customer segments element describes the target groups or market segments of an organisation. This element is central, as the other elements (e.g., value propositions) are tailored to it (H. Chesbrough & Rosenbloom, 2002). Value propositions describe the portfolio of solutions, products, and services that the organisation offers to its customers (Morris, Schindehutte, & Allen, 2005). The value chain element describes the processes and activities, resources, and capabilities needed to generate and distribute the value proposition (Hedman & Kalling, 2003). Finally, the revenue model explains whether and how exactly the business model works from a financial perspective. This includes the cost structures, revenue mechanisms, and revenue sources (Gassmann et al., 2013). BMs can be the basis for innovation: innovative ideas alone do not generate value; it is their commercialisation and adoption in the market that generates value (H. Chesbrough, 2010).

However, BMs are not only the framework for innovation but can themselves be the subject of innovation through reconfiguration (Massa & Tucci, 2013; Schneider & Spieth, 2013). As such, the innovation and reconfiguration of the business model itself promises to be a possible solution for retailers severely impacted by the COVID-19 crisis (Clauss, Breier, Kraus, Durst, & Mahto, 2021; Kraus et al., 2020).

Business model innovation (BMI) refers to the change to one or more elements of an organisation's business model by which competitive advantages can be achieved (Gassmann et al., 2016). BMI does not require the change of all elements, which would mean the implementation of radical changes, instead resulting from the incremental reconfiguration of a few elements. Foss and Saebi (2017) distinguish BMIs on the basis of the dimensions of novelty and scope (Figure 24.1). Novelty refers to the degree of newness, whether a BMI is simply new to the firm or is a novelty to an entire industry. Scope refers to the degree to which the organisation's existing BM is altered by the innovation, i.e., how many elements (value proposition, value chain, customer segments, and revenue model) of the BM are changed. The alteration of one or few elements is termed modular, which can be equated with incremental innovation. If the entire BM—all or the majority of its elements—is altered, the BMI is termed architectural, referring to comparatively radical innovation (Foss & Saebi, 2017).

		Scope	
Novelty		Modular	Architectural
	New to firm	Evolutionary BMI	Adaptive BMI
	New to industry	Focused BMI	Complex BMI

Figure 24.1 Types of business model innovation (adapted from Foss & Saebi, 2017)

Four types of BMI can be derived from the combination of these dimensions. Evolutionary BMI refers to a process of sharpening and fine-tuning. Individual elements of a BM are adjusted, often naturally over time (Demil & Lecocq, 2010). Similar to evolutionary BMI, adaptive BMI involves changing elements that are new to the firm but not to the entire industry. Here, several or all elements of the BM are adapted, e.g., in reaction to changes in environmental conditions and competition (Teece, 2010). Evolutionary and adaptive BMI represents adjustment processes. Focused and complex BMI refers to active and targeted innovation processes carried out by management to disrupt market conditions (Foss & Saebi, 2017). Focused BMI describes the targeted innovation of a single, modular element of the BM to create a competitive advantage. Sourcing a new customer segment while maintaining the original value proposition, value chain, and revenue model is an example of evolutionary or focused BMI, depending on the degree of novelty. Complex BMI refers to the intended renewal of the majority of elements affecting the BM as a whole (Foss & Saebi, 2017). The shift from traditional brick-and-mortar retailing to e-commerce represents a complex BMI, as it not only addresses new customer segments but also substantially changes the value proposition and value chain.

24.5 Risks Associated with BMI

Although BMI appears to be a reasonable and attractive way to strengthen an organisation's competitive advantage, its implementation poses major challenges and risks of failure (Pauwels & Weiss, 2008). These challenges arise for different reasons: uncertainty, complexity, and organisational inertia. First, there is uncertainty as to whether a new BM works with the intended effectiveness (Andries & Debackere, 2007). The second major challenge is rooted in the complexity of BMs, as the various elements and their configurations interact. Therefore, the elements cannot be considered in isolation but only in the entirety of their configurations (Baden-Fuller & Mangematin, 2013). Accordingly, the process of changing or innovating a BM requires a great deal of consideration and anticipation. Particularly in the development of radical changes (i.e., focused and complex BMI), problems can arise if the new BM is developed in parallel with the old BM. Using elements of the old BM can create synergy but can also lead to inertia in the development (Chesbrough & Rosenbloom, 2002). The process of reconfiguration is therefore highly dependent on human factors and leadership to address these challenges. Managers may opt to include new actors or redefine the roles of existing actors for the reconfiguration of resources. Old rules for interaction must be broken and new rules must be created and institutionalised (Koskela-Huotari, Edvardsson, Jonas, Sörhammar, & Witell, 2016). Ramaswamy and Ozcan (2018) label this as ongoing, repetitive, and dynamic processes of 'structuring organizations' and 'agencing engagements,' meaning that organisations are constantly in the process of reconfiguring their value creation by re-arranging the individual components such as people, artifacts, processes, and interfaces. Ideally, this reconfiguration of the business model is evidence-based. Iterative processes such as experimentation and trial-and-error can be used to reduce complexity and guide development (Andries, Debackere, & van Looy, 2013; Sosna, Trevinyo-Rodríguez, & Velamuri, 2010). Additionally, innovations often have to be adapted and refined after implementation (Demil & Lecocq, 2010), which is facilitated by evidence-based rationales.

In summary, the literature provides a solid overview of how companies can respond to crises. Through the reconfiguration of the BM elements, crises can also drive innovation for companies, as past humanitarian crises (e.g., Bessant et al., 2015) and the first findings regarding the COVID-19 crisis have shown (e.g., Netz et al., 2022). However, the question of sustainability remains, i.e., to what extent innovations developed during the crisis are transferred to post-crisis operations.

Research Approach: Multiple-Case Study

25

To investigate innovation and reconfiguration happening in brick-and-mortar retail during the COVID-19 crisis, a multiple-case comparative research strategy was applied (Eisenhardt, 1991). In general, case studies use different perspectives and data sources to illustrate complex phenomena in a real-world context. With the COVID-19 crisis and its impact on retail business models, a unique phenomenon is investigated, making a qualitative, case-based approach highly suitable (Siggelkow, 2007). Multiple-case studies provide an even more powerful base for theory building than single-case studies, as they allow for replication and extension between cases, and thus comparison. The replication of case studies enables the researcher to affirm certain propositions by examining several individual cases. Replication thus helps in identifying patterns and eliminating chance associations. Extension aids in developing theory as different cases emphasise different aspects of a phenomenon (Eisenhardt, 1991), allowing for more detailed and comprehensive consideration. The present research is of an exploratory nature, rather than explanatory or descriptive (Dubé & Paré, 2003; Yin, 2003), seeking to contribute to and advance understandings of existing theory.

Supplementary Information The online version contains supplementary material available at https://doi.org/10.1007/978-3-658-41920-2_25.

M. Perez Mengual, *Designing Physical Interaction Platforms*,
Markt- und Unternehmensentwicklung Markets and Organisations,
https://doi.org/10.1007/978-3-658-41920-2_25

25.1 Research Context

This study takes place in the context of the COVID-19 pandemic and focuses on small and medium-sized retailers in Germany. The COVID-19 virus first officially occurred in Germany in late January 2020 (RKI, 2022). In mid-March 2020, the virus hit Germany hard, with sharply rising infection and death rates. As a result, strict measures were enacted by the German government to contain COVID-19. The first so-called 'lockdown' came into effect on 22 March 2020, bringing about numerous restrictions on public life. This lockdown required the reduction of face-to-face interaction, thereby forcing most retail stores to close. The lockdown lasted for seven weeks, until 4 May 2020 (RKI, 2022). This period was defined by uncertainty and turbulence. Although the German government promised financial aid, the retail sector was nevertheless confronted with a complete and enduring loss of sales at short notice. For small and medium-sized retailers in particular, due to the lack of financial reserves, this posed a major challenge that threatened their very existence. As a result, retailers sought ways to sustain their business through digital, creative, and innovative solutions.

25.2 Research Design

This work seeks to explore the reconfiguration of BM in retail in response to the COVID-19 crisis, which innovations were sustainable, and what can be learned regarding the reconfiguration of retail business models in general. For this reason, this multiple-case study looks at small and medium-sized retailers that have proven to be particularly innovative in order to provide a powerful selection (Figure 25.1).

The identification of cases was done in several steps. First, a preliminary interview study with experts (n = 4) was conducted to identify suitable cases. The expert interviews were conducted with city and retail management officials. From these interviews, initial insights were gathered regarding the handling of the COVID-19 situation, and innovative retailers were identified. This resulted in the creation of a database of case sites that have been described by the experts as particularly innovative (n = 91). The case sites were examined in more detail through desk research and categorised according to the innovations developed. Based on this database, a total of six cases were identified for in-depth case studies. Purposive sampling was used to maximise variation across cases (Suri, 2011). Case studies involve the collection of rich data to capture various perspectives on a phenomenon (Piekkari, Plakoyiannaki, & Welch, 2010). In this study,

1. Expert Interviews

- 4 Interviews with city and retail management officials
- Identification of „innovative“ reactions in retail in response to the COVID-19 crisis
- Identification of „innovative“ retailers

2. Case Database

- Setting up a database with 91 cases from German small- and medium-sized retail
- Categorization of all cases according to product group and "innovative" reactions

3. Case Selection

- Main basis for sampling: heterogeneity of „innovative“ reactions
- 8 cases selected for in-depth case studies

4. Case Study: Interviews (t1)

- Semi-structured interviews with owners and general managers as main data source
- Interviews and desk research took place during and after the first lockdown (April-May 2020)
- Supplementary material includes the analysis of websites and social media channels (April-May 2020)

5. Case Study: Field Visits (t2)

- Conduction of field visits; observations and short interviews with field staff are the main data source
- Short interviews were conducted in August 2020 during the opening hours of the retailers
- Supplementary material includes the analysis of websites and social media channels (August 2020)

Figure 25.1 Research design

cases were selected to facilitate the identification of business model reconfiguration. Therefore, the individual reconfigurations of the retailers' BM (expressed by visible innovation, e.g., new services offered) were used as the main basis for case sampling. As a control mechanism, two cases that showed no visible signs of innovation activities were included in the selection. This was done (1) to identify what reactions and retail innovations were specific to the COVID-19 crisis and (2) to evaluate whether the reconfiguration of the BMs had any impact on dealing with the crisis. Thus, the final selection (n = 8) included six cases in German retail with distinct innovations and two with no visible innovations. The cases showed some variations regarding commodity focus, target audience, and company size. Yet, these variations were not deemed to be extreme enough to prevent cross-case comparisons. Moreover, the broad selection of small and medium-sized retailers contributes to the external generalisability of the findings (Eisenhardt, 1989; Yin, 2013).

25.3 Data Collection

In line with Sarker et al.'s (2013) principle of transparency, this section presents details regarding 'where, when, how, and from whom data was collected' (p. xiii). Data collection in the eight cases was conducted over a period of five months. Primary sources of data were interviews with the managers (t1) and field visits including interviews (t2). This allowed for a comparison of two distinct configuration settings, t1 being during the COVID-19-induced lockdown and t2 being post-lockdown.

t1: The interviews were semi-structured, following a guideline of open-ended questions (see Annex D in the electronic supplementary material), enabling the interviewees to raise issues that were not explicitly asked about (Hesse-Biber & Leavy, 2006). The interviewees were asked to describe solutions developed in response to the COVID-19 pandemic, the development process, and the impacts. Per case, one interview was conducted with the managing director or owner, resulting in eight interviews in total (see table 25.1 for an overview). The interviews took place in April and May 2020. All interviews were recorded and transcribed verbatim. The data material contains 79 pages of single-spaced text.

Table 25.1 Overview of interviews (t1) in the multiple-case study

Name	Number	Interviewed Person	Duration
TTR	1	Owner (TTR-O)	41 min
KUL	2	Managing Director (KUL-MD)	30 min
DBI	3	Managing Director (DBI-MD)	40 min
BJK	4	Managing Director (BJK-MD)	34 min
SEL	5	Owner (SEL-O)	17 min
HLM	6	Owner (HLM-O)	33 min
FAM	7	Owner (FAM-O)	52 min
BLN	8	Owner (BLN-O)	36 min

t2: The field visits were conducted using a field visit protocol. The protocol included guiding questions for short interviews with staff present at the store during the visit. In some cases, these were the same interviewees as during t1, while in other cases these were different interviewees. In total, eight short interviews were conducted in July 2020 during the opening hours of the retailers (see table 25.2 for an overview). The answers to the questions were recorded (handwritten) in a summarised form. In addition, impressions and real-time observations were recorded in the protocol. The protocols were digitised for evaluation purposes. The data from interviews and field visits were supplemented with additional data sources to increase the validity of the findings (Dubé & Paré, 2003). The supplementary material includes the structured analysis of the websites and social media channels of the eight cases over the research period, as well as sales materials.

Table 25.2 Overview of interviews (t2) in the multiple case study

Name	Number	Interviewed Person	Same Person (compared to t1) y/n
TTR	1	Owner (TTR-O)	Yes
KUL	2	Field Staff (KUL-FS)	No
DBI	3	Director Local Store (DBI-DLS)	No
BJK	4	Deputy Director (BJK-DD)	No
SEL	5	Owner (SEL-O)	Yes
HLM	6	Owner (HLM-O)	Yes
FAM	7	Owner (FAM-O)	Yes
BLN	8	Owner (BLN-O)	Yes

25.4 Data Analysis

Each case was individually analysed to discover particularities within the cases. After that, a comparative cross-case analysis was performed to identify patterns and discover similarities and differences between the cases (Eisenhardt, 1989). The data analysis was based on Gioia et al.'s approach (Gioia et al., 2013) and proceeded in three distinct phases, utilising different coding techniques. In the first phase, the researchers familiarised themselves with the data. Open coding was applied to each transcript to identify first-order codes: references to what elements were reconfigured, how innovation took place, and what the impacts were (Corbin & Strauss, 2008; Gioia et al., 2013). During the process, 925 segments were coded from the interviews, and 102 segments were generated from the field visits. In the second phase, the researchers identified more common concepts that emerged from the first-order codes. Twenty-three second-order concepts were created in this phase, paraphrasing the essence of the interviews. In the third phase, the researchers applied systematic combining (Dubois & Gadde, 2002) to link data from the interviews to theoretical knowledge. This was done by relating the second-order concepts to existing knowledge from the literature. Using the business model framework by Gassmann et al. (2013), the innovations that the cases developed during COVID-19 were categorised along the four BM elements presented earlier: *customer segments, revenue model, value propositions, and value chain.*

Additionally, Wenzel et al.'s (2020) framework was used to categorise the crisis-response strategies of the case companies. The third phase of the data analysis took place as an interpretation of the empirical data combined with theory (Van Maanen, Sørensen, & Mitchell, 2007). The trustworthiness of this research is enhanced by establishing a clear chain of evidence from the data collected to the findings. This was achieved by illustrating the findings with 'proof quotes' from the interviews as well as observations from the field visits. Following the recommendation by Pratt (2009), these 'proof quotes' are presented in tables. Furthermore, the transferability of the findings is enhanced by the multiple-case study approach and the clear delimitation of the empirical field (Riege, 2003).

25.5 Case Descriptions

An overview of the cases, as well as the backgrounds of the case companies, is provided in Table 25.3 and the following section, explaining the nature and context of this study (Pratt, 2009). Cases that showed visible innovation are marked with an 'I,' and cases that were included as a control mechanism are marked with a 'C.' A more detailed and narrated description of the cases is provided in Annex E: Detailed Case Descriptions for the Multiple-Case Study in the electronic supplementary material.

Table 25.3 Overview of cases

Name	Innovation (I)/ Control (C)	Retail Product Category	Year of Foundation	No. of Employees
TTR	I	Sports & Outdoors	~ 1985	> 20
KUL	I	Household Goods	~ 1850	> 50
DBI	I	Grocery & Gourmet Food	2014	> 15
BJK	I	Books	~ 1950	> 15
SEL	C	Grocery & Gourmet Food	2005	< 5
HLM	C	Clothing, Shoes, and Jewellery	~ 2005	< 5
FAM	I	Gifts & Handmade	2007	< 5
BLN	I	Baby Clothing & Accessories	2011	> 5

Findings

26

Analysing the data of the eight case companies revealed three major insights answering the following research questions: What were the activities and strategic responses of retailers in reaction to the COVID-19 crisis? and Did these activities and strategic responses lead to sustainable innovation? The insights are as follows: (1) retailers made only changes to the value chain element of their business model, persevering through the crisis. The elements of value proposition, customer segments, and revenue model remained completely untouched. Despite the radical impulse caused by the COVID-19 crisis, only incremental innovation was observed. (2) The changes to the value chain were made using two approaches—either intensification or improvisation. (3) The changes made to the value chain were not sustainable and purely used to overcome the crisis. However, exhibiting innovative activity had a positive effect on post-lockdown revenue recovery. (4) As an additional finding, it was discovered that despite recognising the necessity of innovation, the retailers in this study showed difficulties in implementing innovation, i.e., in not only generating ideas but actually realising them.

26.1 Retailers Only Changed the Value Chain Element of Their Business Model to Persevere Through the Crisis

Changes and adjustments to the business models were observed in the majority of cases (DBI, KUL, TTR, BJK, FAM, BLN). However, all of these changes concerned the value chain dimension. This means that mainly elements of the BM that are necessary to distribute and deliver products were changed. This can be attributed to the pandemic and the circumstances caused by it—the pandemic and the lockdowns made customer interaction in retail almost impossible at peaks.

M. Perez Mengual, *Designing Physical Interaction Platforms*, Markt- und Unternehmensentwicklung Markets and Organisations, https://doi.org/10.1007/978-3-658-41920-2_26

Resulting from that, essential retail functions required reconfiguration and adaptation to new circumstances. Changes to the value chain dimension included a) the transport of goods from the shop to the customer (KUL, TTR, BJK); b) the creation of advisory services via distance, outside the physical sales area (TTR, BLN); c) the product presentation via distance (FAM, BLN); and d) activating and maintaining interaction with customers via distance (e.g., by digital channels) (DBI, TTR, BJK, BLN). Table 26.1 provides an overview of these activities and strategic responses.

Table 26.1 Overview of activities and strategic responses

	Case	1	2	3	4	5	6	7	8
	Retailer	TTR	KUL	DBI	BJK	SEL	HLM	FAM	BLN
	Innovation / Control Group	Innovation	Innovation	Innovation	Innovation	Control	Control	Innovation	Innovation
Strategic responses	Coping Strategy	Perseverance	Perseverance	Perseverance	Perseverance	Retrenchment	Retrenchment	Perseverance	Perseverance
	Business Model Innovation	Evolutionary	Evolutionary	Evolutionary	Evolutionary	-	-	Evolutionary	Evolutionary
Reconfiguration BM Elements	Value Proposition	Same	Same	Same	Same	Same	Same	Same	Same
	Value Chain	Changed	Changed	Changed	Changed	Same	Same	Changed	Changed
	Customer Segments	Same	Same	Same	Same	Same	Same	Same	Same
	Revenue Model	Same	Same	Same	Same	Same	Same	Same	Same
Reconfiguration Process	Built on core competencies	Yes	Yes	Yes	Yes	No	No	Yes	Yes
	Utilized network resources	High	Medium	Low	High	Low	Low	High	High
	Utilized IT infrastructure	Medium	High	High	Medium	Low	Low	Low	High
Impact	Customer Loyalty	Increase	Increase	Increase	Increase	No change	No change	Increase	Increase
	Quick Recovery	Yes	Yes	Yes	Yes	No	Yes	Yes	Yes

However, no changes to the BM elements value proposition, revenue model, or customer segment were observed. None of the cases in this multiple-case study showed signs of more radical innovation or substantial changes to the BM as a reaction to the crisis. When it comes to the business model element of value proposition, the opposite of reconfiguration was observed. Instead of changing existing value propositions, the retailers in this case study focused on their existing value propositions and refined them. This was caused by two aspects. On the one hand, retailers were in most cases aware of the resources and competencies they possess (e.g., TTR, HLM, FAM). They were aware that a new value proposition would require different competencies and resources—which they knew they could not achieve or afford on short notice. On the other hand, operators were also aware of their non-organisational assets. This includes aspects such as their image, values, and (core) customers. It was observed that the retailers in this study focused on their existing assets during the crisis instead of trying to create new ones. The pandemic thus led the retailers to emphasize own strengths and competencies, focusing on what is important for the core business. The majority of the retailers in this case study thus used the perseverance strategy, revolving around maintaining the status quo of a company's operations and mitigating the impact of a crisis. Table 26.2 illustrates these insights by providing quotations from the interviewees.

Table 26.2 Illustrative quotations on activities and strategic responses

Finding	Illustrative Quotation
Changing the value chain BM element	*I have to say that if someone takes on something like this, it should be reasonably professional, otherwise it will go in the wrong direction. […] We had an offer from ten different sites that wanted to help us set up an online store. That would change a complete sales structure for us. Because we wouldn't be able to close it down again after six weeks. Once it's there, it's there. […] You also need the staff. Even a small online store requires an employee who does it full-time. (TTR-O)*
	It's almost impossible to come up with something completely new during a crisis. For us small ones. But some things were already there, had been before. We knew what had to be done. And we simply reinforced that once again. […] Honestly, we don´t do things completely new. So, of course, we will expand our range, because we have always done that. But I have not noticed that we make things completely different now. (KUL-MD)

(continued)

Table 26.2 (continued)

Finding	Illustrative Quotation
Reinforcing existing value propositions and customer segments	*I think it was a great opportunity for everyone to work out their profile and think about exactly who I am, what I am, and where we want to go. (TTR-O)*
	What it showed us, was a bit of the importance of stable regular customer relationships. It was very noticeable that this is important. The many regular customers also recognised the seriousness of the situation and wanted to support the stores. That was a positive insight. [...] The issue of maintaining close communication with regular customers. We have become even more aware that this is very important. That we can communicate with them to maintain communication. In some cases, we have even established our own WhatsApp groups with regular customers, where they also regularly communicate offers and so on via WhatsApp. (DBI-MD)

26.2 Intensification or Improvisation: Two Approaches to Changing the Value Chain

The cross-case analysis revealed two distinct reactions of retailers towards reconfiguration in times of crisis: intensification or improvisation. (1) *Intensification* focuses on utilising existing resources such as IT and developed channels to overcome the crisis. (2) *Improvisation* focuses on ideation and experimentation with new services to tackle challenges. Both approaches are distinguished not only by their organisational resources but also by prerequisites and leadership, as shown in Table 26.3 (p. 152).

Intensification is used by those retailers who can build on a strong existing IT infrastructure, expressed by, e.g., existing online shops, merchandise management systems, payment systems, and cultivated social media channels. This infrastructure enabled two of the case companies (DBI, KUL) to run their business in a hybrid way, sourcing different channels and income sources. Through these prerequisites, they were able to partially compensate for the absence of customer interaction by leaning more towards the digital channels of their existing hybrid business models. As a response to the COVID-19 crisis, improvements were mainly made to the IT infrastructure; in the case of DBI, quantitative metrics were used to identify improvements and evaluate actions.

Table 26.3 Overview two approaches of retailers to changing the value chain

	Intensification	Improvisation
Cases	• DBI • KUL	• TTR • BJK • FAM • BLN
Starting Situation	• Developed IT infrastructure • Multichannel business model	• Existing digital infrastructure • Single-channel business model
Reconfigured Elements	• Minor reconfiguration of the value chain, e.g., by adjusting the online-shop	• Larger reconfiguration of the value chain, e.g., by the development of new services (delivery, customer interaction, etc.)
Reconfiguration Activities	• Targeted adjustment • Relying on defined KPIs to measure success of the reconfiguration (e.g., online shop KPIs, social media metrics, direct customer feedback)	• Execution of several experiments to find suitable solutions • No measurement of reconfiguration, instead relying on 'gut feeling' and direct customer feedback
Recovery	• Quick recovery of customer interaction after lockdown periods • Maintained revenue during the crisis	• Quick recovery of revenue and customer interaction after lockdown periods • Gained experience with new services • Increased customer loyalty
Strategy	• Perseverance	• Perseverance

Improvisation, the second approach to dealing with the COVID-19 crisis, is characterised by high activity and willingness to experiment. To react to the pandemic and compensate for the loss of customer interaction, the improvisation approach relies on creativity. Available resources such as the personal network and employees are used as a source for ideation and implementation. This results in a variety of improvised 'experiments,' such as the development and prototyping of new services, including trying out new channels (e.g., selling via social media in the case of BLN) or changes to the supply chain (e.g., through delivery services in the case of BJK). The case of TTR revealed in interviews and field visits that the effects of these experiments had only a small direct impact on immediate sales but led to increased customer loyalty and thus a rapid recovery and even a post-lockdown increase in sales.

These two approaches show that the retailers in this multiple-case study deliberately did not pursue a more radical approach to innovation. The main reasons given were the limited availability of resources and the high cost of substantial reconfigurations. Instead, minor adjustments were made to the business model to cope with the crisis. This was implemented via a large number of experiments—adaptations to elements of their business models to react to the new situation. These experiments were an expression of the retailers' self-efficacy and willpower to overcome the situation through activity. In companies that followed the improvisation approach (TTR, BJK, FAM, BLN), the analysis showed more varied experiments, i.e., attempts to adapt the BM to the COVID-19 crisis. For example, a vending machine concept was experimented with (FAM) and YouTube channels were founded, bringing product presentation into the digital world (BLN). In IT-heavy companies, change was more likely to take place based on existing technology. For example, DBI's online presence became a virtual storefront by displaying the individual stores' inventory (i.e., available products) online. The experiments carried out during the crisis were not done in a systematic fashion and were not used to advance the business model. The experiments were not properly evaluated, nor was their effect on the business's performance measured. Instead, the majority of retailers relied on their gut feelings in connection with direct, perceived customer feedback for their evaluation. Table 26.4 illustrates these insights by providing quotations from the interviewees.

Table 26.4 Illustrative quotations approaches towards changing the value chain

Finding	Illustrative Quotation
Idea Generation and Implementation	*I don't think about it for very long. So with me, it's a quick idea, a short thought, quick implementation, try it out, and either it works, or it doesn't. [...] I don't have any savings either [...] so I just have to take care of it myself. And I think that's also part of the reason why I think to myself, okay, there has to be a solution. I'll just give it a try. (FAM-O)*
	So, of course, we implemented multiple things faster than we originally planned. (BLN-O)
	As I said, our backbone is our IT, because it is already fully networked. [...] So we look at the customer journeys and form clusters and customer groups [...]. So we simply generate a lot of data and then we try to use it. [...] With an individualised voucher code or an e-mail or whatever, we address specific customers. (DBI-MD)
Measurement of reconfiguration	*Mainly in personal contact, so we talk a lot with our customers, often ask them what they liked, what we could perhaps do better. And we also get a lot of feedback. And that's our key figures. On the one hand, there are certainly likes on social media, and on the other hand, there are simply personal conversations with our customers. (BJK-MD)*
	So, in principle, of course, it's a gut feeling. One is the direct feedback we get. That's not a factor that can be measured in numbers, but when people write in the comments 'how cool it is,' 'how great it is' and 'thank you' [...]. That's the first thing where we say that was successful. (TTR-O)
	So I do a lot according to gut feeling. And yes, it has to feel good, it has to feel right. And you can't pin a lot of things down to direct sales over the next three days. (FAM-O)
	On the one hand, because we talk to the customer. That means we get direct feedback. We also ask: How do you know us and how did you come across us? Then also through direct prompts. Facebook and Instagram in particular are very important for interacting with customers. That means I actively ask the customer to interact with me. Accordingly, I have a direct response and can measure how good or how bad it is. And what goes down well with the customer, what doesn't go down so well with the customer. What interests him, what does not interest him. (BLN-O)

26.3 Changes Made to the Value Chain Were Not Sustainable and Purely Used to Overcome the Crisis

Most of the observed changes to the value chain were implemented on a short-term, temporary basis to overcome the challenges of the COVID-19-induced lockdown. While some of them were maintained in operation after the lockdown periods, this happened with reduced intensity. An example is the bicycle delivery service in case TTR, which regularly delivered goods during the lockdown; this service is now deployed less frequently or discontinued, as the freed personnel resources are needed again for regular operations. However, those reconfigurations that could be implemented with low resource input and matched the core value propositions were more sustainable. This was particularly evident in the case companies that used the COVID-19 crisis to push ahead with the digitisation of their marketing channels (DBI, KUL, TTR, BJK, FAM, BLN). For example, the WhatsApp group with customers in the case of DBI acted and still acts as an easy-to-operate marketing channel while increasing the intimacy of key customer relationships.

Data from the interviews suggests that the activity of innovating itself had an impact on business performance during and after the crisis. The cases that made an active effort to maintain the value chain, i.e., contact with customers (DBI, KUL, TTR, BJK, FAM, BLN) were rewarded with greater attention and loyalty on the part of customers. The process of innovation itself seems to be important, even if the innovations were not sustainably established in the company. It was the exhibition of activity, thus showing that something was happening at all, that caught the attention of customers, not the innovation itself. The cases in this study that acted by improvising or intensifying their efforts recovered far more quickly from the crisis than those that were inactive. Several case companies were even able to exceed the previous year's results (e.g., TTR, FAM). Table 26.5 illustrates these insights by providing quotations from the interviewees.

Table 26.5 Illustrative quotations on sustainability of innovation

Finding	Illustrative Quotation
Sustainability of innovation	*Online (Zoom) readings will no longer take place in this form. However, a hybrid solution is to be offered; Social channels: continue as usual and are increasingly used; Bicycle delivery service: only 2 times a week, as all employees are needed on-site and only from a minimum order value. (observation; field notes of in-store interview) (BJK-MD)*
	The online store continues, but the care is no longer as intensive because the employees are no longer flexibly available. (observation; field notes of in-store interview) (KUL-MD)
	Regular customer relationships have become even more intimate; loyalty and gratitude of customers have been particularly noticeable during the crisis, now thanking them after the lockdown (observation; field notes of in-store interview; BJK-DD)
	WhatsApp group for regular customers is looked after even more closely; Maintaining even stronger contact with (regular) customers à Founding of 'Local Supporters Club,' conveying even more emotionality and personal connection to customers and thus selling the value of the product (observation; field notes of in-store interview; DBI-DLS)
Activity as a cause for business success	*So it's more or less, the many regular customers have also recognised the seriousness of the situation a little bit, and have then also wanted to support the branches exactly, so to speak, and have also done that, and that was exactly a positive realisation, which I now times, especially also the digital offers were and are still actually very well accepted. (DBI-MD)*
	In fact, in all three stores, will achieve the same sales as last year or the previous years, as it looks like. Even have more sales. Despite empty city centres. The turnover is no longer distributed on Saturdays but is distributed over the week. (TTR-O)
	We have now opened, the first days, only five customers were allowed in at a time, but we have had sales in the direction of almost Christmas. (FAM-O)

26.4 Retailers in This Study Showed Difficulties in Implementing Innovation, Not Only Generating Ideas But Realising Them

The COVID-19 crisis has provided an initial impetus for retailers to question their own BM. It was repeatedly emphasised during the case interviews that a reaction to the crisis requires a great deal of flexibility, that agility is essential, and that cooperation among peer retailers is regarded as important. Some retailers (TTR, FAM) said that they aim to maintain these creative spaces and phases of experimentation in the future. Observations during the post-lockdown field visits, however, contrast this, as little experimentation was observed. The case companies tended to return to existing values, value propositions, and resources instead of reacting in an agile and flexible manner. Furthermore, while they were praised in the first few weeks of the crisis, dealer retailer networks lost a great deal of their dynamism due to declining participation.

The case analysis indicates that there is a general openness for more substantial innovation, but retailers themselves are not capable of handling it. The case companies like BLN, KUL, TTR, and BJK find it difficult to organise innovation as resources are tied up elsewhere. While aspects such as networking with other actors, holistic thinking, and the bundling of resources were emphasised, the data of this case study suggested that external impulses are required or desired for accomplishing experimentation and innovation, either by triggering or reinforcing. In particular, there have been calls for a central agent to orchestrate and manage networks and to put ideas into practice. Such a central agent is expected to provide leadership and directionality, driving joint activities and innovation. Table 26.6 illustrates these insights by providing quotations from the interviewees.

Table 26.6 Illustrative quotes on difficulties of implementing innovation

Finding	Illustrative Quotation
Attitude towards innovation	*The pandemic affected us. We've already started to think about how we can perhaps do this more often during the year, out-of-the-box breaks, so to speak, where we can reflect from a distance. [...] It's just that in everyday life, you often become blinded or somehow don't really take this creativity or the time for creative ideas, but instead just do your routine tasks. (BJK-MD)*
	For example, I simply take the freedom to do things. [...] Because I think it has to run smoothly. You can't work just for yourself, but I'm in favour of a lot of networking. (FAM-O)
	Flexibility as to the be-all and end-all à no longer plan everything 10 days in advance but act more flexibly and agile (observation; field notes of in-store interview; BLN-O)
Need for Orchestration	*I try to do that with networks, with regulars' tables [...]. And that is a bit of our problem, where someone is missing. We no longer have a city management. That's a crucial point because I'd like to have one. That would be the task of a city manager. To take people by the hand and organise them. Showing them digital ways of doing business, of networking. Let them talk to each other. Because very few people figure it out on their own. (BLN-O)*
	Yes, we need a functioning city to be able to adequately operate the areas and the people we employ. That's very important. And that's where we're continuing to work now. For example, we have an initiative called [...]. We now meet publicly in small circles. To simply see what can be done, and what needs to be done. (KUL-MD)
	What I would find interesting is if you had such a delivery service. You can package that quite nicely. Two people drive around every day and deliver things home from the stores. Maybe I should suggest that to the city, it just occurred to me, because I also have a good connection there. (TTR-O)
	We are also very dependent on walk-in customers. And if no one comes to the city centre because it's no longer attractive, then we'll have a huge problem. And that's why we're interested in making sure that our neighbours are doing well around us. (BJK-MD).

27 Discussion and Implications

Based on the case study of eight retailers with data from the COVID-19 crisis peak and after, the strategic responses and activities of retailers in reaction to the COVID-19 crisis were explored. Further, whether these strategic responses and activities led to sustainable innovation was investigated. The findings showed that the COVID-19 crisis triggered the reconfiguration of the retailers' business models, which aligns with the literature stating that organisations adapt their BMs when facing threats (Foss & Saebi, 2017). However, this reconfiguration referred exclusively to the value chain. Also, this reconfiguration was temporary and purely used to compensate for the omitted customer interaction (resulting from lockdowns). As such, some of the reconfigurations were successful measures in mitigating the detrimental effects of the crisis and securing survival. However, the reconfigurations were not sustainable and did not lead to the self-renewal of the retailers in the case study. This was due to the following two reasons: 1) the limited resources available to the small- and medium-sized retailers and 2) 'surviving' as a main objective of the innovation activities carried out during the COVID-19 crisis. Based on these results, the findings of this multiple-case study are discussed in the following paragraphs.

27.1 Perseverance as Main Strategic Response to the COVID-19 Crisis

Only temporary reconfiguration of the value chain to tackle the challenges posed by the crisis (limited possibilities for customer interaction) was observed. In contrast to more complex BMI, temporary BMI is closely aligned with a company's strategy and core competencies, building on the ability of the company to reuse existing capabilities (Prahalad & Hamel, 1997). This corresponds with the more

M. Perez Mengual, *Designing Physical Interaction Platforms*, Markt- und Unternehmensentwicklung Markets and Organisations, https://doi.org/10.1007/978-3-658-41920-2_27

defensive strategies the case companies adopted during the crisis. Some retailers in this case study (SEL, HLM) pursued the retrenchment strategy (Robbins & Pearce, 1993) and reduced costs, i.e., by putting their staff on part-time hours. Most of the case companies (TTR, KUL, DBI, BJK, FAM, BLN), however, adopted the perseverance strategy (Wenzel et al., 2021) in that they tried to keep the business running, focusing on the business's key strengths. This was demonstrated by retailers in the present case study sharpening their profiles and value propositions instead of changing their strategies (cf. Stieglitz et al., 2016). Thus, all case companies used short-term strategies that could lead to a loss of valuable resources and capabilities in the long term (Wenzel et al., 2021).

27.2 No Complex Business Model Innovation Resulting from the COVID-19 Crisis

Unlike other studies that observed the impact of COVID-19 on small- and medium-sized enterprises (SMEs) (Clauss et al., 2021), it was not observed that retailers changed more than one element of their business model (going beyond the reconfiguration of their value chain). In other studies on reactions to COVID-19, SMEs (e.g., catering, consulting, and manufacturing) changed their revenue model or sold different products and services in reaction to the pandemic, thus changing their value propositions (cf. Clauss et al., 2021). Their BMs were thus changed in an architectural scope (Foss & Saebi, 2017). However, the retailers in our case study all stayed close to their original BM and only innovated in a limited, modular scope (Foss & Saebi, 2017). One possibility to explain this behaviour lies in low learned strategic flexibility, i.e., 'the ability to identify innovation opportunities, commit resources to new courses of action, or reverse unproductive resource deployment' (Bock, Opsahl, George, & Gann, 2012, p. 279). Strategic flexibility is an antecedent to business model innovation (Bock et al., 2012). However, this flexibility has to be learned, for example, through repeated and continuous BMI activities (Schneider & Spieth, 2014).

27.3 Scarce Resources Limited the Retailers' Ability to Innovate

The findings showed that the retailers are restricted in their ability to innovate by limited resources, personnel capacities, and skills at their disposal. As a result, few complex changes were observed overall, and even those identified have not been permanently implemented. This can be explained by the lack of slack resources that are needed for architectural BMI (Foss & Saebi, 2017). The resources that were freed up during the COVID-19 crisis were only temporarily available. They were not resources planned for innovation ventures but resources needed for retail operations.

Nevertheless, the retailers in this study have demonstrated the ability to improvise with scarce resources, similar to frugal innovators. Frugal innovations are simplified, low-cost solutions that serve needs efficiently, often in creative ways (Weyrauch & Herstatt, 2017). Existing resources were identified and resource fungibility (Danneels, 2011) was recognised. In doing so, the retailers used opportunistic means. For example, they used their networks and personal contacts to design solutions (e.g., TTR used its network to produce YouTube videos for professional marketing purposes; FAM used its network to find new and unrestricted points of sale). Parallels can be drawn here to a study in the maker movement by Corsini, Dammicco, and Moultrie (2021). Like the makers in that study, retailers in this study have demonstrated the ability to identify, produce, and implement solutions locally, based on their own needs and constraints. They can therefore use existing resources efficiently but are nevertheless restricted in their innovation activities by resource scarcity.

27.4 No Sustainable Innovation From the COVID-19 Crisis

The retail sector requires strategic renewal (Agarwal, Breschi, & Devillard-Hoellinger, 2017; Reinartz, 2019). The COVID-19 pandemic has dramatically intensified this situation (Fairlie, 2020). Since crises can trigger innovation, this study investigated what can be learned from the reactions to the crisis for regular retail operations, similar to reverse innovation (Govindarajan & Euchner, 2012). However, none of the retailers in this case study used the crisis as an opportunity for strategic renewal, i.e., by exploring new alternatives, expanding business activities into new sectors, or reflecting on new ways of doing business (Wenzel et al., 2021). The observed temporal reconfigurations of the BMs were aimed purely at the survival of the companies.

A strategic renewal, however, aims for a lasting competitive advantage. That means innovating and expanding business activities. The changes are more complex and affect several elements of the business model (Foss & Saebi, 2017). The change processes in the company are therefore also more comprehensive. Existing structures, organisational inertia, and conceptual fixation need to be surpassed (Schreyögg & Kliesch-Eberl, 2007). Complex BMI, i.e. strategic renewal, requires cognitive effort and conscious commitment on the part of the organisation and its members (Eggers & Kaplan, 2013; Prahalad & Bettis, 1986). It requires long-term engagement and, most importantly, slack resources. These factors were not present among the retailers in this multiple-case study during the COVID-19 pandemic. Nevertheless, a question arises—if such a radical impulse does not trigger sustainable innovation, what will?

27.5 Managerial Implications

Two types of managerial implications can be derived from this multiple-case study: (1) direct implications for retail innovation and, on this basis, (2) design principles for the sustainable design of PIPs in general.

27.5.1 Managerial Implications for Retail Innovation

The COVID-19 crisis did not bring sustainable innovation to the retail industry. Most retailers have adhered to their traditional BMs. This study and discussion of the results highlight the reasons for this—resource scarcity as well as little commitment and strategic intent for complex BMI. From this, the derived mutually dependent conditions reveal the requirements for complex BMI and strategic renewal in retail.

(1) *Trigger for innovation activity:* In the course of the COVID-19 crisis, the retail sector showed that it has the ability to innovate. However, to overcome organisational inertia in stable business conditions, external impulses are still needed to stimulate innovation activities, especially when it comes to complex BMI.
(2) *Strategic flexibility of the organisation:* Retailers must acquire the ability to seize innovation opportunities. At the same time, they must also show commitment to deploying their resources for new courses of action (cf. Bock et al., 2012).
(3) *Availability of slack resources:* Resource scarcity was one of the main reasons for limited innovation effort—resources are usually tied up in day-to-day operations. To carry out complex BMI, excess resources in terms of personnel and cash (cf. Kim & Bettis, 2014) are needed that can be used for strategic ventures and innovation activities.

(4) *Guidance and structure in the innovation process:* For complex BMI, strategic direction is needed to set out development steps. Retailers started experimenting during COVID-19. This approach needs to be pursued more consistently and purposefully (cf. McGrath, 2010).
(5) *Formation of a retail innovation ecosystem:* In the case study, the retailers focused on the core business, not seizing opportunities to innovate. Nevertheless, the need to innovate was recognised, and some voices called for 'someone who orchestrates innovation.' Although it is still unclear who should take on this role, third-party input seems necessary for retail innovation on a broad scale.

27.5.2 Design Principles for Sustainable PIP Design

Based on the empirical observations of this case study, design principles ensuring the sustainable design of PIPs were derived. Design principles are explicit instructions regarding how an artifact, or a class of artifacts, should be designed (Gregor & Hevner, 2013; Gregor & Jones, 2007; Sein, Henfridsson, Purao, Rossi, & Lindgren, 2011). They convey design knowledge by describing 'what an artifact should enable users to do and how it should be built in order to do so' (Chandra, Seidel, & Gregor, 2015, p. 4043). In order to meet these general requirements, design principles are purposefully described in an abstract way (Gregor & Jones, 2007). Four principles for sustainable PIP design were formulated based on the implications of this multiple-case study.

(1) *PIP innovation needs to be considered early:* Innovation is essential for platforms (Memon, 2021; Parker et al., 2016; Thomas et al., 2021). When designing and implementing new PIPs, it should be considered that the PIP may require renewal during its lifecycle. Appropriate precautions for this should be taken during the development of the PIP.
(2) *PIP innovation continues after the market launch*: PIPs should express strategic flexibility to respond to changing conditions. This includes (1) the continuous sensing and seizing of innovation opportunities and (2) continuous learning cycles consisting of experimentation and evaluation.
(3) *PIP innovation requires scheduling slack resources*: Resources for innovating the PIP should be included in the financial planning during the initial PIP design. The experimentation and evaluation necessary for PIP innovation require resources, as does the implementation of an advanced PIP concept.

(4) *PIP innovation benefits from third-party input*: It seems necessary to bring in third parties to break fixation on an original concept. This approach has been tried and tested with digital platforms, where innovations are not generated by the platform provider but by complementors (Cennamo, 2018; Deilen & Wiesche, 2021; McIntyre & Srinivasan, 2017). The creation of opportunities for third parties to complement the PIP should be part of the initial design of a PIP.

Summary and Outlook 28

This research looked at retailer reactions and activities during the COVID-19 pandemic to understand innovation under extraordinary conditions. Employing a multi-case approach with two survey points, this study shed light on whether this crisis-driven innovation was sustainable.

The analysis revealed that innovation in retail triggered by the COVID-19 pandemic was not sustainable for several reasons, as follows: (1) when innovating, the existing business model must not be jeopardised by the innovation but support the core values and value proposition of the innovating retailer; (2) resources for innovation are scarce—to innovate beyond incremental adaptions or short-term alternations, additional resources and capabilities are required; (3) due to a lack of experience with experimenting, retailers ask for networked guidance and orchestration, a source of inspiration and trigger for innovation.

Insights from this study hold implications for retail innovation and PIP design in general. Derived from the findings, four design principles for sustainable PIP design were formulated. These principles should be considered at the beginning of a PIP design process to create the basis for the continuous innovation of PIPs.

This multiple-case study relies on eight cases from a central German city and looks at cases known for their general openness to innovation. Additional studies with a broader selection of cases in similar or different settings would be helpful to validate and enrich the current findings, just as a follow-up quantitative study would. The study highlights business model reconfigurations in the short and mid-term, fostering insights on sustained innovative behaviour. The effects of the COVID-19 crisis on retail business models, in the long run, have not been explored and could be subject to future research.

The insights generated during this multiple-case study have implications for the remainder of this dissertation. The findings indicate that the ability for continuous innovation must be considered early in a PIP design process. PIP design

M. Perez Mengual, *Designing Physical Interaction Platforms*, Markt- und Unternehmensentwicklung Markets and Organisations, https://doi.org/10.1007/978-3-658-41920-2_28

does not end with a launch but requires continuous innovation after the launch. This finding needs to be resembled in the PIP design process (cf. Figure 21.2). The findings from Part V complement Parts III and IV by looking beyond the phase of PIP concept development and operationalisation. Taken together, the findings from Parts III to V highlight various aspects that need to be considered in the initial design of a PIP, from the early phase of ideation to the ability to innovate. They thus represent a toolkit for PIP design. Part VI introduces and evaluates this toolkit in the context of a PIP design process.

Part VI

A Toolkit for Designing PIPs: An Action Research Study to Apply and Evaluate this Dissertation's Insights

Objectives and Structure 29

This dissertation seeks to explore *how a physical interaction platform (PIP) can be designed in a systematic and structured way.* Part VI supports this objective by evaluating the findings and artifacts developed in this dissertation's empirical studies (Parts III–V). Furthermore, by applying the findings and artifacts in an actual PIP design project, this study also synthesizes the findings and demonstrates how a PIP can be designed in a systematic and structured way.

In design research, evaluating artifacts is a pivotal activity to provide feedback for further development (Gregor & Hevner, 2013; Sonnenberg & vom Brocke, 2012). According to Venable, Pries-Heje, and Baskerville (2016), this study presents a naturalistic evaluation of these artifacts. Naturalistic evaluation analyses the performance of artifacts in natural environments, in this case, an actual PIP design process. Naturalistic evaluation methods typically lean towards an interpretive paradigm, including, e.g., case studies, field studies, and action research (Venable et al., 2016).

Since an evaluation should demonstrate the usefulness of the artifacts (Prat et al., 2015), a 14-month action research study was conducted. Based on the approach of Coghlan & Brannick (2005), two complete AR cycles were executed, consisting of the following phases: 1) diagnosing, 2) planning action, 3) taking action, and 4) evaluating action. (Coghlan & Brannick, 2005). The AR study occurred in the context of developing the 'Future Retail Store,' a new to-be-designed PIP. This study formulated one research question relating to the demonstration and the evaluation of the artifacts as follows:

Part VI of this dissertation builds upon and extends a contribution, which was presented and discussed at the doctoral colloquium of the 6th SIG Design Theory Tutorial in Paris, France (Perez Mengual, 2022).

M. Perez Mengual, *Designing Physical Interaction Platforms*, Markt- und Unternehmensentwicklung Markets and Organisations, https://doi.org/10.1007/978-3-658-41920-2_29

RQ 7: *Are the developed artifacts (from Parts III–V) applicable (ease of use) and useful (perceived usefulness) for the design process of a PIP?*

Part VI is structured as follows. Chapter 30 briefly summarises the artifacts from Parts III to V, relating them to each other and scholarly work. Chapter 31 provides background details about the study's particular AR project. Following this, Chapter 32 describes the first AR cycle and its results. Chapter 33 describes the second AR cycle. Finally, Chapter 34 discusses the results of Part VI and puts the derived insights into the context of the entire dissertation. The structure of Part VI is shown in Figure 29.1.

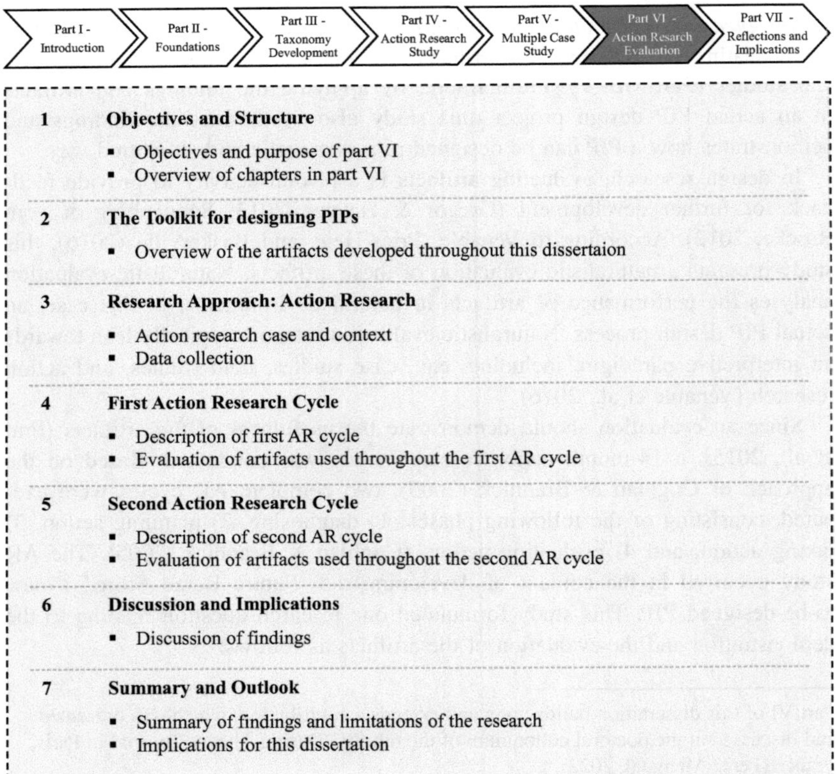

Figure 29.1 Structure of Part VI

30 The Toolkit for Designing PIPs

The artifacts developed throughout this dissertation resemble a toolkit for designing PIPs. They contain knowledge about PIP design and address the issues arising from using more generic innovation processes.

A common issue is that extant innovation processes are generic, typically consisting of stages such as idea generation, idea screening, business analysis, forming cross-functional teams, testing and validation, and market launch (Alam, 2006; Cooper, 2008). From this, three problems arise: (1) these innovation processes are very general, reducing their acceptance by practitioners (Menschner, Peters, & Leimeister, 2011). (2) They over-emphasise a sequential and systematic approach (Alam, 2006; Bowers, 1989; Scheuing & Johnson, 1989) while containing little knowledge on how a service should be designed (cf. Gregor & Hevner, 2013). (3) They are still an evolution of product-centric design, building on the seminal groundwork by Booz Allen Hamilton (1982); they focus on developing the service itself, with little consideration of systems and ecosystems, business models, strategies, and organisational fit (Böhmann, Leimeister, & Möslein, 2014), which are essential for the sustainable deployment of services.

M. Perez Mengual, *Designing Physical Interaction Platforms*,
Markt- und Unternehmensentwicklung Markets and Organisations,
https://doi.org/10.1007/978-3-658-41920-2_30

To address the abovementioned issues and in line with the engaged-scholarship paradigm (Van de Ven, 2007), the artifacts in this dissertation were derived from empirical studies aiming to solve real-world problems. Accordingly, the artifacts' intended purpose is to address the wicked problems encountered when designing PIPs (Coyne, 2005; Lönngren & van Poeck, 2021; Pries-Heje & Baskerville, 2008). Most complex problems are 'wicked,' expressed by two properties: 1) formulating the problem itself already depends on the perspective (Coyne, 2005). In the context of developing a PIP, for example, someone with a marketing background will likely have different expectations of designing the PIP than an innovation manager. 2) For wicked problems, there is no single solution, and testing the validity of a solution must take place in a practical context (Coyne, 2005; Elia & Margherita, 2018). Based on the insights from the previous studies, the wicked problems of designing PIPs concern the activities of (1) initiating, (2) sustaining, (3) conceptualising, and (4) operating PIPs.

- **Initiating a PIP** refers to setting up and initiating a PIP design process. This wicked problem is evident in the first AR cycle of Part VI, which explores the development of the Fraunhofer ENIQ. The 'wickedness' in initiating the design process comes from contrasting views of the stakeholders regarding what the PIP is intended to do.
- **Conceptualising a PIP** refers to concept development, e.g., designing the business model and selecting coherent design characteristics. Part III of this dissertation examined the design characteristics of PIPs, illustrating the various trajectories PIP development can take. Conceptualising a PIP is wicked, as there are various possibilities of combining design characteristics.
- **Operating a PIP** refers to operationalisation, i.e., how the PIP can be brought to life., which includes the design of operational processes and organisational structure. This is illustrated in the second AR cycle of Part VI. Ultimately, operating a PIP is wicked, as several stakeholders want to influence how it is done.
- **Sustaining a PIP** relates to the economic sustainability of PIPs. Part V of this dissertation highlighted that environmental factors (e.g., the COVID-19 pandemic or changing actor demands) make the reconfiguration of PIPs necessary. The 'wickedness' of sustaining a PIP lies in developing and testing possible solutions while the PIP is in operation.

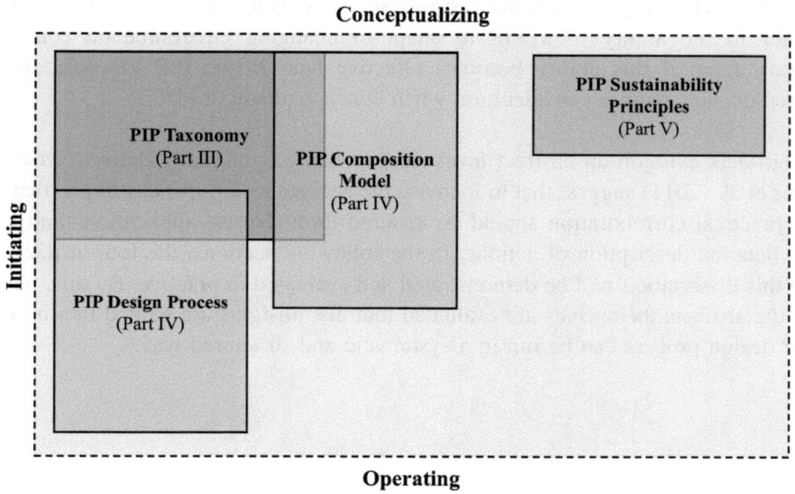

Figure 30.1 Artifacts related to the wicked problems of PIP design

The artifacts developed in this dissertation are intended to solve these wicked problems as illustrated in Figure 30.1. The artifacts offer different perspectives and applications for the PIP design process as follows:

- **Part III—PIP taxonomy:** The taxonomy (cf. Figure 13.1) can be used as a tool to initiate a PIP design process. IT provides an overview of design dimensions and characteristics necessary for sustainable PIP operation. Additionally, it can be extended to other design characteristics to create consistent and comprehensive PIP concepts.
- **Part IV—PIP composition model:** This model (cf. Figure 21.1) addresses the organisational anchoring of a PIP. The PIP composition model highlights the importance of the team and organisational infrastructure relationship. The model can be used at later stages of concept development and significantly impacts operationalisation.
- **Part IV—PIP design process:** The process model (cf. Figure 21.2) depicts a structured PIP design process. It illustrates design steps from early conceptualisation to implementation, i.e., opening a PIP.

- **Part V—Design principles for sustainable PIP design:** The design principles refer to the ability of a PIP to adapt to changing environmental conditions. Even if this ability becomes effective later in the PIP lifecycle, the prerequisites require consideration when conceptualising a PIP.

The artifacts exist on an abstract level, despite being empirically derived. Menschner et al. (2011) suggest that to increase the acceptance of artifacts in practice, their practical corroboration should be ensured through case applications and a more detailed description of actions. In the following sections, the four artifacts from this dissertation will be demonstrated and evaluated in practice. By this, not only the artifacts themselves are evaluated, but also insights are gained into how a PIP design process can be run in a systematic and structured way.

31 Research Approach

A large body of knowledge on evaluating artifacts is found in the literature on design science. As building and evaluating artifacts resembles the core of design science, with numerous contributions explaining how and why to evaluate (e.g., Hevner, 2007; Prat et al., 2015; Venable et al., 2016), this study draws on rich scholarly information. A distinction can be made between the demonstration and evaluation of artifacts (Peffers, Tuunanen, Rothenberger, & Chatterjee, 2007). Demonstration seeks to prove that the artifact works by using it to solve one or more problems (Gregor & Jones, 2007; Prat et al., 2015). The demonstration is followed by a more formal evaluation, which examines the usefulness of the artifact (Hevner, March, Park, & Ram, 2004).

To choose the right evaluation strategy, the FEDS framework provides guidance (Venable et al., 2016). The FEDS framework distinguishes evaluation strategies based on their functional purpose (formative or summative) and paradigm (artificial or naturalistic). Formative evaluation seeks to improve the outcome of the artifact, whereas summative evaluation assesses the extent to which the artifact matches the expectations of the involved stakeholders (Venable et al., 2016). However, any evaluation activity may hold evidence that can be used both formatively and summatively, as the difference between the two is purposive. As its second dimension, the FEDS framework distinguishes between artificial and naturalistic evaluation. Artificial evaluation can be empirical or non-empirical but is always positivist and reductionist. Typical methods for artificial evaluation include laboratory experiments, simulations, theoretical arguments, or mathematical proofs (Sonnenberg & vom Brocke, 2012; Venable et al., 2016). In contrast, naturalistic evaluation assesses the performance of an artifact in natural environments, ideally within organisations. It is always empirical and the

M. Perez Mengual, *Designing Physical Interaction Platforms*,
Markt- und Unternehmensentwicklung Markets and Organisations,
https://doi.org/10.1007/978-3-658-41920-2_31

methods applied lean towards interpretivism, including case studies, field studies, hermeneutic methods, and action research (Venable et al., 2016; Venable, 2006).

An action research approach was chosen to demonstrate and evaluate the artifacts generated in the previous parts (III–V) of this dissertation. Action research is one of the methods that allow for a practice-based evaluation of an artifact's usefulness (Prat et al., 2015). The method represents a naturalistic evaluation (Venable et al., 2012, 2016) characterised by real users utilising real artifacts to solve real problems (Sun & Kantor, 2006). It 'aims to contribute both to the practical concerns of people in an immediate problematic situation and to the goals of social science by joint collaboration' (Rapoport, 1970, p. 499).

31.1 Evaluation Approach: Action Research

Similar to the study featured in Part IV, this research follows the cyclical approach of Coghlan and Brannick (2005), who draw upon the canonical action research method of Susman and Evered (1978). Their method is iterative, rigorous, and oriented towards a collaborative process and has been applied in high-ranking research (Davison, Martinsons, & Kock, 2004; Lindgren et al., 2004). The cyclical approach is described in four phases as follows:

- **Diagnosis stage:** This first phase begins with an assessment of the situation as it is (e.g. an assessment of the starting situation of the PIP design project). Researchers and practitioners identify issues and challenges.
- **Planning-action stage:** Based on the analysis in the diagnosis phase, the action expected to improve the issues and challenges is specified. In the context of this study, this refers to the selection of the appropriate artifact.
- **Taking-action stage:** In the taking-action phase, previously planned actions are implemented. In the context of this study, this refers to the demonstration of the artifacts.
- **Evaluating-action stage***:* In the evaluation phase, the results of the actions are jointly evaluated by researchers and practitioners. In the present study, this relates to evaluating the artifacts' ease of use and usefulness during the PIP design process.

31.2 Evaluation Criteria

In contrast to the study in Part IV, the purpose of this action research is not to explore a PIP design process. Instead, it aims to demonstrate and evaluate how the artifacts developed in this dissertation can support a PIP design process. As Venable et al. (2016) have stated, formative evaluation should be conducted as early as practicable in an evaluation strategy to identify difficulties and areas for improvement. Given the variety of artifact evaluations, it is essential to specify the criteria by which the artifact should be evaluated. Following Prat et al. (2015), this AR study seeks to qualitatively evaluate (1) the ease of use of the artifacts and (2) their usefulness during the design process of a PIP, thereby focusing on highlighting areas for improvement.

31.3 The Action Research Context: Building a Future Retail Store

The demonstration and evaluation of the artifacts takes place in the context of developing a 'Future Retail Store' (FRS). This FRS is a collaborative PIP development project between the Fraunhofer IIS and two project partners (hereinafter referred to as Company A and Company B). The FRS follows the objectives of a PIP for advancing brick-and-mortar retail. As discussed in Part V, brick-and-mortar retail is under intense pressure to innovate its business model (Agarwal et al., 2017; Reinartz, 2019). Therefore, the FRS project aims to develop a mechanism that enables the innovation of brick-and-mortar retail business models, compensating for the resource disadvantages through the provision of a) funding, b) technology, and c) expertise on innovation and prototyping. The FRS is intended to be the platform that connects innovative retailers, researchers, technology providers and customers. The project was initially started in 2019 but halted in early 2020 in the wake of the COVID-19 pandemic. The project was resumed in mid-2021 but required some adjustments since the pandemic had led to new insights, i.e. regarding retailers' ability to innovate (cf. Part V).

31.4 Demonstration and Evaluation Process

Two action research cycles (Coghlan & Brannick, 2005) were conducted over 14 months, from June 2021 to August 2022. The AR cycles focused on (1) revisiting and refining the original FRS concept from early 2020 and (2) designing organisation and defining roles for the sustainable operation of the FRS.

The first AR cycle was completed within 11 months (July 2021–May 2022). The goal of this cycle was to revisit and further develop the original FRS concept from 2020. In this process, the PIP taxonomy from Part III was applied to aid the refinement of the FRS concept (demonstration of the artifact). In addition, insights from this AR cycle were used to evaluate the PIP taxonomy's ease of use and usefulness.

The second AR cycle was completed within three months (June 2022–August 2022), focusing on the design of the FRS's organisational structure. This AR cycle draws on the PIP composition model from Part IV and the design principles regarding the sustainability of PIPs in Part V. Insights from the second AR cycle were used to evaluate the ease of use and usefulness of both PIP composition model and design principles.

The FRS project did not follow precisely the PIP design process developed in Part IV (cf. Figure 21.2), as early concepts of the FRS date back to 2020. The PIP design process is intended more to guide PIP design in its entirety, from early ideation to implementation. Nonetheless, the FRS project partly draws on insights from the PIP design process.

31.5 Data Collection

Collaboration between practitioners and researchers is fundamental for a rigorous and successful AR project (Coghlan & Brannick, 2005; Ollila & Yström, 2020; Susman & Evered, 1978). Therefore, to develop the FRS, representatives of Company A and researchers from the Fraunhofer IIS formed a joint development team, as highlighted in Table 31.1. This development team planned and implemented the design steps for creating the FRS in collaboration.

Table 31.1 Composition of the FRS development team

FRS Development Team		
Project partner	Company A (practitioners) Background: retail	Fraunhofer IIS (researchers) Background: innovation research
Development team members	• Chairperson of the board • Chairperson of the advisory board	• Professor of digital business • Head of the department • Head of the group • Senior researcher

The data collection supporting this development process consisted of workshop sessions (both with external expert participants and internal workshops), various meetings, observations, and written project documentation such as meeting minutes, e-mails, presentations, and workshop protocols, as illustrated in Table 31.2.

Table 31.2 Data material for the FRS development

AR Cycle	**Purpose**	**Artifacts used**	**Data material**
First AR cycle	Refining and finalising the initial FRS concept	• PIP taxonomy	• Two expert workshops • One development team workshop • Development team meetings • Researchers' meetings (bi-weekly) • Observations • Written project documentation (Meeting minutes, workshop protocols, e-mails, presentations, calculations)
Second AR cycle	Designing organisation and defining roles	• PIP composition model • Design principles for sustainable PIP design	• Development team meetings • Researchers' meetings (bi-weekly) • Observations • Written project documentation (Meeting minutes, workshop protocols, e-mails, presentations, calculations)

To ensure the evaluation of the artifacts, additional reflections with two other more experienced researchers took place regularly (bi-weekly). Following Walsham's notion (2006, p. 325) that 'the researcher's best tool for analysis is his or her own mind, supplemented by the minds of others when work and ideas are exposed to them,' the evaluation of the artifacts was based on interpreting the impact of the artifacts during the AR project. This step was conducted to explore the artifacts' perceived usefulness. Both the demonstration and evaluation of the artifacts are described in the following sections.

32 First Action Research Cycle

The first AR cycle began in July 2021. The goal for the first AR cycle was to revisit and further develop the original FRS concept from 2020. For this purpose, an overview of possible design characteristics should be compiled. The PIP taxonomy was used to structure the design characteristics, forming the foundation for the concept development.

32.1 Diagnosing Phase

The idea for the FRS already came to life in 2020. Inspired by the open innovation laboratory JOSEPHS (cf. Figure 14.1), a PIP for the future of retail was to be created. Although the development team had already formulated some initial thoughts, the COVID-19 pandemic resembled a 'concept reset', and a clear vision of the FRS was lacking. Therefore, the main objective was to develop a coherent concept for the FRS, to start with the operationalisation of the concept, i.e., the physical implementation of the FRS.

32.2 Planning-action Phase

To address the objective outlined above, the development team agreed first to collect possible design characteristics of the FRS and then distil them into a coherent concept. This process should use the PIP taxonomy, extending it with additional design characteristics. To achieve this, several actions were planned accordingly, as follows:

M. Perez Mengual, *Designing Physical Interaction Platforms*, Markt- und Unternehmensentwicklung Markets and Organisations, https://doi.org/10.1007/978-3-658-41920-2_32

Identifying design characteristics: Existing design characteristics were to be identified from the original concept (2020 version) and used to expand the taxonomy. The design characteristics of the FRS were to be discussed and extended together with experts from retail, research, administration, and politics to uncover their requirements and expectations of the FRS (similar to step 3 'identify actor requirements' in the PIP design process; cf. Figure 21.2). In particular, current challenges in brick-and-mortar retail and possible solutions were to be discussed.

Expanding the taxonomy: The solutions outlined were to be analysed and translated into possible design characteristics for the FRS. These should provide the basis for the final design of the concept. The taxonomy (Part III) should be used and expanded to capture the design characteristics in their entirety.

Drafting the FRS concept: Finally, a coherent concept for the Future Retail Store should be created based on the previously identified design characteristics. Supporting the development of the concept, the taxonomy from Part III was to be used (1) to ensure that design characteristics relevant for value creation are considered in the PIP concept and (2) to uncover contradictions and problems arising from the various actor requirements.

32.3 Taking-action Phase

Identifying design characteristics: Fraunhofer IIS and Company A initiated two expert workshops with non-development team participants. The workshop participants were recruited from retail, science, administration, and politics to ensure heterogeneous perspectives on retail challenges and possible solutions. The participants represented actors that would later use the FRS (retail and science) or support its implementation and operation (administration and politics). An overview of the workshop participants is provided in Table 32.1.

As planned, the expert workshops addressed current challenges the retail sector faces, as well as possible solutions to these challenges. The workshops started with impulses and systematic elaboration of the problem situation. Based on this, solutions were developed with guiding questions such as 'What can the participants in the city ecosystem do to enable new retail business models?' and 'What services/infrastructure would enable new retail business models?' Finally, the results of these discussions were captured using specifically designed canvas (workshop methods), as illustrated in Figure 32.1.

Table 32.1 Participants of the first (July 2021) and second expert workshop (October 2021)

ID	Profession
Expert workshop 1 (July 2021)	
WS1-P1	Chairperson of the Board—Company A
WS1-P2	Professor of digital business—Fraunhofer IIS
WS1-P3	Senior researcher—Fraunhofer IIS
WS1-P4	Head of regional economic support—Municipality
WS1-P5	Chairman of the expert committee for trade and services—Chamber of Commerce
WS1-P6	Head of Trade and Services—Chamber of Commerce
WS1-P7	Chairperson of the Board—Regional Retail Association
WS1-P8	Owner and managing director—Local Retail Company
WS1-P9	Owner and managing director—Local Retail Company
WS1-P10	Managing director—Local Retail Company
WS1-P11	Professor of urban management—University
Expert workshop 2 (October 2021)	
WS2-P1	Chairperson of the Board—Company A
WS2-P2	Chairperson of the advisory board—Company A
WS2-P3	Professor of digital business—Fraunhofer IIS
WS2-P4	Senior researcher—Fraunhofer IIS
WS2-P5	Head of regional economic support—Chamber of Commerce
WS2-P6	Owner and managing director—Local Retail Company
WS2-P7	Owner and managing director—Local Retail Company
WS2-P8	Regional economic support—Municipality
WS2-P9	Managing director—Retail Association
WS2-P10	Managing director—Local Retail Company
WS2-P11	Head of Cultural and Creative Business—Municipality
WS2-P12	Owner and managing director—Local Retail Company
WS2-P13	Expert for Urban Development—Center for Entrepreneurship
WS2-P14	Director of the Department for Trade and Services—State Ministry

Through the identification and discussion of possible solutions by the participants, design characteristics of the FRS were deductively derived. The workshops were concluded with follow-up work by two experienced researchers, who synthesised the challenges and solutions identified by the participants into design characteristics for the FRS, as illustrated by Figure 32.1.

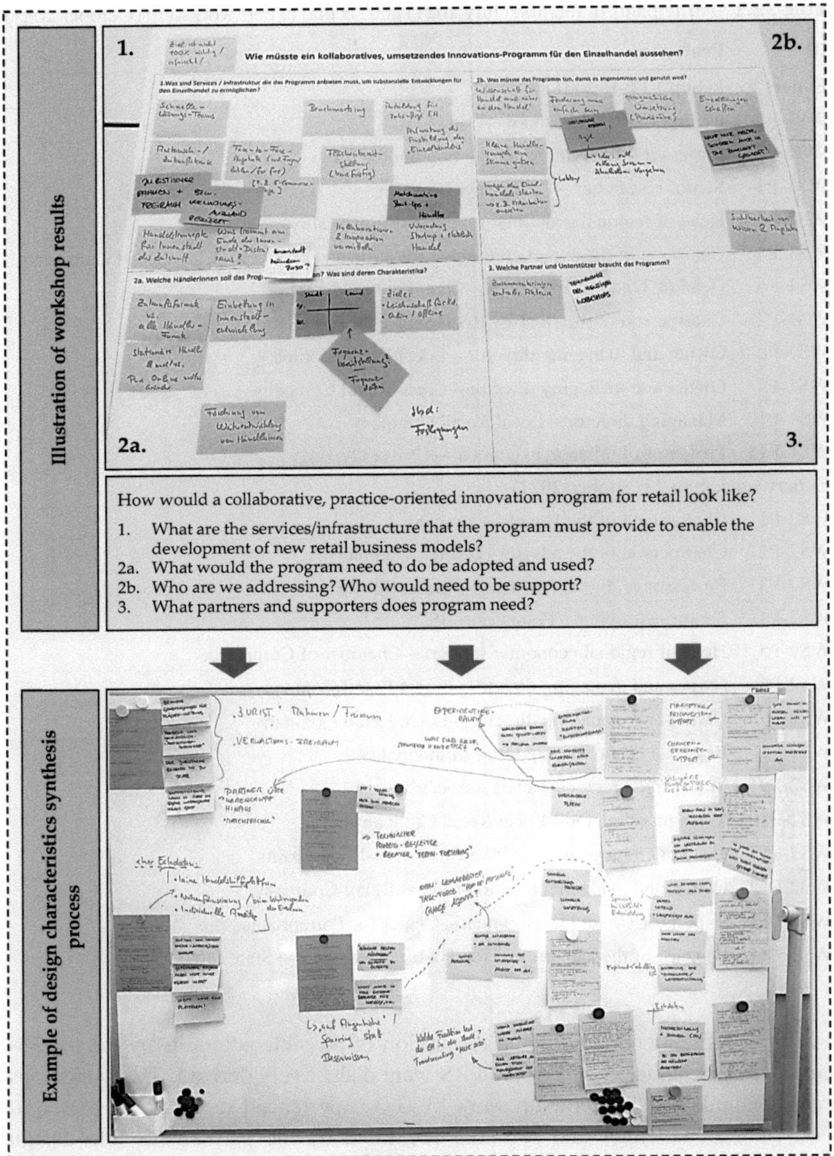

Figure 32.1 Illustration of workshop results and the design characteristics synthesis process

Expanding the taxonomy: Based on the results of the two expert workshops, the taxonomy developed in Part III was adapted and extended to the context of retail innovation, as illustrated in Figure 32.2. As a result, this extended taxonomy is more granular—meaning that new design dimensions and corresponding design characteristics were added. For example, to 'platform actors,' the dimensions of 'retailers' and 'additional partners' were added, describing the target group of the FRS (experienced retailers or retail start-ups) and other key stakeholders (e.g., city administration, property management). The taxonomy is, therefore, no longer universal, nor does it correspond to Nickerson et al.'s (2013) conditions. Instead, it assists in obtaining an overview of all possible design characteristics, enabling the development team to establish a fit between the identified actor requirements and the possible solutions.

	Dimension	Characteristics		
Physical Architecture	*Engagement*	Temporary	Continuous	
	Position	Stationary	Mobile	
	Accessibility to public	Open	Controlled	Closed
Added from Workshops	*Location*	City centre	Rural area	Both (two locations)
	Property	Independent property	Existing retail space	
	Retail space	High frequency retail space	Low frequency retail space	
Platform Actors	*Actor segments**	B2B	B2C	C2C
	Industry focus	Vertical	Horizontal	
Added from Workshops	*Retailer*	Retail start-ups	Experienced retailers	
	Additional partners	City administration	Retail associations	Start-ups
		Property management	Research facilities	Technology provider
		Citizens	Consultancies	Retail foundations

Figure 32.2 The expanded FRS taxonomy

Key Value Propositions	*Platform role**	Market Creation	Operation	Co-Creation			
Key Value Propositions	*Core activity**	Transaction	Innovation	Matchmaking / Networking	Co-Working	Service Provision	
Key Value Propositions	*Monetary incentives**	Cost reduction	Additional sales	Performance increase	Decreased time-to-market	No incentive	
Key Value Propositions	*Non-monetary incentives**	Access	User experience	Social exchange	Visibility	Information / Scouting	
Key Value Propositions	*Non-monetary incentives**	Testing/quality control	Organisational transformation	Inspiration	No incentive		
Added from Workshops	*Resources provided by FRS*	Retail space	Technology	Expert knowledge			
Added from Workshops	*Resources provided by FRS*	Temporary workforce	Financial resources	No resources			
Added from Workshops	*Activities implemented by the FRS*	Guiding development BM processes	Providing temporary workforce	Creating legal freedom	Supporting administrative processes		
Added from Workshops	*Activities implemented by the FRS*	Providing space for experimenting with new BM´s	Evaluating experiments with new BM´s	Initiating dialogue with property management	Providing financial support (e.g., rental costs)		
Added from Workshops	*Activities implemented by the FRS*	Trend scouting retail technologies ("Retail 2030")	Trend scouting city development ("City 2030")	Lobbying			
Added from Workshops	*Activities implemented by the FRS*	Providing technology expertise	Supporting marketing & outreach	Offering training			
Added from Workshops	*Activities implemented by the FRS*	Providing inspiration (Innovation-safaris, etc.)	Matchmaking with start-ups/technology providers	[...]			

Value Creation	Ecosystem	*Ecosystem dimension*	Local	Regional	National	International	
Value Creation	Ecosystem	*Platform sides*	One-sided	Two-sided	Multi-sided		
Value Creation	Governance	*Owner*	Single organisation	Multi-Organisation	Community		
Value Creation	Governance	*IP control*	Proprietary	Open access			
Value Creation	Governance	*Content-control*	Responsible for content	Partially responsible for content	Not responsible for content		

Revenue Logic	*Profit orientation*	Non-profit	For-profit				
Revenue Logic	*Pricing policy*	Symmetric	Asymmetric	No Pricing			
Revenue Logic	*Revenue mechanism**	Transaction fee	Subscriptions	Direct Selling	Project-based	Third-party funding	
Revenue Logic	*Key performance indicator**	Revenue	Number of interactions	Productivity increase	Media coverage	Ecosystem growth	PIP utilisation
Added from Workshops	*Provider*	Spin-off	Consortial project	Operator model	Existing organisation		
Added from Workshops	*Funding (Initial) of the FRS via:*	Governmental support	Private sector funding	Public Private Partnership	Cooperative		
Added from Workshops	*Funding (Permanent) of the FRS via:*	Consulting services	Sponsoring	Profit-sharing			

Figure 32.2 (continued)

Drafting the FRS concept: Creating the final FRS concept took place in an internal workshop with members of the development team, consisting of representatives of Fraunhofer IIS and Company A, as depicted in Table 32.2. The fact that the final concept was designed with this team and not on a larger scale with other stakeholders resulted from the insights gained during the PIP design process illustrated in Part IV. At a certain point in the design process of a PIP, informed decisions must be made by a dedicated team so that the individual interests of various (external) actors do not dilute the final PIP concept.

Table 32.2 Participants of the third workshop (May 2022)

ID	Profession
Development team workshop (May 2022)	
WS3-P1	Chairperson of the Board—Company A
WS3-P2	Chairperson of the advisory board—Company A
WS3-P3	Professor of digital business—Fraunhofer IIS
WS3-P4	Head of the Department—Fraunhofer IIS
WS3-P5	Head of Group—Fraunhofer IIS
WS3-P6	Senior researcher—Fraunhofer IIS
WS3-P7	Retail Expert

The workshop commenced by reviewing the overall development process (since 2020) and the actor requirements the FRS is about to address. Based on this 'design briefing,' the extended taxonomy served as the basis for setting up various scenarios for the FRS. These scenarios were crafted and discussed using a canvas consisting of the dimensions place/location, operation, activities, and partner. In these dimensions, the individual design characteristics from the extended FRS taxonomy were inserted and discussed thoroughly, weighing each characteristic's advantages, disadvantages, and feasibility. An illustration of this process is provided in Figure 32.3. The workshop resulted in the design of a consistent FRS concept, consisting of the following design characteristics (derived from the FRS taxonomy, cf. Figure 32.2): *continuous, stationary, open, city centre, independent property, high-frequency retail space, B2C, horizontal; experienced retailer, market creation and operation; transaction and innovation, access, visibility and inspiration, retail space, technology and expert knowledge, regional, two-sided, multi-organisation, open access, responsible for content, non-profit, asymmetric, third-party funding, revenue and pip utilization, spin-off, private sector funding.* The selection of some design characteristics, such as additional partners and activities, was scheduled for the operationalisation phase of the FRS.

Illustration of FRS final concept development process

1. Place / Location (of the FRS)
2. Operation (of the FRS)
3. Activities (of the FRS)
4. Partners (of the FRS)

Figure 32.3 Illustration of FRS final concept development process

32.4 Evaluating-action Phase

The outcomes of the taxonomy's implementation during the FRS concept-development process were assessed by two senior researchers regarding the criteria of ease of use and usefulness.[1] For this assessment, the two researchers used observations from the FRS design process and comparative data from other PIP design projects (e.g., the ENIQ, cf. Part IV; or the JOSEPHS, cf. Part III). Based on this, implications for the future use of the artifact were derived:

[1] The variables (perceived) ease of use and (perceived) usefulness are derived from the Technology Acceptance Model (TAM; Davis, 1989). Prat et al. (2015) list these variables as possible criteria for the evaluation of design artifacts. While the TAM also includes the variables 'attitude toward using' and 'behavioral intention to use', these variables were not addressed in this evaluation.

Ease of use of the artifact during the development process: Overall, the taxonomy can be rated as easy to use. Nevertheless, there are limitations and opportunities for improvement.

- The use of the taxonomy confirmed two of the requirements Nickerson et al. (2013) formulated (extendable and explanatory). The taxonomy was easily extendable to design characteristics at a more granular level. Further, the taxonomy proved to be explanatory, with its design dimensions and characteristics providing practical explanations on how to design PIPs (.e.g, by highlighting the importance of value propositions, revenue model and KPIs).
- Depending on the particular PIP context, the taxonomy needs adaptation to be used in the PIP design process. The taxonomy can provide an impulse in its original form but would not function as a universal tool. Therefore, the identification of additional design characteristics in the particular PIP context is a necessary step. Using the taxonomy as a tool to structure PIP design processes should thus take place in conjunction with additional (creative) methods, as illustrated in the above section.

Usefulness of the artifact for the development process: Overall, the taxonomy's application during the design process of the FRS can be evaluated positively in terms of its usefulness:

- The adapted and expanded taxonomy was used to illustrate the solution space, showing all possible design characteristics of the FRS. This laid the foundation for making important decisions about the FRS's final design. It has to be noted that the taxonomy was not used for a combinatorial approach. The final FRS concept was not created by top-down running through the taxonomy's design dimensions, picking design characteristics along the way. The taxonomy should be understood as a tool supporting creativity but not restricting it.
- The taxonomy enabled testing the coherence of various FRS concepts—constellations of different design characteristics (e.g., should the FRS address retail start-ups or established retailers). It allowed for the identification of interdependencies of design characteristics and inconsistencies early in the development process.

Insights on improving the practice of the artifact: Potential for improvement is seen in using the taxonomy as a workshop method. With additional effort, the (extended) taxonomy could be more engaging, as it is currently too static for application in development workshops. First considerations entail printing out the individual design characteristics as cards. Combined with a canvas (similar to the canvas illustrated in Figure 32.3), this could be an easy tool for creating new PIP concepts.

33 Second Action Research Cycle

The second AR cycle started in June 2022, intending to design the organisation of the FRS. The findings from Part IV (cf. Figure 21.1) indicate that a PIP needs to be designed on three levels—operation, team, and infrastructure. While the operation level was defined in the previous AR cycle, the second AR cycle focused on the latter, as illustrated in Figure 33.1.

33.1 Diagnosis Phase

Two issues were identified by the development team to be addressed in the second AR cycle. First, drawing on the PIP composition model, both the operator-team (provider) and the organisational infrastructure (owner) needed clarification. The relationship between both must be harmonised to support the actual value-creating interaction (operation-level) between consumer and producer in the PIP. Second, as Part V shows, there may be organisational inertia towards innovation once a PIP is in operation, preventing the self-renewal of the PIP. This circumstance should be anticipated early, answering the question of how the PIP's sustainable, continuous operation and innovation can be achieved throughout and beyond the project duration.

33.2 Planning-action Phase

Following the insights gained from the diagnosing phase, four actions were planned by the development team to address the outlined challenges accordingly.

M. Perez Mengual, *Designing Physical Interaction Platforms*, Markt- und Unternehmensentwicklung Markets and Organisations, https://doi.org/10.1007/978-3-658-41920-2_33

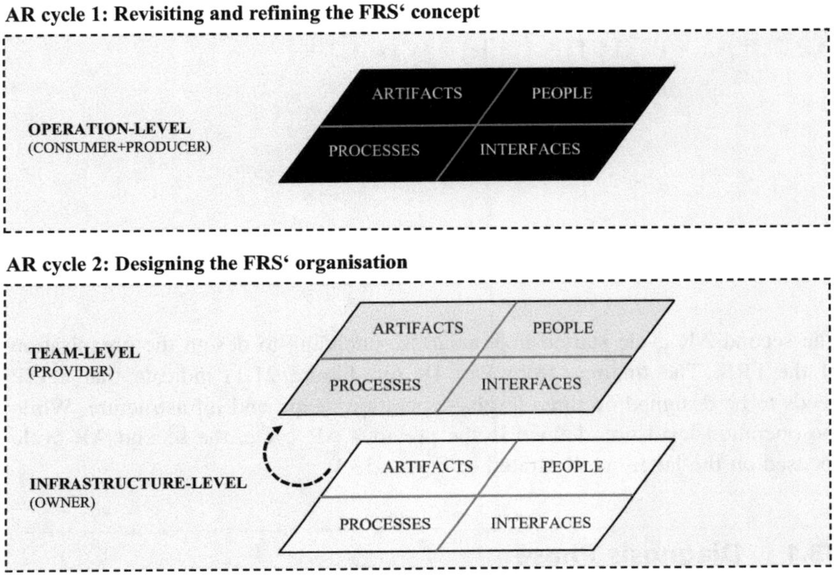

Figure 33.1 Development challenge illustrated using the PIP composition model

Clarifying ownership: Following the insights gained from Part IV and the PIP design process (cf. Figure 21.2), funding and ownership require early clarification. This is the central point of departure so that all further design activities—and even more critical, the PIP implementation—can build on a reliable foundation.

Crafting the team: The second action was planned to focus on the design of the FRS' team (provider), ensuring the operation of the FRS. This includes selecting team members, crafting value propositions for the team, and clarifying internal processes and roles.

Ensuring harmony between team and owner: Third, action was planned to align the three levels: infrastructure (owner), team (provider) and operation (consumer and producer) to ensure smooth implementation and operation of the PIP (i.e., resource flows, coordination, documentation).

Providing a sustainable perspective: Based on the findings of Part V, the fourth action intended to explore options of continuing the FRS beyond the project duration. This should be clarified early, not only to ensure the PIP's sustainability but also to create prospects for the team (provider) and the infrastructure (owner).

33.3 Taking-action Phase

Clarifying ownership: Several scenarios of varying actor constellations were created and evaluated. Their creation and evaluation took place in meetings and workshops with the development team. The development process of the scenarios is illustrated in Figure 33.2. In summary, the development team discussed whether to form a new company (RELAB) to create more operational autonomy and minimise risk or if Fraunhofer IIS should carry out the FRS as a project.

Crafting the team: Concerning the team composition, several scenarios were created, illustrating possibilities for operating the FRS. First, an assessment was made regarding the required personnel resources. This was followed by a discussion, where the personnel resources would be allocated (at Fraunhofer IIS or the newly founded RELAB company). Figure 33.2 shows the various scenarios and how they are evaluated regarding their feasibility and attractiveness for the actors involved.

Ensuring harmony between team and owner: The third action was to check whether the constellations were feasible for implementation (relating to step 5 in the PIP design process, cf. Figure 21.1). It was verified that the FRS's concept and business model would align with the participating organisation's (Fraunhofer IIS, Company A and Company B) objectives and business models. In addition, attention was paid to several criteria, including legal and financial aspects, team fit, and career prospects. Based on this, possible scenarios for the FRS' implementation were selected.

Providing a sustainable perspective: The prospects of the project beyond its three-year duration were openly discussed by the development team. This discussion resulted in the commitment of all participating companies to continue the FRS if it was deemed successful. From the beginning of the project, a dedicated work package with sufficient resources was scheduled, exploring possibilities for adapting and continuing the FRS after project duration. This includes monitoring the project's activities and (creatively) identifying potential for continuation. It is taken into account that the PIP can take on new forms if continuing in the current form is not promising.

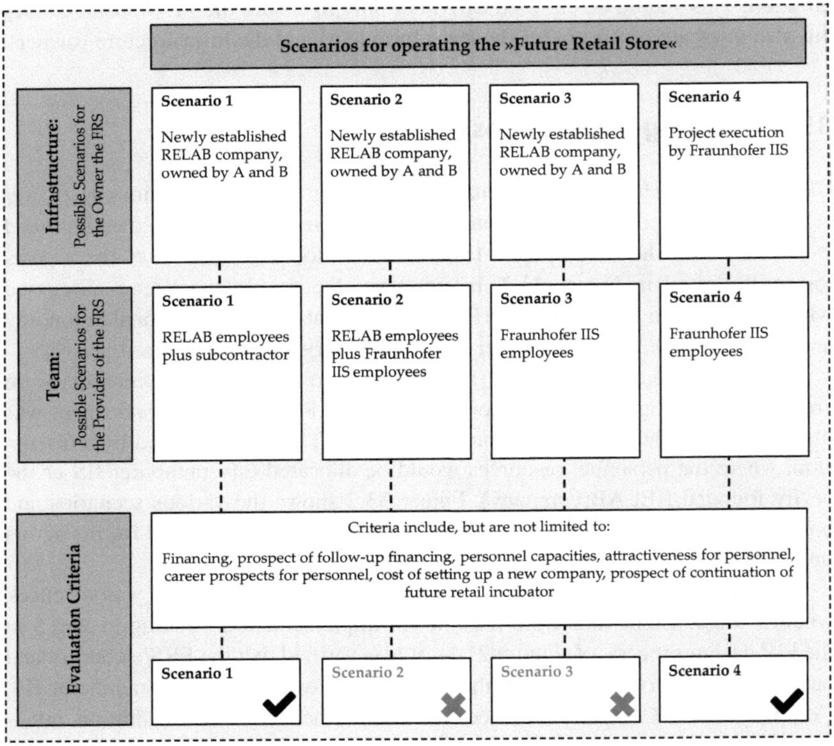

Figure 33.2 Overview of team and infrastructure scenarios

33.4 Evaluating-action Phase

The implementation of the artifacts (PIP composition model, PIP design process, design principles) during the second AR cycle of the FRS project was assessed by two senior researchers with regard to the criteria of ease of use and usefulness, as in the first AR cycle. Based on this, implications for the future use of the artifacts were derived.

Ease of use of the artifacts during the development process:

- The PIP composition model was shown to be particularly valuable in shaping the operational structure of a PIP by highlighting the necessary interdependence between the three levels. However, being rather abstract, it may not be understood as a practical workshop tool. Instead, it serves to structure a design process, pinpointing necessary discussions.
- Despite its solid theoretical foundation (cf. Ramaswamy & Ozcan, 2018), the model is easy to understand. However, the models' understandability refers more to the three levels and their interrelation and less to the APPI components.
- The design of the APPI components as part of the PIP composition model was not a planned activity during the design process of the FRS. However, most of the APPI components were defined automatically when the team and operation levels and their interrelation were designed. This refers to, for example, contracts and project plans (artifacts), role assignments (people), workflows (processes), advisory board meetings, and public outreach (interfaces).
- The design principles for sustainable PIP design are easy to understand. The content is comprehensible and illustrates the challenge of innovation many PIPs have to answer during their life cycle. Incorporating these design principles during the initial PIP design lays the foundation for self-renewal of the PIP at a later stage in its lifecycle.

Usefulness of the artifact for the development process: Overall, the application of the PIP composition model and the design principles for sustainable PIP design can be evaluated positively in terms of their usefulness:

- The PIP composition model highlighted the importance of early clarification of roles and relationships between the team and the organizational infrastructure. This was an essential step in the FRS design process, leading to a high degree of planning certainty regarding human and financial resources. In addition, early clarification enabled the PIP concept to be tailored specifically to the people involved and their requirements. As reported by the development team, a good fit between the team (provider) and the organizational infrastructure (owner) is essential—not only from a conceptual perspective but also on a personal level.
- The knowledge conveyed by the design principles for sustainable PIP design was considered relevant by all stakeholders. Several possibilities for sustaining the FRS after the project period were discussed extensively among the development team and incorporated into the project, illustrating the design principles' usefulness.

Insights on improving the practice of the artifacts: The FRS design process has provided valuable insights into the artifacts' ease of use and usefulness. At the same time, this is not only an evaluation of single artifacts but also of their interaction as a toolkit in a PIP design process. The following presents insights on how the toolkit can be improved to facilitate PIP design processes.

- Overall, the alignment between operation, team and infrastructure needs to be emphasized. Every change on one level has repercussions on the other levels. The PIP composition model illustrates this mutual dependency. However, the model does not show how exactly harmonization between the levels can occur. Clear communication, negotiations, good relationships and trust are essential when harmonizing the interrelation between the levels. Formalizing these 'invisible' harmonisation steps could further enhance the utility of the PIP composition model and the entire toolkit for designing PIPs.
- Planning resources for the continuous development of a PIP is central to its sustainability. Therefore, the PIP process model should be extended by a further stage, emphasising that designing a PIP is not linear but requires continuous monitoring and improvement throughout the operation.

34 Discussion and Implications

This study presented the toolkit for designing PIPs—a compilation of the artifacts created in the empirical studies of this dissertation. To ensure the ease of use and the usefulness of the toolkit, a naturalistic evaluation (Venable et al., 2016) consisting of an AR project (Coghlan & Brannick, 2005) was executed. The contributions of this study are manifold. As a theoretical contribution, the study demonstrated the viability of AR as a method for evaluating artifacts. As a practical contribution, the study synthesised the overall findings from this dissertation (Parts III-V) into *the toolkit for designing PIPs*. The study showed that the toolkit was perceived to add value in a PIP design process and highlighted implications for improvement and future use of the toolkit. These contributions are discussed below.

Action research as a method for artifact evaluation: This study utilised AR as an evaluation method for artifacts. AR and design science have often been compared to each other (Collatto, Dresch, Lacerda, & Bentz, 2018; Goldkuhl, 2013; Iivari & Venable, 2009). However, an AR evaluation is rarely seen in practice, with most publications using illustrative scenarios or case studies for evaluation (Peffers et al., 2007). These evaluations often focus on the technological view of an artifact, paying little attention to the organisational context (Sein et al., 2011). This study demonstrated that AR is a viable method for artifact evaluation but differs in which properties of the artifacts are evaluated. Using AR, it is difficult to focus on artifact properties such as completeness and understandability, as Prat et al. (2015) suggested. Instead, an AR evaluation focuses more on the impact that the artifacts have on an organisation—in this case, the design of a PIP. This supports the notion that authenticity in applying the artifact is more critical than a controlled setting offering a neutral view on the artifact itself (Iivari, 2003; Sein et al., 2011).

M. Perez Mengual, *Designing Physical Interaction Platforms*, Markt- und Unternehmensentwicklung Markets and Organisations, https://doi.org/10.1007/978-3-658-41920-2_34

Applying the toolkit for designing PIPs: This study showed how the developed artifacts could be used, highlighting the importance of the organisational context. The artifacts only generate value for the PIP design process if they are actively utilised and adapted. For example, the taxonomy must be modified to the respective PIP context. Furthermore, inferences must be drawn from the PIP composition model and the principles for sustainable PIP design. Following Orlikowski and Iacono (2001), the toolkit and the context in which it is used should be understood as 'ensemble.' Sein et al. (2011, p. 38) state that 'designing ensemble artifacts involves dimensions beyond the technological, because they result from the interaction of design efforts and contextual factors throughout the design process'. Ensemble artifacts thus evolve through adaptation to the organisational context (Alter, 2015; Sein et al., 2011). This also applies to using the toolkit in a PIP design process. While this dissertation provided the initial design of the artifacts, their true form is 'dynamic and emerge[s] from the contexts of both their initial design and continual redesign via organizational use' (Sein et al., 2011, p. 52)

PIP design as a continuous process: The toolkit and the artifacts are tailored explicitly towards PIP design, guiding organisations seeking to design PIPs. In contrast to extant generic innovation processes (Alam, 2006; Cooper, 2008), the toolkit for designing PIPs considers aspects essential for successful PIP implementation, such as business models and organisational fit. Thereby, the toolkit responds to the requests made by Böhmann et al. (2014), who call for more actionable knowledge for systematically designing systems, such as PIPs. Next, the design principles in the toolkit emphasise PIP design as a continuous process. Designing PIPs should be understood as continuous service development, a cyclical approach embracing continuous learning in line with Johnson, Menor, Roth, and Chase (2000) and Yu and Sangiorgi (2018).

Formalised platform design knowledge: The artifacts are ingrained with knowledge from the design of digital platforms. They convey essential insights into how platforms should be designed, such as the importance of the roles of owner and provider and governance mechanisms for the platform ecosystem (Parker et al., 2016; Tiwana, 2014). The toolkit, with its encompassing artifacts, thus formalises knowledge, giving prescriptions for design and action (Gregor, 2006; Gregor & Hevner, 2013). PIP designers can directly apply these artifacts without having to be platform experts in advance.

35 Summary and Outlook

This research synthesised the artifacts developed throughout this dissertation into the *toolkit for designing PIPs*. In addition, the study evaluated the artifacts' regarding their ease of use and usefulness during a PIP design process. The evaluation was executed in the context of the design process of a real to-be-designed PIP—the Future Retail Store.

The evaluation highlighted several aspects: (1) evaluating artifacts in a real-world context generated insights (e.g., regarding the adaptation of the artifacts) that would not have been possible in a more controlled evaluation. (2) Just as a PIP development process is dynamic, the artifacts should also be used and adapted dynamically. (3) PIP design should be perceived as a continuous process. The artifacts can form the basis for this; for example, the PIP taxonomy can be constantly expanded and revisited, e.g., to generate new ideas through combination. (4) The toolkit contains formalised knowledge about platforms. Similar to the Business Model Canvas (Osterwalder, 2004), designers can apply this knowledge without having obtained it previously.

There are limitations to this research which could spark future research. First, this study evaluated the artifacts from this dissertation according to a single AR project. While the evaluation of this toolkit was positive overall, additional evaluations in different PIP design projects would be desirable to verify and, if necessary, complement the evaluation results. Second, this evaluation took an interpretivist approach to analyse the data arising from the nature of the AR method. Nevertheless, triangulation with other approaches towards evaluation could be interesting in future research. Third, the evaluation results concerning the ease of use revealed that not all artifacts' properties were used (e.g., the APPI

M. Perez Mengual, *Designing Physical Interaction Platforms*, Markt- und Unternehmensentwicklung Markets and Organisations, https://doi.org/10.1007/978-3-658-41920-2_35

components of the PIP composition model). Although easily comprehensible, the artifacts could be made more accessible and interactive, accentuating their use as 'ensemble' (Goldkuhl, 2012b; Sein et al., 2011). To achieve this, implications from the literature around design thinking (e.g., Meinel & Leifer, 2011; Stickdorn et al., 2017) or business model innovation (e.g. Osterwalder, 2004) could be used as inspiration to advance the toolkit for designing PIPs.

Part VII

Reflections and Conclusion: Designing Physical Interaction Platforms

Objectives and Structure 36

This dissertation seeks to explore *how a physical interaction platform (PIP) can be designed in a systematic and structured way*. As the final section of this dissertation, Part VII summarises the research, lists limitations and avenues for further research, and concludes this dissertation.

Part VII is organised as follows: Chapter 37 summarizes Parts I–VI, consisting of the introduction (Part I), the theoretical background (Part II), and the empirical studies (Parts III–VI). Chapter 38 pinpoints the limitations of the empirical studies, followed by highlighting avenues for future research. Finally, Chapter 39 closes this dissertation with a final reflection. The overall structure of Part VII is illustrated in Figure 36.1.

M. Perez Mengual, *Designing Physical Interaction Platforms*,
Markt- und Unternehmensentwicklung Markets and Organisations,
https://doi.org/10.1007/978-3-658-41920-2_36

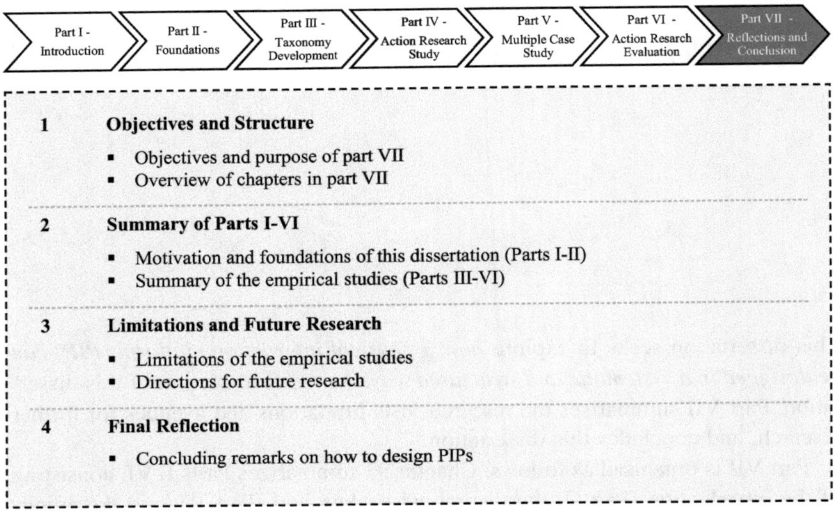

Figure 36.1 Structure of *Part VII*

Summary of Parts I–VI 37

This chapter summarises Parts I–VI of this dissertation. The short summaries capture the essence of the individual parts, i.e., which insights were generated, thereby representing the executive summary of this dissertation.

37.1 Summary of Part I

Chapter 1 introduced the academic and practical relevance of the topic of this dissertation. The motivation explained the importance of physical spaces for interactive value creation. It introduced the many conceptualisations of such spaces that prevail in the literature—e.g., innovation labs, incubators, co-working spaces, and innovative retail concepts (cf. Hossain et al., 2019; Kraus et al., 2022; Roth et al., 2014). From these various conceptualisations, two challenges arise. First, from an academic perspective, it is increasingly difficult to distinguish between the different concepts (Bogers et al., 2017; Enkel, Bogers, & Chesbrough, 2020). Second, from a practical perspective and despite widespread academic attention, there is little guidance regarding how to build such spaces. Therefore, Chapter 1 introduced the term *physical interaction platform (PIP)*. In essence, all the outlined spaces are platforms that enable interaction between actors (Bessant, 2020; Yablonsky, 2018). This insight provides a new perspective on such spaces and allows for a structured approach to their design. As a critical challenge for practitioners lies in the design of such spaces, this dissertation aims to shed light on *how a physical interaction platform (PIP) can be designed in a systematic and structured way*. Addressing this overall objective, Chapter 2 formulated the following research questions, following the logic of a platform lifecycle from first conceptualisation and birth to continuous innovation and self-renewal (Moore, 1993; Teece, 2017):

M. Perez Mengual, *Designing Physical Interaction Platforms*, Markt- und Unternehmensentwicklung Markets and Organisations, https://doi.org/10.1007/978-3-658-41920-2_37

RQ 1: *What are the design dimensions of PIPs that enable interactive value creation?*
RQ 2: *How can these design dimensions be grouped to provide a useful tool for designers of PIPs?*
RQ 3: *How can a PIP systematically be designed?*
RQ 4: *What are the challenges and turning points in the design process of a PIP?*
RQ 5: *What were strategic responses and activities of retailers in reaction to the COVID-19 crisis?*
RQ 6: *Did these strategic responses and activities lead to sustainable innovation?*
RQ 7: *Are the developed artifacts (from Parts III–V) applicable (ease of use) and useful (perceived usefulness) for the design process of a PIP?*

Following the formulation of the research questions, Chapter 3 introduced the research paradigm and research design. This dissertation follows a pragmatist research paradigm (Göran Goldkuhl, 2012a; Wahyuni, 2012) and embraces the engaged scholarship approach (Van de Ven, 2007). Both paradigm and approach are geared towards this dissertation's objective of constructing knowledge that is useful in action, i.e., for the design of PIPs (Goldkuhl, 2012). Chapter 4 provided an overview of the structure of this dissertation.

37.2 Summary of Part II

Part II presented relevant theoretical foundations to illustrate this dissertation's perspective on PIPs. Chapter 5 provided an overview of the objectives and structure of Part II, highlighting that this dissertation's empirical research on PIPs builds upon concepts found in three distinct streams of literature—(1) service dominant logic (SDL) and interactive value creation, (2) (platform) business models, and (3) approaches to the systematic design of platforms.

Chapter 6 introduced an understanding of value and value creation. This was done by explaining a paradigm of value creation, initially forwarded and publicised by Vargo and Lusch (2004) as the Service-Dominant-Logic (SDL). SDL emphasises the role of the customer or user as a co-creator of value (Vargo et al., 2008). It proposes that value creation is an interactive process between two or more actors (Vargo & Lusch, 2017; Vargo et al., 2008). These interactions are enabled by some sort of place, space, or interface. For example, in surroundings like a retail PIP, interactions are enabled by items on display and consultation through retail staff or reviews in an online shop. This thought is continued by Ramaswamy and Ozcan (2018), who propose that value creation is determined by so-called platformed interactions, focusing on the interactional dimension of value creation.

Chapter 7 elaborated on the theoretical foundations regarding the concept of platforms. It delineated this dissertation's understanding of the term platform, based on definitions prevalent in the academic literature (cf. Anderson & Coate, 2005; Evans, 2003; Parker & Van Alstyne, 2005; Schiff, 2003). A platform is defined by (1) enabling the connection of two or more sides of actors (D. S. Evans, 2003), and (2) the presence of network effects is the unifying basis of many definitions of the term platform (McIntyre & Srinivasan, 2017). In addition, the distinct characteristics of operating platform business models were presented. Operating platforms requires various skills, such as orchestrating a platform's actor ecosystem, determining governance rules to balance platform control, and providing value creation and value-appropriation mechanisms leading actors to engage with the platform (Gawer & Cusumano, 2014; Ghazawneh & Henfridsson, 2013; Parker et al., 2016). Lastly, the platform lifecycle was depicted, highlighting the importance of innovation activities during the platform's maturity (Moore, 1993; Teece, 2017). Without innovation, platforms run the risk of overthrow and obsolescence due to high competition (Thomas et al., 2021).

Chapter 8 focused on the design process, leading to the creation of PIPs (Tura et al., 2018). Therefore, strategies for designing and launching were introduced, as forwarded by, e.g. Evans and Schmalensee (2016), Memon (2021), Parker et al. (2016), and Reillier and Reillier (2017). Following this, design theory was presented to elaborate on the structure and reasoning in design processes. This led to additional insights for the platform, such as the idea that platform design is a structured exploration of alternatives (Le Masson et al., 2009), and to effectively approach a design process, the decomposition of a problem, i.e., a design task, into smaller sub-problems is essential (Bender & Gericke, 2021).

Finally, Chapter 9 summarised the key concepts introduced, highlighting the value of these three concepts concerning the systematic and structured design of sustainably successful PIPs.

37.3 Summary of Part III

Part III contains the first empirical study of this dissertation. The study focused on identifying design dimensions of PIPs that enable interactive value creation and are essential for the design and sustainable operation of PIPs. It answered the first and the second research questions formulated in this dissertation. Chapter 10 introduced the objectives and structure of the study.

Chapter 11 provided an overview of the research approach—Nickerson et al.'s (2103) taxonomy development method. A taxonomy is a uniform model by which objects can be classified using defined criteria, categories, or classes. Taxonomies can help to structure the complex knowledge of research fields to explain similarities and differences between objects of interest (Nickerson et al., 2013; Wand et al., 1995). The method formulates two preliminary instructions to be followed before starting the taxonomy development process. First, taxonomies are purposefully created; therefore, researchers must define a meta-characteristic that shapes the development process. The meta-characteristic in this research was defined as *relevant for the design and description of value creation on physical interaction platforms*. Second, Nickerson et al. (2013) formulate ending conditions (objective and subjective) that determine the completion of the taxonomy-building process.

Chapter 12 described the taxonomy development process based on the outlined research approach. Using Nickerson et al.'s (2013) method, the study used and transferred conceptual knowledge and empirical evidence in an iterative process. Five iterations were performed: (1) an initial screening of PIPs, (2) an expert workshop and systematic literature reviews on (3) platform classifications and (4) on platform-mediated value creation, as well as (5) a taxonomy evaluation by practitioners. Each iteration added or modified design dimensions and characteristics of the PIP taxonomy. After the fifth iteration, all ending conditions were satisfied, causing the taxonomy building process to be terminated.

Chapter 13 revealed and detailed the results of the development process. The resulting PIP taxonomy comprises 18 design dimensions summarised according to five groups: physical architecture, platform actors, key-value propositions, value creation, and revenue logic. Each design dimension contains a subset of characteristics describing PIPs. Chapter 14 illustrated the usefulness of the developed taxonomy in describing physical interaction platforms. Two examples were used to show that the taxonomy worked for several manifestations of PIPs—both JOSEPHS as an open innovation (OI) lab and WeWork as a co-working space are classified along the 18 dimensions of the PIP taxonomy.

Chapter 15 discusses the implications of the taxonomy. It contributes with (1) a tangible framework for PIP concept development, building on established design dimensions from the platform, business model, and value creation literature. (2) It emphasises criteria that require thorough reflection in the design phase (e.g., IP rights), which enables practitioners to address critical issues early. Therefore, practitioners and designers of PIPs can benefit from the taxonomy as a basis for applying the morphological analysis and systematic exploration of ideas and concepts (Geum, Jeon, & Lee, 2016; Le Masson et al., 2009). Chapter 16 provided a summary of the study, depicting limitations and implications for the remainder of this dissertation. An overview of the main aspects of the taxonomy development study is presented in Table 37.1.

Table 37.1 Summary of the taxonomy development

Aspect	Description
Presented in	Part III
Research need	Identifying design dimensions relevant for the design and description of value creation on physical interaction platforms (PIPs).
Research questions	RQ 1: What are the design dimensions of PIPs that enable interactive value creation? RQ 2: How can these design dimensions be grouped to provide a useful tool for designers of PIPs?
Research method	Taxonomy development method according to Nickerson et al. (2013)
Data collection and analysis	Five iterations: (1) screening of PIPs (online directories), (2) expert workshop, systematic literature reviews on (3) platform classifications (14 articles for full analysis) and (4) on platform-mediated value creation (12 articles for full analysis), and (5) a taxonomy evaluation by practitioners (5 interviews).
Key findings	The taxonomy contains 18 core dimensions, each with a subset of characteristics describing PIPs. The dimensions are grouped under the categories physical architecture (*engagement, position, accessibility to public*), customers (*actor segments, industry focus*), key value propositions (*platform role, core activity, monetary incentives, non- monetary incentives*), value creation (*ecosystem dimension, platform sides, owner, IP control, content-control*), and revenue logic (*profit orientation, pricing policy, revenue mechanism, key performance indicator*).
Theoretical contributions	The taxonomy provides a tool for scholars to classify different types of PIPs based on design characteristics. The taxonomy development process also showed that many design dimensions of online platforms can be transferred to physical platforms but must be interpreted differently.
Implications for practitioners	Building on established design dimensions from well-known business model and value creation literature, the taxonomy offers a simple and tangible approach towards PIP design, emphasising design aspects that are necessary for the creation of sustainable and permanently successful spaces.

37.4 Summary of Part IV

Part IV presented an action research study focusing on exploring the design process of a PIP, from first conceptualisations to final implementation. Chapter 17 introduced the objectives and structure of the study. While Part III explored design characteristics relevant to interactive value creation in a PIP, it was argued that a development process is needed that leads to the selection and choice of these individual characteristics. The action research is built on theoretical foundations introduced in Part II, seeking to answer the third and fourth research question of this dissertation.

Chapter 18 described the research approach of action research—a method where researchers use their knowledge to assist practitioners in solving real-world problems (Coghlan & Brannick, 2005; Susman & Evered, 1978). The research took place in the context of a PIP design project (the Fraunhofer ENIQ), from early conceptualisation to implementation. Two action research cycles were conducted throughout an overall period of 19 months. During this time, the researcher was deeply involved with the project team to plan, execute, and evaluate development steps. The data consists of desk research data, a review of project-related documents, stakeholder interviews, and, as a primary source of information, meeting minutes, e-mails, calculations, and cost structures for the PIP, pinpointing challenges and turning points during the design process.

Chapter 19 described the results of the first action research cycle (August 2019–June 2020). This cycle aimed to develop a concept and business model for the PIP. The evaluation of the development steps was positive, and a concept and business model was established. However, some challenges were revealed concerning the implementation of the developed concept. With an understanding of these challenges, a second AR cycle was initiated. Chapter 20 described the second AR cycle (July 2020 – February 2021). The focus of the development steps in the second AR cycle was on, e.g., the definition of workflows, team building, interior design, procurement processes, and internal and external communication. The evaluation of the second AR cycle highlighted challenges arising during implementation as well as approaches which made it possible to overcome these challenges.

Chapter 21 summarised and discussed key insights from both AR cycles. Building on these insights, the PIP composition model and the PIP design process were proposed. Chapter 22 provided a summary of the study, listing limitations and implications for the remainder of the dissertation. An overview of the main aspects of the action research study is presented in Table 37.2.

Table 37.2 Summary of the Action Research

Aspect	Description
Presented in	Part IV
Research need	Creating a process that structures the development of a PIP and overcomes / foresees possible challenges.
Research questions	RQ 3: How can a PIP systematically be designed? RQ 4: What are the challenges and turning points in the design process of a PIP?
Research method	Action Research according to Coghlan & Brannick (2005)
Data collection and analysis	Desk research to structure the PIPs design process: a review of project-related documents and interviews with the members of the development team. Evaluation of the development process along of meeting minutes, e-mails, reflections with team member as well as and written project documentation.
Key findings	(1) As PIPs are bound to the physical realm, a development process cannot start entirely from scratch, as there will always be the central factor of location. (2) The organisational implementation of a PIP needs careful attention. 'Soft' challenges such as, e.g., team dynamics are essential for a PIPs success. (3) The transition from the concept development phase to implementation requires special attention. Team roles and responsibilities must be defined at an early stage for a frictionless transition.
Theoretical contributions	The PIP composition model, suggesting that a PIP needs to be built on three levels: operation-, team- and infrastructure-level. These three levels show that value-creating interactions are taking place on each level. However, the three levels must be aligned with each other to ensure that the PIP functions optimally.
Implications for practitioners	Combining the PIP composition model with practical insights from the project, a design process consisting of seven stages (from defining preconditions to implementation) is proposed. In each phase, a distinction is made between the levels of operation, team, and infrastructure, illustrating required actions.

37.5 Summary of Part V

Part V contains the third empirical study of this dissertation, which focused on the reconfiguration and self-renewal of PIPs. This was examined in the context of the COVID-19 crisis, where retail PIPs were challenged by suspended customer interaction due to lockdowns. The study answered the fifth and sixth research question formulated in the dissertation. Chapter 23 introduced the objectives and structure of the study.

Chapter 24 added to the theoretical background introduced in Part II by providing scholarly work necessary to understand the self-renewal of retail PIPs. It provided an introduction to the innovation challenges that brick-and-mortar retail faces and the impact of the COVID-19 crisis. Furthermore, strategic responses in dealing with crises were described. Following this, the 'innovation' response, similar to self-renewal (cf. Teece, 2017; Wenzel et al., 2021), was enriched with business model literature.

Chapter 25 described the research approach. A multiple-case study was conducted, according to Eisenhardt (1989) and Yin (2003). Eight cases from the German retail sector were examined. The data collection took place over a period of five months. Primary data sources consisted of interviews with the managers (t1) and field visits including interviews (t2). The data analysis was based on Gioia et al.'s (2013) approach.

Chapter 26 showed the findings of the multiple-case study. Overall, despite the radical impulse from the COVID-19 crisis, no signs of self-renewal, in a strategic sense, were observed. The main findings were as follows: (1) retailers made only changes to the value chain element of their business model, persevering through the crisis; (2) the changes to the value chain were made by using two approaches: either intensification or improvisation; (3) the changes were not sustainable beyond the crisis; and (4) retailers showed difficulty in implementing innovation, i.e., not only generating ideas but realising them.

Chapter 27 discussed these key insights. Finally, Chapter 28 provided a summary of the study, listing limitations and implications for the remainder of this dissertation. Additionally, design principles for sustainable PIP operation were formulated. An overview of the main aspects of the multiple-case study is presented in Table 37.3.

Table 37.3 Summary of the Multiple Case Study

Aspect	Description
Presented in	Part V
Research need	Exploring continuous innovation of PIPs.
Research questions	RQ 5: What were strategic responses and activities of retailers in reaction to the COVID-19 crisis? RQ 6: Did these strategic responses and activities lead to sustainable innovation?
Research method	Multiple-case study according to Eisenhardt (1989) and Yin (2003)
Data collection and analysis	Examination of 8 cases from the German retail sector. The data collection took place over a period of 5 months. Primary sources of data were interviews with the managers (t1) and field visits including interviews (t2). The data analysis is based on Gioia et al.'s approach (2013).
Key findings	(1) Retailers made only changes to the value chain element of their business model, persevering through the crisis. (2) The changes to the value chain were made by using two approaches: either intensification or improvisation. (3) The changes were not sustainable beyond the crisis. (4) Retailers showed difficulties in implementing innovation, i.e., not only generating ideas, but actually realising them.
Theoretical contributions	Continuous innovation of PIPs requires more than improvisation. Innovation and self-renewal require long-term planning, resources and commitment.
Implications for practitioners	The study formulates design principles for sustainable PIP operation.

37.6 Summary of Part VI

Part VI contains the fourth empirical study of this dissertation, which applied and evaluated the 'toolkit for designing PIPs'. Chapter 29 presented the objectives and structure of the study. Chapter 30 introduced the toolkit, which consists of the artifacts developed in this dissertation as follows: (1) the PIP taxonomy, (2) the PIP composition model, (3) the PIP design process, and (4) design principles for sustainable PIP design.

Chapter 31 described the research approach. In order to provide a naturalistic evaluation of the artifacts (Venable et al., 2016; Venable, 2006), an AR approach was applied. Similar to the study featured in Part IV, this research followed the cyclical approach of Coghlan and Brannick (2005). The AR took place in the context of designing a new PIP—the Future Retail Store (FRS). Two AR cycles (Coghlan & Brannick, 2005) were conducted over 14 months, focusing on (1) revisiting and refining the original FRS concept and (2) designing organisation and defining roles for the sustainable operation of the FRS. The data material consisted of workshop sessions, various meetings, observations, and written project documentation such as meeting minutes, e-mails, presentations, and workshop protocols.

Chapter 32 described the results of the first AR cycle (July 2021–May 2022). The goal of this cycle was to design the concept for the FRS. In this process, the PIP taxonomy from Part III was applied. Insights from this AR cycle were used to evaluate the PIP taxonomy's ease of use and usefulness. Chapter 33 described the second AR cycle (June 2022–August 2022), which focused on the design of the FRS's organisational structure and team roles. This AR cycle drew on the PIP composition model from Part IV and the design principles regarding the sustainability of PIPs in Part V. Insights from the second AR cycle were used to evaluate the ease of use and usefulness of both the PIP composition model and the design principles for sustainable PIP design.

Chapter 34 discussed the insights from both AR cycles, i.e., the evaluation of the artifacts comprising the toolkit for designing PIPs. The evaluation regarding ease of use and usefulness of the toolkit was positive overall. Some areas of improvement were identified regarding the use of the artifacts as workshop methods. Chapter 35 provided a summary of the study and listed limitations. An overview of the main aspects of the AR artifact evaluation is presented in Table 37.4.

Table 37.4 Summary of the Action Research Evaluation

Aspect	Description
Presented in	Part VI
Research need	Evaluating the artifacts supporting PIP design which were developed throughout this dissertation.
Research questions	RQ 7: Are the developed artifacts (from Parts III–V) applicable (ease of use) and useful (perceived usefulness) for the development process of a PIP?
Research method	Action research according to Coghlan & Brannick (2005), supplemented by implications from evaluation in design science (Prat et al., 2015; Venable et al., 2016).
Data collection and analysis	Data on the demonstration of the artifacts consists of workshop sessions (both workshops with external expert participants and internal workshops), various meetings, observations, and written project documentation such as meeting minutes, e-mails, presentations, and workshop protocols. Additionally, reflections between senior researchers took place bi-weekly for evaluation of the artifacts.
Key findings	The toolkit for designing PIPs is useful, as it illuminates factors that are essential for successful PIP development, such as value creating design characteristics, organisational structure and team roles as well as the ability to innovate during maturity of the PIP. The artifacts require to be adapted and actively worked with during PIP development. Therefore, future research could address the ease of use of the toolkit as a workshop method.
Theoretical contributions	The study demonstrated the usefulness and applicability of AR as a method for artifact evaluation.
Implications for practitioners	The study introduced the toolkit for designing PIPs and demonstrated its application. All in all, the study showed how a PIP can be designed in a systematic and structured way.

Limitations and Future Research 38

The findings of the empirical studies presented in this dissertation are subject to consideration in light of their limitations. This chapter highlights the shortcomings of the studies from Parts III to VI, thereby opening up avenues for future research. In the following, shortcomings and future research are presented chronologically. An overview is provided in Table 38.1.

Limitations of Part III: The first empirical study of this dissertation employed Nickerson et al.'s (2013) taxonomy development method to create a taxonomy for PIPs. As described by Nickerson et al. (2013), a taxonomy is never exhaustive. Instead, it is purposefully developed towards its intended audience and usefulness, according to the selected meta-characteristic. This meta-characteristic therefore determines the entire development process. The selection of a different meta-characteristic will likely lead to different results. Further, Nickerson et al.'s (2013) taxonomy development method is an iterative process. The iterations presented in Part III consisted of various methods, including two systematic literature reviews (iterations three and four) as well as an interview-based evaluation with practitioners (iteration five). From this, several limitations arose. It is acknowledged that the SLRs were limited by the selection of the database (Scopus), the search-string and keyword selection, article selection criteria, and the subjective selection process of title and abstract screening. Therefore, both SLRs might not have provided an exhaustive collection of all published academic work relevant for the description of value creation for PIPs. For the taxonomy's evaluation in iteration five, a qualitative approach in the form of expert interviews was deliberately chosen. Despite a selection of interview partners from heterogeneous PIPs with different orientations, the choice remained limited. It cannot be ruled out that an increase in the number of interviews would reveal additional characteristics.

M. Perez Mengual, *Designing Physical Interaction Platforms*,
Markt- und Unternehmensentwicklung Markets and Organisations,
https://doi.org/10.1007/978-3-658-41920-2_38

Future research avenues from Part III: Despite the limitations, the plasticity of the taxonomy was emphasised, and researchers are strongly encouraged to adapt it according to their own purposes and research findings. Future researchers are encouraged (1) to define other meta-characteristics, creating taxonomies emphasising different aspects of PIPs (e.g., tools and methods used for interaction); (2) to review the concepts of PIPs from theoretical perspectives other than interactive value creation; (3) to validate the PIP taxonomy using more interviews and interviewees with other backgrounds; and (4) to use a quantitative approach for taxonomy valuation, e.g., by creating a database with numerous PIPs, examining whether new characteristics can be found.

Limitations of Part IV: The second empirical study of this dissertation employed an AR approach (Coghlan & Brannick, 2005). This research builds on a single action research project (Fraunhofer ENIQ). Although the ENIQ design process is a powerful example, the scope for generalisations remains limited. Furthermore, the study is framed by the subjective perspective of the participating actors (the researchers and the project team). Therefore, the findings from the study, e.g., the stages of the design process, require replication and validation.

Future research avenues from Part IV: The PIP composition model (cf. Figure 27.1) and the PIP design process (cf. Figure 27.2) highlight that PIP development is a complex endeavour. The AR study focused on identifying the organisational levels and stages in the design process. This resulted in two identified future research avenues: (1) The interrelationships between the levels of operation, team, and organisation could be an exciting area of research, both from the perspective of the individual and the organisation. (2) The stages of the design process could benefit from more elaboration, providing more comprehensive overviews of tools and methods that can be used. Overall, condensing the insights from Part IV into a toolkit (similar to, e.g., the Business Model Canvas) could greatly assist practitioners in designing value-creating PIPs.

Limitations of Part V: The third empirical study of this dissertation used a multiple case study approach (Eisenhardt, 1989; Yin, 2013). The study was carried out in the context of German retail. From this, several limitations arose. First, it provided only the perspective of selected German small and medium-sized brick-and-mortar retailers. Generalising the results to other contexts, economic (e.g., larger organisations or other orientations such as innovation labs) or cultural (e.g., other countries), is difficult. Second, the German government financially supported the retail sector during the lockdown periods. This may have weakened the need to innovate or adapt, as discussed previously. Similar studies in other countries might produce different results. Additionally, the COVID-19 pandemic posed a unique scenario. It is uncertain whether the findings apply to retail PIPs in general.

Future research avenues from Part V: From the limitations listed above, several possibilities for future research arise: (1) Examining self-renewal in other PIP scenarios (e.g., innovation labs, co-working spaces) could provide a valuable perspective on the self-renewal processes of PIPs in general. (2) The replication of the study in more common (non-crisis) settings could provide interesting results, especially as the challenges facing brick-and-mortar retail will most likely intensify in the near future (Agarwal et al., 2017; Alexander & Blazquez Cano, 2020). Self-renewal process and innovation will be essential for brick-and-mortar retail. Future research could address starting points, development paths, and success factors of such self-renewal processes.

Limitations of Part VI: The fourth empirical study, for a second time, employed an AR approach (Coghlan & Brannick, 2005). This study evaluated the artifacts from this dissertation in the content of a PIP design process. While the evaluation of these artifacts was positive overall, additional evaluations in different development contexts would be desirable to verify and, if necessary, complement the evaluation results. In addition, this evaluation took an interpretivist approach to analyse the data arising from the nature of the AR method. Therefore, the evaluation is framed by the subjective perspective of the development team.

Future research avenues from Part VI: The AR study on designing the Future Retail Store was context-specific. Therefore, to better understand the ease of use and usefulness of the developed artifacts, the toolkit should be applied and evaluated in other PIP design projects, ideally in other industries. Applying the taxonomy in the FRS project showed that the artifact had to be adapted to the retail context. Future research could explore the possibilities of creating more holistic, context-specific taxonomies (e.g. containing design dimensions specific to co-working and innovation).

Overall, the empirical research in this dissertation was carried out with the attitude of an engaged scholar (Van de Ven, 2007, 2018). Engaged scholarship blends academic work with practice, and a vital part of the research process is to make clear connections between real-world problems and academically supported solutions. Especially in the context of PIPs, future research should embrace this to advance our understanding of what leads to sustainable and prosperous PIPs.

Table 38.1 Overview of limitations an avenues for future research

Referring to	Limitation	Avenue for future research
Part III	Definition of the meta-characteristic, guiding the development process	Definition of other meta-characteristics, creating a taxonomy emphasising different aspects of PIPs.
Part III	Iterations 3-4 SLR: Database, keyword selection, article selection criteria, subjective screening process (title, abstract)	Identification of other relevant keywords; use of other databases; Inclusion of other literature
Part III	Iteration 5 Interviews: Selection of experts for the evaluation of the taxonomy	Validating the taxonomy using more interviews; interviewees with other (international) backgrounds
Part III	Iteration 5 Interviews: Qualitative approach towards taxonomy evaluation	Quantitative approach towards taxonomy valuation, e.g., by creating a database with PIPs.
Part IV	Single case approach	Replication and validation of the results
Part IV	Generalisation of AR findings	Extension of researched cases
Part V	Selection of cases in multiple case study	Increase of variety in selection, e.g., from other geographical regions or with larger company sizes
Part V	Focus on retail-PIPs	Examining self-renewal in other PIP scenarios (e.g., innovation labs, co-working spaces)
Part V	Generalisation of case study findings	Extension of researched cases
Part V	Uniqueness of the COVID-19 setting	Replication in more common settings
Part VI	Evaluating the toolkit during a single case AR project	Application and evaluation of the toolkit in other PIP design projects, ideally in other industries
Part VI	Artifacts in the toolkit require adaptation to a specific PIP context (.e.g the taxonomy)	Development of context-specific artefacts (e.g. the taxonomy for co-working PIPs)

39 Final Reflection

In the context of research on PIPs, this dissertation explored an essential and hitherto understudied topic: *how a physical interaction platform (PIP) can be designed in a systematic and structured way*. Along the lifecycle of a PIP, this dissertation uncovered which characteristics are essential for the value creation and sustainable operation of PIPs (Part III), which steps constitute a PIP design process, and at which organisational levels this process needs to take place (Part IV), as well as what can be learned about the renewal of PIPs (Part V). This dissertation harnessed the results of a taxonomy development method (Part III), action research (Part IV), and a multiple-case study (Part V). Fulfilling the aspiration of a practitioner, the results were evaluated in the context of a PIP design project, the design of the Future Retail Store, highlighting their usefulness (Part VI). As a result, this dissertation not only explored how a PIP can be designed in a systematic and structured way—it simultaneously contributed to the design and implementation of a new, value-creating PIP. In the spirit of engaged scholarship, academic work and practical problems were combined to create something of relevance and sustainable impact. As a final reflection, six significant insights can be derived from this dissertation that PIP designers should embrace in their quest to design prosperous and sustainable spaces for interaction.

(1) PIP design is business model design: Part III emphasized that for understanding value creation in PIPs, design dimensions and characteristics of platform business models can be utilized. Following this, it is suggested that designing PIPs should be understood as a process similar to business model design (Van Alstyne & Parker, 2017). This involves designing value propositions for the (multiple) PIP actors, designing the value creation mechanism, and ensuring long-term operation by designing a revenue model.

M. Perez Mengual, *Designing Physical Interaction Platforms*, Markt- und Unternehmensentwicklung Markets and Organisations, https://doi.org/10.1007/978-3-658-41920-2_39

(2) The location and the PIP design are mutually dependent: A PIP's physical location should be the design's central starting point. The physical location determines which groups of actors can be addressed (in terms of PIP accessibility), thereby determining which interaction can take place in the PIP. Not every PIP concept can be realised everywhere (e.g., an Open Innovation lab based on a self-selection of visitors will likely not work in a remote industrial area). Therefore, either (1) the PIP concept must be tailored to fit an available location, or (2) a suitable location for a developed PIP concept needs to be identified.

(3) Value propositions for owner and provider need to be clearly defined: PIPs are not predominantly about market control and rapid scaling, unlike digital platforms. Accordingly, it is essential to define the expectations raised towards a PIP or what value the PIP is expected to deliver to the 'owning' organization and the operating team. This determines not only the KPIs by which PIP success can be measured but also the acceptance and commitment of the commissioning organisation towards the PIP.

(4) A PIP's ability to innovate is shaped during initial PIP design: As laid out by scholarly contributions (Memon, 2021; Parker et al., 2016; Thomas et al., 2021), innovation is essential for platforms. When designing and implementing new PIPs, it should be considered that the PIP will require renewal during its lifecycle. This entails allocating appropriate budget or funding, as both experimenting with new ideas as well as implementing an advanced PIP concept requires substantial resources.

(5) Forming a core design team is vital: PIP design processes can be demanding. Therefore, creating a capable, dedicated design team that is up to the challenge is essential. This team will have to make crucial decisions on the direction and implementation of the PIP. While PIP design requires the design team to identify and discuss requirements from other stakeholders, care must be taken not to lose track in light of manifold interests. Different stakeholders have different interests. The PIP will not satisfy all of them, and the core design team will eventually need to balance interests and defend the PIP design concept.

(6) PIPs are an innovation by themselves: PIPs are a business model innovation for those who operate the PIPs. This should not be underestimated as it has two implications. (1) If the owner of the PIP is a larger organization (e.g., in the case of innovation labs), unleashing and harnessing the value generated by the PIP requires a certain degree of organizational and role-specific transformation. The PIP needs to be integrated into organizational routines, and that implies change and change management. (2) For smaller PIP operators (e.g., retailers), the implication is that innovation has a high impact on the overall business model, i.e., direct consequences for operations.

As a final note, it is hoped that the findings of this dissertation will be found helpful by both academics and practitioners alike. I am looking forward to see how my work will contribute to the creation of a whole new set of sustainable PIPs that harness the value created by rich, physical interactions.

References

Abdelkafi, N., Raasch, C., Roth, A., & Srinivasan, R. (2019). Multi-sided platforms. *Electronic Markets, 29*(4), 553–559.

Agarwal, P., Breschi, R., & Devillard-Hoellinger, S. (2017). How the mall business can reinvent itself for the digital age. *McKinsey & Company*, 1–5. Retrieved from https://www.mckinsey.com/business-functions/marketing-and-sales/our-insights/how-the-mall-business-can-reinvent-itself

Agogue, M., & Cassotti, M. (2013). Understanding fixation effects in creativity: A design-theory approach. *Proceedings of the International Conference on Engineering Design, ICED, 2 DS75–02*(August), pp. 103–112.

Ahuja, S. B. (2019). Why innovation labs fail, and how to ensure yours doesn't. *Harvard Business Review, 22.*

Alam, I. (2006). Service innovation strategy and process: A cross-national comparative analysis. *International Marketing Review, 23*(3), 234–254. https://doi.org/10.1108/02651330610670433

Alexander, B., & Blazquez Cano, M. (2020). Store of the future: Towards a (re)invention and (re)imagination of physical store space in an omnichannel context. *Journal of Retailing and Consumer Services, 55*, 101913. https://doi.org/10.1016/j.jretconser.2019.101913

Almirall, E., Lee, M., & Wareham, J. (2012). Mapping Living Labs in the Landscape of Innovation Methodologies. *Technology Innovation Management Review, 2*(9), 12–18. https://doi.org/10.22215/timreview603

Alter, S. (2015). The concept of "IT artifact" has outlived its usefulness and should be retired now. *Information Systems Journal, 25*(1), 47–60. https://doi.org/10.1111/isj.12048

Alves, C., Oliveira, J., & Jansen, S. (2018). Understanding governance mechanisms and health in software ecosystems: A systematic literature review. In S. Hammoudi, M. Smialek, O. Camp, & J. Filipe (Eds.), *Enterprise information systems* (pp. 517–542). https://doi.org/10.1007/978-3-319-93375-7_24

Anderson, S. P., & Coate, S. (2005). Market provision of broadcasting: A welfare analysis. *Review of Economic Studies, 72*(4), 947–972. https://doi.org/10.1111/0034-6527.00357

Andries, P., & Debackere, K. (2007). Adaptation and performance in new businesses: Understanding the moderating effects of independence and industry. *Small Business Economics, 29*(1–2), 81–99. https://doi.org/10.1007/s11187-005-5640-2

M. Perez Mengual, *Designing Physical Interaction Platforms*,
Markt- und Unternehmensentwicklung Markets and Organisations,
https://doi.org/10.1007/978-3-658-41920-2

Andries, P., Debackere, K., & van Looy, B. (2013). Simultaneous experimentation as a learning strategy: Business model development under uncertainty. *Strategic Entrepreneurship Journal, 7*(4), 288–310. https://doi.org/10.1002/sej.1170

Archibugi, D., Filippetti, A., & Frenz, M. (2012). *SSRN Electronic Journal.* https://doi.org/10.2139/ssrn.2001486

Arreola González, A., Pfaff, M., & Krcmar, H. (2019). Value modeling for ecosystem analysis. *Computers, 8*(3), 1–15. https://doi.org/10.3390/computers8030068

Aryan, V., Bertling, J., & Liedtke, C. (2021). Topology, typology, and dynamics of commons-based peer production: On platforms, actors, and innovation in the maker movement. *Creativity and Innovation Management, 30*(1), 63–79. https://doi.org/10.1111/caim.12392

Avison, D. E., Davison, R. M., & Malaurent, J. (2018). Information systems action research: Debunking myths and overcoming barriers. *Information and Management, 55*(2), 177–187. https://doi.org/10.1016/j.im.2017.05.004

Baden-Fuller, C., & Mangematin, V. (2013). Business models: A challenging agenda. *Strategic Organization, 11*(4), 418–427. https://doi.org/10.1177/1476127013510112

Bailey, K. D. (1994). *Typologies and taxonomies.* https://doi.org/10.4135/9781412986397

Baron, S., & Warnaby, G. (2008). Individual customers' use and integration of resources: Empirical findings and organizational implications in the context of value co-creation. *Otago Forum 2: Academic Papers, Paper No: 6*, pp. 62–78. Retrieved from https://citeseerx.ist.psu.edu/viewdoc/download?doi=10.1.1.510.7860&rep=rep1&type=pdf

Baskerville, R., & Wood-Harper, A. T. (1998). Diversity in information systems action research methods. *European Journal of Information Systems, 7*(2), 90–107. https://doi.org/10.1057/palgrave.ejis.3000298

Baskerville, Richard, & Pries-Heje, J. (2010). Explanatory design theory. *Business & Information Systems Engineering, 2*(5), 271–282. https://doi.org/10.1007/s12599-010-0118-4

Bason, C. (2018). *Leading public sector innovation: Co-creating for a better society.* Retrieved from https://books.google.de/books?hl=de&lr=&id=0v9oDwAAQBAJ&oi=fnd&pg=PR1&dq=Bason,+C.+2010.+Leading+public+sector+innovation:+Co-creating+for+a+better+society.+Bristol:+Policy+Press&ots=ryFYYuJNc_&sig=li_zGqFeFE7QvLN_R4_zK6WEJVY

Bender, B., & Gericke, K. (Eds.) (2021). *Pahl/Beitz Konstruktionslehre.* https://doi.org/10.1007/978-3-662-57303-7

Berbegal-Mirabent, J. (2021). What do we know about co-working spaces? Trends and challenges ahead. *Sustainability (Switzerland), 13*(3), 1–30. https://doi.org/10.3390/su13031416

Berengian, A. (2017). It's time to ditch your innovation lab. *Venture Beat.* Retrieved from https://venturebeat.com/2017/03/22/its-time-to-ditch-your-innovation-lab/

Berger, A., & Brem, A. (2016). Innovation hub how-to: Lessons from Silicon Valley. *Global Business and Organizational Excellence, 35*(5), 58–70. https://doi.org/10.1002/joe.21698

Bergvall-Kåreborn, B., Ihlström Eriksson, C., Ståhlbröst, A., & Svensson, J. (2009). A milieu for innovation—Defining living labs. *ResearchGate.* Retrieved from https://www.researchgate.net/publication/228676111_A_Milieu_for_Innovation-Defining_Living_Labs

Bernstein, R. J. (2010). *The pragmatic turn.* Cambridge, UK: Polity Press.

Bessant, J. (2020). Creating the creative open lab. In A. Fritzsche, J. M. Jonas, A. Roth, & K. M. Möslein (Eds.), *Innovating in the open lab* (pp. 191–202). https://doi.org/10.1515/9783110633665-017

Bessant, J., Rush, H., & Trifilova, A. (2015). Crisis-driven innovation: The case of humanitarian innovation. *International Journal of Innovation Management, 19*(6), 1–23. https://doi.org/10.1142/S1363919615400149

Betts, A., & Bloom, L. (2014). *Humanitarian innovation: The state of the art*. New York: United Nations Office for the Coordination of Humanitarian Affairs (OCHA). t

Blaschke, M., Haki, K., Aier, S., & Winter, R. (2019). Taxonomy of digital platforms: A platform architecture perspective. *14th International Conference on Wirtschaftsinformatik*, 15. Retrieved from https://www.researchgate.net/publication/331904829

Bloom, L., & Faulkner, R. (2016). Innovation spaces: lessons from the United Nations. *Third World Quarterly, 37*(8), 1371–1387. https://doi.org/10.1080/01436597.2015.1135730

Bock, A. J., Opsahl, T., George, G., & Gann, D. M. (2012). The effects of culture and structure on strategic flexibility during business model innovation. *Journal of Management Studies, 49*(2), 279–305. https://doi.org/10.1111/j.1467-6486.2011.01030.x

Bogers, M., Zobel, A. K., Afuah, A., Almirall, E., Brunswicker, S., Dahlander, L., … Ter Wal, A. L. J. (2017). The open innovation research landscape: Established perspectives and emerging themes across different levels of analysis. *Industry and Innovation, 24*(1), 8–40. https://doi.org/10.1080/13662716.2016.1240068

Bogner, A., Littig, B., & Menz, W. (2009). Introduction: Expert interviews—An introduction to a new methodological debate. *Interviewing Experts*, 1–13. https://doi.org/10.1057/978 0230244276_1

Böhmann, T., Leimeister, J. M., & Möslein, K. (2014). Service systems engineering. *Business and Information Systems Engineering, 6*(2), 73–79. https://doi.org/10.1007/s12599-014-0314-8

Bollweg, L., Lackes, R., Siepermann, M., Sutaj, A., & Weber, P. (2016). Digitalization of Local Owner Operated Retail Outlets: The Role of the Perception of Competition and Customer Expectations, in *PACIS 2016 Proceedings*, Chiayi, Taiwan.

Bollweg, L., Lackes, R., Siepermann, M., & Weber, P. (2020). Drivers and barriers of the digitalization of local owner operated retail outlets. *Journal of Small Business and Entrepreneurship, 32*(2), 173–201. https://doi.org/10.1080/08276331.2019.1616256

Booz Allen Hamilton. (1982). *New products management for the 1980s*. Booz, Allen & Hamilton Inc. New York.

Boudreau, K. J., & Hagiu, A. (2009). Platform rules: Multi-sided platforms as regulators. *Platforms, Markets and Innovation, 1*, 163–191. https://doi.org/10.4324/9780203926994

Bouncken, R., & Aslam, M. M. (2019). Understanding knowledge exchange processes among diverse users of coworking-spaces. *Journal of Knowledge Management, 23*(10), 2067–2085. https://doi.org/10.1108/JKM-05-2018-0316

Bouncken, R. B., Laudien, S. M., Fredrich, V., & Görmar, L. (2018). Coopetition in coworking-spaces: value creation and appropriation tensions in an entrepreneurial space. *Review of Managerial Science, 12*(2), 385–410. https://doi.org/10.1007/s11846-017-0267-7

Bouncken, R. B., & Reuschl, A. J. (2018). Coworking-spaces: how a phenomenon of the sharing economy builds a novel trend for the workplace and for entrepreneurship. *Review of Managerial Science, 12*(1), 317–334. https://doi.org/10.1007/s11846-016-0215-y

Bowers, M. R. (1989). Developing new services: Improving the process makes it better. *Journal of Services Marketing, 3*(1), 15–20. https://doi.org/10.1108/EUM0000000002478

Brannick, T., & Coghlan, D. (2007). In defense of being "native": The case for insider academic research. *Organizational Research Methods, 10*(1), 59–74. https://doi.org/10.1177/1094428106289253

Breier, M., Kallmuenzer, A., Clauss, T., Gast, J., Kraus, S., & Tiberius, V. (2021). The role of business model innovation in the hospitality industry during the COVID-19 crisis. *International Journal of Hospitality Management, 92*, 102723. https://doi.org/10.1016/j.ijhm.2020.102723

Buck, R. C., & Hull, D. L. (1966). The logical structure of the Linnaean Hierarchy. *Systematic Zoology, XV*, 97–111.

Buhalis, D., Andreu, L., & Gnoth, J. (2020). The dark side of the sharing economy: Balancing value co-creation and value co-destruction. *Psychology & Marketing, 37*(5), 689–704. https://doi.org/10.1002/mar.21344

Caccamo, M. (2020). Leveraging innovation spaces to foster collaborative innovation. *Creativity and Innovation Management*, (November 2019), 178–191. https://doi.org/10.1111/caim.12357

Capdevila, I. (2015). Co-working spaces and the localised dynamics of innovation in Barcelona. *International Journal of Innovation Management, 19*(3). https://doi.org/10.1142/S1363919615400046

Capdevila, I. (2019). Joining a collaborative space: Is it really a better place to work? *Journal of Business Strategy, 40*(2), 14–21. https://doi.org/10.1108/JBS-09-2017-0140

Cappellaro, F., Cutaia, L., Innella, C., Meloni, C., Pentassuglia, R., & Porretto, V. (2019). Investigating circular economy urban practices in Centocelle, Rome district. *Environmental Engineering and Management Journal, 18*(10), 2145–2153.

Castilho, M. F., & Quandt, C. O. (2017). Technology innovation management review. *Technology Innovation Management Review, 7*(12), 32–43.

Catlin, T., Scanlan, J., & Willmott, P. (2015). Raising your digital quotient. *McKinsey Quarterly*, 3, 30–43.

Cennamo, C. (2018). Building the value of next-generation platforms: The paradox of diminishing returns. *Journal of Management, 44*(8), 3038–3069. https://doi.org/10.1177/0149206316658350

Chandler, J. D., & Vargo, S. L. (2011). Contextualization and value-in-context: How context frames exchange. *Marketing Theory, 11*(1), 35–49. https://doi.org/10.1177/1470593110393713

Chandra, L., Seidel, S., & Gregor, S. (2015). Prescriptive knowledge in IS research: Conceptualizing design principles in terms of materiality, action, and boundary conditions. *Proceedings of the Annual Hawaii International Conference on System Sciences, 2015-March*, 4039–4048. https://doi.org/10.1109/HICSS.2015.485

Chasin, F., von Hoffen, M., Cramer, M., & Matzner, M. (2018). Peer-to-peer sharing and collaborative consumption platforms: A taxonomy and a reproducible analysis. *Information Systems and E-Business Management, 16*(2), 293–325. https://doi.org/10.1007/s10257-017-0357-8

Chesbrough, H. (2010). Business model innovation: Opportunities and barriers. *Long Range Planning, 43*(2–3), 354–363. https://doi.org/10.1016/j.lrp.2009.07.010

Chesbrough, H., & Rosenbloom, R. S. (2002). The role of the business model in capturing value from innovation: Evidence from Xerox Corporation's technology spin-off companies. *Industrial and Corporate Change, 11*(3), 529–555. https://doi.org/10.1093/icc/11.3.529

Chesbrough, H. W. (2003). The era of open innovation. *MIT Sloan Management Review.* https://doi.org/10.1371/journal.pone.0015090

Chronéer, D., Ståhlbröst, A., & Habibipour, A. (2019). Urban Living Labs: Towards an integrated understanding of their key components. *Technology Innovation Management Review, 9*(3), 50–62. https://doi.org/10.22215/timreview/1224

Clauss, T., Breier, M., Kraus, S., Durst, S., & Mahto, R. V. (2021). *Temporary business model innovation—SMEs' innovation response to the Covid-19 crisis,* 1–19. https://doi.org/10.1111/radm.12498

Clayton, P., Feldman, M., & Lowe, N. (2018). Behind the scenes: Intermediary organizations that facilitate science commercialization through entrepreneurship. *Academy of Management Perspectives, 32*(1), 104–124. https://doi.org/10.5465/amp.2016.0133

Coghlan, D., & Brannick, T. (2005). *Doing action research in your own organization.* 2nd ed. London: Sage

Coghlan, D., & Shani, A. B. (2021). Abductive reasoning as the integrating mechanism between first- second- and third-person practice in action research. *Systemic Practice and Action Research, 34*(4), 463–474. https://doi.org/10.1007/s11213-020-09542-9

Cohendet, P., Grandadam, D., Simon, L., & Capdevila, I. (2014). Epistemic communities, localization and the dynamics of knowledge creation. *Journal of Economic Geography, 14*(5), 929–954. https://doi.org/10.1093/jeg/lbu018

Coll-Martínez, E., & Méndez-Ortega, C. (2020). Agglomeration and coagglomeration of co-working spaces and creative industries in the city. *European Planning Studies, 0*(0), 1–22. https://doi.org/10.1080/09654313.2020.1847256

Collatto, D. C., Dresch, A., Lacerda, D. P., & Bentz, I. G. (2018). Is action design research indeed necessary? Analysis and synergies between action research and design science research. *Systemic Practice and Action Research, 31*(3), 239–267. https://doi.org/10.1007/s11213-017-9424-9

Cooper, R. (2008). Perspective: The Stage-Gate idea to launch process—Update, what's new and nexgen systems. *Journal of Product Innovation Management, 25*(3), 213–232. https://doi.org/10.1111/j.1540-5885.2008.00296.x

Cooper, R. G. (1990). New products: What distinguishes the winners? *Research-Technology Management, 33*(6), 27–31. https://doi.org/10.1080/08956308.1990.11670699

Corbin, J., & Strauss, A. (2008). Basics of qualitative research (3rd ed.): Techniques and procedures for developing grounded theory. In *AMCIS 2017—America's Conference on Information Systems: A Tradition of Innovation* (Vol. 2017–August). https://doi.org/10.4135/9781452230153

Corsini, L., Dammicco, V., & Moultrie, J. (2021). Frugal innovation in a crisis: The digital fabrication maker response to COVID-19. *R and D Management, 51*(2), 195–210. https://doi.org/10.1111/radm.12446

Coyne, R. (2005). Wicked problems revisited. *Design Studies, 26*(1), 5–17. https://doi.org/10.1016/j.destud.2004.06.005

Cruz, E., Orts-Escolano, S., Gomez-Donoso, F., Rizo, C., Rangel, J. C., Mora, H., & Cazorla, M. (2019). An augmented reality application for improving shopping experience in large retail stores. *Virtual Reality, 23*(3), 281–291. https://doi.org/10.1007/s10055-018-0338-3

Curtis, S. K., & Mont, O. (2020). Sharing economy business models for sustainability. *Journal of Cleaner Production, 266*, 121519. https://doi.org/10.1016/j.jclepro.2020.121519

Cusumano, M. A., Gawer, A., & Yoffie, D. B. (2019). *The business of platforms: Strategy in the age of digital competition, innovation, and power*. Harper Business.

Dachs, B., & Peters, B. (2020). ZEW policy brief. *ZBW Leibniz Information Centre for Economics, 2*(7), 1–7.

Dahlke, J., Bogner, K., Becker, M., Schlaile, M. P., Pyka, A., & Ebersberger, B. (2021). Crisis-driven innovation and fundamental human needs: A typological framework of rapid-response COVID-19 innovations. *Technological Forecasting and Social Change, 169*, 120799. https://doi.org/10.1016/j.techfore.2021.120799

Dam, N. A. K., Le Dinh, T., & Menvielle, W. (2020). Customer Co-creation through the lens of service-dominant logic: A literature review. *AMCIS 2020 Proceedings*, 10. Retrieved from https://aisel.aisnet.org/amcis2020/data_science_analytics_for_decision_support/data_science_analytics_for_decision_support/29/

Danneels, E. (2011). Trying to become a different type of company: Dynamic capability at Smith Corona. *Strategic Management Journal, 32*(1), 1–31. https://doi.org/10.1002/smj.863

Danzinger, F., Schmidt, R., Memmert, F., & Pichlbauer, M. (2020). 5 open lab functionalities in offline-retail—A step towards future retail? In A. Fritzsche, J. M. Jonas, A. Roth, & K. M. Möslein (Eds.), *Innovating in the Open Lab* (pp. 49–70). https://doi.org/10.1515/9783110633665-005

Davis, F. D. (1989). Perceived usefulness, perceived ease of use, and user acceptance of information technology. *MIS Quarterly: Management Information Systems, 13*(3), 319–339. https://doi.org/10.2307/249008

Davison, R. M., Martinsons, M. G., & Kock, N. (2004). Principles of canonical action research. *Information Systems Journal, 14*(1), 65–86. https://doi.org/10.1111/j.1365-2575.2004.00162.x

de Oliveira, D. T., & Cortimiglia, M. N. (2017). Value co-creation in web-based multisided platforms: A conceptual framework and implications for business model design. *Business Horizons, 60*(6), 747–758. https://doi.org/10.1016/j.bushor.2017.07.002

de Reuver, M., Sørensen, C., & Basole, R. C. (2018). The digital platform: A research agenda. *Journal of Information Technology, 33*(2), 124–135. https://doi.org/10.1057/s41265-016-0033-3

Deilen, M., & Wiesche, M. (2021). The role of complementors in platform ecosystems. *Wirtschaftsinformatik 2021 Proceedings*. Retrieved from http://aisel.aisnet.org/icis2008%0Ahttp://aisel.aisnet.org/icis2008/53

Dell'Era, C., Altuna, N., Magistretti, S., & Verganti, R. (2017). Discovering quiescent meanings in technologies: Exploring the design management practices that support the development of technology epiphanies. *Technology Analysis and Strategic Management, 29*(2), 149–166. https://doi.org/10.1080/09537325.2016.1210785

Dell'Era, C., & Landoni, P. (2014). Living Lab: A methodology between user-centred design and participatory design. *Creativity and Innovation Management, 23*(2), 137–154. https://doi.org/10.1111/caim.12061

Demil, B., & Lecocq, X. (2010). Business model evolution: In search of dynamic consistency. *Long Range Planning, 43*(2–3), 227–246. https://doi.org/10.1016/j.lrp.2010.02.004

Di Fiore, A., & Vetter, J. (2016). Why B2B companies struggle with collaborative innovation. *Harvard Business Review.*

Diniz, E. H., Siqueira, E. S., & van Heck, E. (2019). Taxonomy of digital community currency platforms. *Information Technology for Development, 25*(1), 69–91. https://doi.org/10.1080/02681102.2018.1485005

Doorley, S., & Witthoft, S. (2012). *Make space: How to set the stage for creative collaboration* (1st ed.). Wiley.

Dubé, L. & Paré, G. (2003). Rigor in information systems positivist case research: Current practices, trends, and recommendations. *MIS Quarterly, 27*(4), 597. https://doi.org/10.2307/30036550

Dubois, A., & Gadde, L. E. (2002). Systematic combining: An abductive approach to case research. *Journal of Business Research, 55*(7), 553–560. https://doi.org/10.1016/S0148-2963(00)00195-8

Duryee, T. (2015). Nordstrom shrinks Innovation Lab, reassigns employees in shakeup of tech initiatives. *GeekWire.* Retrieved from https://www.geekwire.com/2015/nordstrom-shrinks-innovation-lab-reassigns-employees-shakeup-tech-intiatives/

Ebersberger, B., & Kuckertz, A. (2021). Hop to it! The impact of organization type on innovation response time to the COVID-19 crisis. *Journal of Business Research, 124*(July 2020), 126–135. https://doi.org/10.1016/j.jbusres.2020.11.051

Edvardsson, B., Kristensson, P., Magnusson, P., & Sundström, E. (2012). Customer integration within service development: A review of methods and an analysis of insitu and exsitu contributions. *Technovation, 32*(7–8), 419–429. https://doi.org/10.1016/j.technovation.2011.04.006

Eggers, J. P., & Kaplan, S. (2013). Cognition and capabilities: A multi-level perspective. *Academy of Management Annals, 7*(1), 295–340. https://doi.org/10.1080/19416520.2013.769318

Eggert, A., Ulaga, W., Frow, P., & Payne, A. (2018). Conceptualizing and communicating value in business markets: From value in exchange to value in use. *Industrial Marketing Management, 69*, 80–90. https://doi.org/10.1016/j.indmarman.2018.01.018

Eisenhardt, K. M. (1989). Building theories from case study research. *The Academy of Management Review, 14*(4), 532. https://doi.org/10.2307/258557

Eisenhardt, K. M. (1991). Better stories and better constructs: The case for rigor and comparative logic. *Academy of Management Review*, 16, pp. 620–627. https://doi.org/10.5465/amr.1991.4279496

Elia, G., & Margherita, A. (2018). Can we solve wicked problems? A conceptual framework and a collective intelligence system to support problem analysis and solution design for complex social issues. *Technological Forecasting and Social Change, 133*(March), 279–286. https://doi.org/10.1016/j.techfore.2018.03.010

Elmquist, M., Ollila, S., & Yström, A. (2016). Beyond intermediation: The open innovation arena as an actor enabling joint knowledge creation. *International Journal of Technology Management, 72*(4), 273–295. https://doi.org/10.1504/IJTM.2016.081573

Engels, F., Wentland, A., & Pfotenhauer, S. M. (2019). Testing future societies? Developing a framework for test beds and living labs as instruments of innovation governance. *Research Policy, 48*(9), 103826. https://doi.org/10.1016/j.respol.2019.103826

Enkel, E., Bogers, M., & Chesbrough, H. (2020). Exploring open innovation in the digital age: A maturity model and future research directions. *R and D Management*, *50*(1), 161–168. https://doi.org/10.1111/radm.12397

EUREF. (2021). Retrieved from https://euref.de/

Evans, D. S. (2003). Some empirical aspects of multi-sided platform industries in: *Review of Network Economics*, *2*(3), 191–209. https://www.degruyter.com/view/journals/rne/2/3/article-rne.2003.2.3.1026.xml.xml?tab_body=pdf-74962

Evans, D. S., & Schmalensee, D. (2016). *Matchmakers: The new economics of multisided platforms*. Harvard Business Review Press.

Evans, D. S., & Schmalensee, R. (2005). *The industrial organization of markets with two-sided platforms*. Retrieved from https://www.nber.org/papers/w11603

Evans, D. S., Schmalensee, R., Noel, M. D., Chang, H. H., & Garcia-Swartz, D. D. (2011, December 17). *Platform economics: Essays on multi-sided businesses*.

Evans, J. R. (2011). Retailing in perspective: The past is a prologue to the future. *International Review of Retail, Distribution and Consumer Research*, *21*(1), 1–31. https://doi.org/10.1080/09593969.2011.537817

Fairlie, R. (2020). The impact of COVID-19 on small business owners: Evidence from the first three months after widespread social-distancing restrictions. *Journal of Economics and Management Strategy*, *29*(4), 727–740. https://doi.org/10.1111/jems.12400

Filippetti, A., & Archibugi, D. (2011). Innovation in times of crisis: National systems of innovation, structure, and demand. *Research Policy*, *40*(2), 179–192. https://doi.org/10.1016/j.respol.2010.09.001

Fink, A. (2020). *Conducting research literature reviews: From internet to paper*. Los Angeles: SAGE Publications, Inc.

Fiorentino, S. (2019). Different typologies of 'co-working spaces' and the contemporary dynamics of local economic development in Rome. *European Planning Studies*, *27*(9), 1768–1790. https://doi.org/10.1080/09654313.2019.1620697

Foss, N. J., & Saebi, T. (2017). Fifteen years of research on business model innovation: How far have we come, and where should we go? *Journal of Management*, *43*(1), 200–227. https://doi.org/10.1177/0149206316675927

Fricke, G. (1996). Successful individual approaches in engineering design. *Research in Engineering Design*, (8), 151–165.

Friedman, K. (2003). Theory construction in design research criteria: Approaches and methods. *Design Studies*, *24*(6), 507–522. https://doi.org/10.1016/S0142-694X(03)00039-5

Fritzsche, A., Jonas, J. M., Roth, A., & Möslein, K. M. (2020). *Innovating in the Open Lab. The new potential for interactive value creation across organizational boundaries*. Berlin: De Gruyter Oldenbourg.

Gassmann, O., Frankenberger, K., & Csik, M. (2013). *The St. Gallen Business Model Navigator*. Retrieved from https://www.alexandria.unisg.ch/224941/7/BusinessModelNavigatorworkingpaper.pdf

Gassmann, O., Frankenberger, K., & Sauer, R. (2016). *Exploring the field of business model innovation: New theoretical perspectives*. Springer.

Gatautis, R. (2017). The rise of the platforms: Business model innovation perspectives. *Engineering Economics*, *28*(5), 585–591. https://doi.org/10.5755/j01.ee.28.5.19579

Gawer, A., & Cusumano, M. A. (2014). Industry platforms and ecosystem innovation. *Journal of Product Innovation Management, 31*(3), 417–433. https://doi.org/10.1111/jpim.12105

Gericke, K., & Blessing, L. (2012). An analysis of design process models across disciplines. *Proceedings of International Design Conference, DESIGN, DS 70*, 171–180.

Geum, Y., Jeon, H., & Lee, H. (2016). Developing new smart services using integrated morphological analysis: Integration of the market-pull and technology-push approach. *Service Business, 10*(3), 531–555. https://doi.org/10.1007/s11628-015-0281-2

Ghazawneh, A., & Henfridsson, O. (2013). Balancing platform control and external contribution in third-party development: The boundary resources model. *Information Systems Journal, 23*(2), 173–192. https://doi.org/10.1111/j.1365-2575.2012.00406.x

Gioia, D. A., Corley, K. G., & Hamilton, A. L. (2013). Seeking qualitative rigor in inductive research: Notes on the Gioia methodology. *Organizational Research Methods, 16*(1), 15–31. https://doi.org/10.1177/1094428112452151

Glass, R. L., & Vessey, I. (1995). Contemporary application: Domain taxonomies. *IEEE Software, 12*(4), 63–76.

Goldkuhl, Goran. (2013). Action research vs. design research: Using practice research as a lens for comparison and integration. *Workshop on IT Artefact Design & Workpractice Improvement*, (October), 1–23.

Goldkuhl, Göran. (2012a). Pragmatism vs interpretivism in qualitative information systems research. *European Journal of Information Systems, 21*(2), 135–146. https://doi.org/10.1057/ejis.2011.54

Goldkuhl, Göran. (2012b). What is an Ensemble Artifact? *International Workshop on IT Artefact Design & Workpractice Intervention*, 1–19.

Gomes, L. A. de V., Facin, A. L. F., Salerno, M. S., & Ikenami, R. K. (2018). Unpacking the innovation ecosystem construct: Evolution, gaps and trends. *Technological Forecasting and Social Change, 136*, 30–48. https://doi.org/10.1016/j.techfore.2016.11.009

Goodman, D. (1989). Enlightenment salons: The convergence of female and philosophic ambitions. *Eighteenth-Century Studies, 22*(3), 329. https://doi.org/10.2307/2738891

Govindarajan, V., & Euchner, J. (2012). Reverse innovation. *Research-Technology Management, 55*(6), 13–17. https://doi.org/10.5437/08956308x5506003

Gregor, S. (2006). The nature of theory in information systems. *MIS Quarterly: Management Information Systems, 30*(3), 611–642. https://doi.org/10.2307/25148742

Gregor, S., & Hevner, A. R. (2013). Positioning and presenting design science research for maximum impact. *MIS Quarterly, 37*(2), 337–355. https://doi.org/10.25300/MISQ/2013/37.2.01

Gregor, S., & Jones, D. (2007). The anatomy of a design theory. *Journal of the Association for Information Systems, 8*(5), 312–335. https://doi.org/10.17705/1jais.00129

Greve, K., Martinez, V., Jonas, J., Neely, A., & Möslein, K. (2016). *Facilitating co-creation in living labs : The JOSEPHS study*. Retrieved from https://cambridgeservicealliance.eng.cam.ac.uk/resources/Downloads/MonthlyPapers/2016MayPaper_FacilitatingCoCreationinLivingLabs.pdf

Grewal, D., Noble, S. M., Roggeveen, A. L., Nordfalt, J., & Noble, S. M. (2020). *The future of in-store technology*. 96–113.

Grönroos, C. (2011). A service perspective on business relationships: The value creation, interaction and marketing interface. *Industrial Marketing Management, 40*(2), 240–247. https://doi.org/10.1016/j.indmarman.2010.06.036

Grubbauer, M. (2013). Mainstreaming urban interventionist practices: The case of the BMW Guggenheim lab in Berlin. *Footprint*, (13), 123–130.

Gryszkiewicz, L., Lykourentzou, I., & Toivonen, T. (2016). Innovation labs: Leveraging openness for radical innovation? *Journal of Innovation Management, 4*(4), 68–97. https://doi.org/10.24840/2183-0606_004.004_0006

Hagberg, J., Sundstrom, M., & Egels-Zandén, N. (2016). The digitalization of retailing: an exploratory framework. *International Journal of Retail and Distribution Management, 44*(7), 694–712. https://doi.org/10.1108/IJRDM-09-2015-0140

Halkier, B. (2011). Methodological practicalities in analytical generalization. *Qualitative Inquiry, 17*(9), 787–797. https://doi.org/10.1177/1077800411423194

Hatchuel, A. (2001). Towards design theory and expandable rationality: The unfinished program of Herbert Simon. *Journal of Management and Governance, 5*(3/4), 260–273. https://doi.org/10.1023/1014044305704

Hatchuel, A., Le Masson, P., & Weil, B. (2011). Teaching innovative design reasoning: How concept-knowledge theory can help overcome fixation effects. *Artificial Intelligence for Engineering Design, Analysis and Manufacturing: AIEDAM, 25*(1), 77–92. https://doi.org/10.1017/S089006041000048X

Hatchuel, A., & Weil, B. (2003). A new approach of innovative design: An introduction to C-K theory. *International Conference on Engineering Design, 19*, 1–15.

Hausman, A., & Johnston, W. J. (2014). The role of innovation in driving the economy: Lessons from the global financial crisis. *Journal of Business Research, 67*(1), 2720–2726. https://doi.org/10.1016/j.jbusres.2013.03.021

Hedman, J., & Kalling, T. (2003). The business model concept: Theoretical underpinnings and empirical illustrations. *European Journal of Information Systems, 12*(1), 49–59. https://doi.org/10.1057/palgrave.ejis.3000446

Helkkula, A., Kelleher, C., & Pihlström, M. (2012). Characterizing value as an experience: Implications for service researchers and managers. *Journal of Service Research, 15*(1), 59–75. https://doi.org/10.1177/1094670511426897

Hermes, S., Kaufmann-Ludwig, J., Schreieck, M., Weking, J., & Böhm, M. (2020). A taxonomy of platform envelopment: Revealing patterns and particularities. *AMCIS 2020 Proceedings*, 10. Retrieved from https://aisel.aisnet.org/amcis2020/strategic_uses_it/strategic_uses_it/17

Hesse-Biber, S. N., & Leavy, P. (2006). *Emergent methods in social research.* Sage.

Hevner, A., March, S. T., Park, J., & Ram, S. (2004). Design science in IS research. *MIS Quarterly, 28*(1), 75–105.

Hevner, A. R. (2007). A three cycle view of design science research. *Scandinavian Journal of Information Systems, 19*(2), 1–6. Retrieved from http://aisel.aisnet.org/sjis/vol19/iss2/4

Hodapp, D., Remane, G., Hanelt, A., & Kolbe, L. M. (2019). Business models for internet of things platforms: Empirical development of a taxonomy and archetypes. *14th International Conference on Wirtschaftsinformatik*, 15. Retrieved from https://www.researchgate.net/publication/330759288

Holland, C. P., & Gutiérrez-Leefmans, M. (2018). A taxonomy of SME e-commerce platforms derived from a market-level analysis. *International Journal of Electronic Commerce, 22*(2), 161–201. https://doi.org/10.1080/10864415.2017.1364114

Hossain, M., Leminen, S., & Westerlund, M. (2019). A systematic review of living lab literature. *Journal of Cleaner Production, 213*, 976–988. https://doi.org/10.1016/j.jclepro.2018.12.257

Howcroft, D., & Bergvall-Kåreborn, B. (2019). A typology of crowdwork platforms. *Work, Employment and Society, 33*(1), 21–38. https://doi.org/10.1177/0950017018760136

Huang, H. B. (2010). What is good action research?: Why the resurgent interest? *Action Research, 8*(1), 93–109. https://doi.org/10.1177/1476750310362435

Hunke, F., Engel, C., Schüritz, R., & Ebel, P. (2019). Understanding the anatomy of analytics-based services—A taxonomy to conceptualize the use of data and analytics in services. *27th European Conference on Information Systems (ECIS2019)*. Retrieved from https://aisel.aisnet.org/ecis2019_rp/25/

Iivari, J. (2003). The IS Core–VII: Towards information systems as a science of meta-artifacts. *Communications of the Association for Information Systems, 12*, 568–581. https://doi.org/10.17705/1cais.01237

Iivari, J. (2007). A paradigmatic analysis of information systems as a design science. *Scandinavian Journal of Information Systems, 19*(2), 39–64.

Iivari, J., & Venable, J. (2009). Action research and design science research: Seemingly similar but decisively dissimilar. *Ecis, Paper 73*(2009), 1–13. https://doi.org/10.1097/01.WOX.0000411817.24011.93

Inman, J. J., & Nikolova, H. (2017). Shopper-Facing Retail Technology: A Retailer Adoption Decision Framework Incorporating Shopper Attitudes and Privacy Concerns. *Journal of Retailing, 93*(1), 7–28. https://doi.org/10.1016/j.jretai.2016.12.006

Jansson, D. G., & Smith, S. M. (1991). Design fixation. *Design Studies, 12*(1), 3–11.

Johnson, S. P., Menor, L. J., Roth, A. V., & Chase, R. B. (2000). A critical evaluation of the new service development process: Integrating service innovation and service design. In *New service development: Creating memorable experiences* (pp. 1–32). https://doi.org/10.4135/9781452205564.n1

Josephson, A., Schrank, H., & Marshall, M. (2017). Assessing preparedness of small businesses for hurricane disasters: Analysis of pre-disaster owner, business and location characteristics. *International Journal of Disaster Risk Reduction, 23*, 25–35. https://doi.org/10.1016/j.ijdrr.2017.03.013

Jullien, B., & Pavan, A. (2019). Information management and pricing in platform markets. *The Review of Economic Studies, 86*(4), 1666–1703. https://doi.org/10.1093/restud/rdy040

Kaiser, U., & Wright, J. (2006). Price structure in two-sided markets: Evidence from the magazine industry? *International Journal of Industrial Organization, 24*(1), 1–28. https://doi.org/10.1016/j.ijindorg.2005.06.002

Karimi, S., Pohl, S., Scholer, F., Cavedon, L., & Zobel, J. (2010). Boolean versus ranked querying for biomedical systematic reviews. *BMC Medical Informatics and Decision Making, 10*(58). https://doi.org/10.1186/1472-6947-10-58

Katzy, B. (2012). Designing Viable Business Models for Living Labs. *Technology Innovation Management Review, 2*(9), 19–24. https://doi.org/10.22215/timreview604

Kaushik, V., & Walsh, C. A. (2019). Pragmatism as a researcKaushik, V. and Walsh, C. A. (2019). Pragmatism as a research paradigm and its implications for social work research. *Social Sciences, 8(9)*. doi: https://doi.org/10.3390/socsci8090255.h paradigm and its implications for Social Work research. *Social Sciences*, *8*(9), 1–17.

Ketchen, D. J., Ireland, R. D., & Snow, C. C. (2007). Strategic entrepreneurship, collaborative innovation, and wealth creation. *Strategic Entrepreneurship Journal*, *1*(3–4), 371–385. https://doi.org/10.1002/sej.20

Kim, C., & Bettis, R. A. (2014). Cash is surprisingly valuable as a strategic asset. *Strategic Management Journal*, *35*(13), 2053–2063. https://doi.org/10.1002/smj.2205

Kim, & Min. (2019). Supplier, tailor, and facilitator: Typology of platform business models. *Journal of Open Innovation: Technology, Market, and Complexity*, *5*(3), 57. https://doi.org/10.3390/joitmc5030057

Konietzko, J., Bocken, N., & Hultink, E. J. (2019). Online Platforms and the Circular Economy. In N. Bocken, P. Ritala, L. Albareda, & R. Verburg (Eds.), *Innovation for Sustainability* (pp. 435–450). https://doi.org/10.1007/978-3-319-97385-2_23

Korte, R. F. (2009). Engaged scholarship: A guide for organizational and social research. *Human Resource Development International*, *12*(2), 233–239. https://doi.org/10.1080/13678860902764191

Koskela-Huotari, K., Edvardsson, B., Jonas, J. M., Sörhammar, D., & Witell, L. (2016). Innovation in service ecosystems: Breaking, making, and maintaining institutionalized rules of resource integration. *Journal of Business Research*, *69*(8), 2964–2971. https://doi.org/10.1016/j.jbusres.2016.02.029

Kraus, S., Bouncken, R. B., Görmar, L., González-Serrano, M. H., & Calabuig, F. (2022). Coworking spaces and makerspaces: Mapping the state of research. *Journal of Innovation and Knowledge*, *7*(1). https://doi.org/10.1016/j.jik.2022.100161

Kraus, S., Clauss, T., Breier, M., Gast, J., Zardini, A., & Tiberius, V. (2020). The economics of COVID-19: Initial empirical evidence on how family firms in five European countries cope with the corona crisis. *International Journal of Entrepreneurial Behavior & Research*, *26*(5), 1067–1092. https://doi.org/10.1108/IJEBR-04-2020-0214

Kuhlmann, S., & Rip, A. (2018). Next-generation innovation policy and Grand Challenges. *Science and Public Policy*, *45*(4), 448–454. https://doi.org/10.1093/SCIPOL/SCY011

Le Glatin, M., Le Masson, P., & Weil, B. (2017). Generative action and preference reversal in exploratory project management. *CERN IdeaSquare Journal of Experimental Innovation*, *1*(2), 39–46. https://doi.org/10.23726/cij.2017.539

Le Masson, P., Weil, B., & Hatchuel, A. (2009). Platforms for the design of platforms: Collaborating in the unknown. *Platforms, Markets and Innovation*, (January), 273–305. https://doi.org/10.4337/9781849803311.00019

Le Masson, P., Weil, B., & Hatchuel, A. (2017). Design theory: Methods and organization for innovation. In *Design Theory: Methods and Organization for Innovation*. https://doi.org/10.1007/978-3-319-50277-9

Leipziger Messe. (n.d.). Retrieved June 26, 2022, from https://www.leipziger-messe.de/de/unternehmen/portrait/geschichte/

Leminen, S. (2013). Coordination and Participation in Living Lab Networks. *Technology Innovation Management Review*, *3*(11), 5–14. https://doi.org/10.22215/timreview740

Leminen, S., & Westerlund, M. (2017). Categorization of innovation tools in Living Labs. *Technology Innovation Management Review*, *7*(1), 15–25. https://doi.org/10.22215/timreview1046

Leminen, S., Westerlund, M., & Nyström, A. A.-G. (2012). Living Labs as open-innovation networks. *Technology Innovation Management Review*, *2*(September), 6–11. https://doi.org/10.22215/timreview602

Lewin, K. (1946). Action research and minority problems. *Journal of Social Issues*, *2*(4), 34–46. https://doi.org/10.1111/j.1540-4560.1946.tb02295.x

Lewis, M., & Moultrie, J. (2005). The organizational innovation laboratory. *Creativity and Innovation Management*, *14*(1), 73–83. https://doi.org/10.1111/j.1467-8691.2005.00327.x

Li, M., Ramaswamy, K., & Pécherot Petitt, B. S. (2006). Business groups and market failures: A focus on vertical and horizontal strategies. *Asia Pacific Journal of Management*, *23*, 439–452. https://doi.org/10.1007/s10490-006-9016-1

Li, S., & Tallman, S. (2011). MNC strategies, exogenous shocks, and performance outcomes. *Strategic Management Journal*, *32*(10), 1119–1127. https://doi.org/10.1002/smj.918

Lindgren, Henfridsson, & Schultze. (2004). Design principles for competence management systems: A synthesis of an action research study. *MIS Quarterly*, *28*(3), 435. https://doi.org/10.2307/25148646

Lis, D., & Otto, B. (2021). Towards a taxonomy of ecosystem data governance. *Proceedings of the 54th Hawaii International Conference on System Sciences*, *0*, 6067–6076. https://doi.org/10.24251/hicss.2021.733

March, S. T., & Smith, G. F. (1995). Design and natural science research on information technology. *Decision Support Systems*, *15*(4), 251–266. https://doi.org/10.1016/0167-9236(94)00041-2

Massa, L., & Tucci, C. (2013). Business model innovation. In *The Oxford handbook of innovation management*.

Mathiassen, L., & Nielsen, P. A. (2008). Engaged scholarship in IS research. *Scandinavian Journal of Information Systems*, *20*(2), 3–20.

Matzner, M., Büttgen, M., Demirkan, H., Spohrer, J., Alter, S., Fritzsche, A., … Neely, A. (2018). Digital Transformation in Service Management. *Journal of Service Management Research*, *2*(2), 3–21. https://doi.org/10.15358/2511-8676-2018-2-3

Mazzucato, M. (2018). Mission-oriented innovation policies: Challenges and opportunities. *Industrial and Corporate Change*, *27*(5), 803–815. https://doi.org/10.1093/icc/dty034

McCrory, G., Schäpke, N., Holmén, J., & Holmberg, J. (2020). Sustainability-oriented labs in real-world contexts: An exploratory review. *Journal of Cleaner Production*, *277*. https://doi.org/10.1016/j.jclepro.2020.123202

McGann, M., Blomkamp, E., & Lewis, J. M. (2018). The rise of public sector innovation labs: experiments in design thinking for policy. *Policy Sciences*, *51*(3), 249–267. https://doi.org/10.1007/s11077-018-9315-7

McGrath, R. G. (2010). Business models: A discovery driven approach. *Long Range Planning*, *43*(2–3), 247–261. https://doi.org/10.1016/j.lrp.2009.07.005

McIntyre, D. P., & Srinivasan, A. (2017). Networks, platforms, and strategy: Emerging views and next steps. *Strategic Management Journal*, *38*(1), 141–160. https://doi.org/10.1002/smj.2596

Meinel, C., & Leifer, L. (2011). *Design thinking* (C. Meinel, L. Leifer, & H. Plattner, Eds.). https://doi.org/10.1007/978-3-642-13757-0

Memon, T. (2021). *Effective platform product management*. Packt Publishing.

Menschner, P., Peters, C., & Leimeister, J. M. (2011). Engineering knowledge-intense, person-oriented services: A state of the art analysis. *19th European Conference on Information Systems, ECIS 2011*, (2011).

Meuser, M., & Nagel, U. (2009). Experts and changes in knowledge production. In *Interviewing experts* (pp. 17–43). London: Palgrave Macmillan.

Meyer, P., Jonas, J. M., & Roth, A. (2020). Frontline Employees' Acceptance of and Resistance to Service Robots in Stationary Retail – An Exploratory Interview Study. *Journal of Service Management Research, 4*(1), 21–34. https://doi.org/10.15358/2511-8676-2020-1-21

Moore, J. F. (1993). Predators and prey: A new ecology of competition. *Harvard Business Review, 71*(3), 75–86.

Morgan, D. L. (2014). Pragmatism as a paradigm for social research. *Qualitative Inquiry, 20*(8), 1045–1053. https://doi.org/10.1177/1077800413513733

Moriset, B. (2014). Building new places of the creative economy. The rise of co-working spaces, *2nd Geography of Innovation International Conference 2014 Utrecht University, Utrecht, 23–25 January 2014*, 24.

Morris, M., Schindehutte, M., & Allen, J. (2005). The entrepreneur's business model: Toward a unified perspective. *Journal of Business Research, 58*(6), 726–735. https://doi.org/10.1016/j.jbusres.2003.11.001

Mortara, L., & Parisot, N. (2018). How do Fab-spaces enable entrepreneurship? Case studies of 'makers': Entrepreneurs. *International Journal of Manufacturing Technology and Management, 32*(1), 16–42. https://doi.org/10.1504/IJMTM.2018.089465

Mukhopadhyay, S., & Bouwman, H. (2019). Orchestration and governance in digital platform ecosystems: A literature review and trends. *Digital Policy, Regulation and Governance, 21*(4), 329–351. https://doi.org/10.1108/DPRG-11-2018-0067

Narsalay, R., Kavathekar, J., & Light, D. (2016). A hands-off approach to open innovation doesn't work. *Harvard Business Review*.

Nestle, V., Glauner, P., & Plugmann, P. (2021). *Creating innovation spaces* (1st ed.). V. Nestle, P. Glauner, & P. Plugmann, eds.). https://doi.org/10.1007/978-3-030-57642-4

Netz, J., Reinmoeller, P., & Axelson, M. (2022). Crisis-driven innovation of products new to firms: The sensitization response to COVID-19. *R and D Management*, 407–426. https://doi.org/10.1111/radm.12522

Nickerson, R. C., Varshney, U., & Muntermann, J. (2013). A method for taxonomy development and its application in information systems. *European Journal of Information Systems, 22*(3), 336–359. https://doi.org/10.1057/ejis.2012.26

Niehm, L. S., Fiore, A. M., Jeong, M., & Kim, H.-J. (2007). Pop-up Retail's Acceptability as an Innovative Business Strategy and Enhancer of the Consumer Shopping Experience. *Journal of Shopping Center Research, 13*(2), 1–30.

O'Hern, M. S., & Rindfleisch, A. (2010). Customer co-creation: A typology and research agenda. *WisconsInnovation: Thoughts on Innovation from the Wisconsin School of Business*. https://doi.org/10.1108/S1548-6435(2009)0000006008

Ollila, S., & Yström, A. (2016). Exploring design principles of organizing for collaborative innovation: The case of an open innovation initiative. *Creativity and Innovation Management, 25*(3), 363–377. https://doi.org/10.1111/caim.12177

Ollila, S., & Yström, A. (2020). Action research for innovation management: Three benefits, three challenges, and three spaces. *R and D Management, 50*(3), 396–411. https://doi.org/10.1111/radm.12407

Olsson, A., Paredes, K. M. B., Johansson, U., Olander Roese, M., & Ritzén, S. (2019). Organizational climate for innovation and creativity–a study in Swedish retail organizations. *International Review of Retail, Distribution and Consumer Research, 29*(3), 243–261. https://doi.org/10.1080/09593969.2019.1598470

Orel, M. (2019). Coworking environments and digital nomadism: balancing work and leisure whilst on the move. *World Leisure Journal, 61*(3), 215–227. https://doi.org/10.1080/16078055.2019.1639275

Orel, M., & Kubátová, J. (2019). Coworking as a model for conscious business. *Journal of Global Responsibility, 10*(3), 257–270. https://doi.org/10.1108/JGR-11-2018-0068

Orlikowski, W. J., & Iacono, C. S. (2001). Research commentary: Desperately seeking the 'IT' in IT research: A call to theorizing the IT artifact. *Information Systems Research, 12*(2), 121–134. https://doi.org/10.1287/isre.12.2.121.9700

Osorio, F., Dupont, L., Camargo, M., Palominos, P., Peña, J. I., & Alfaro, M. (2019). Design and management of innovation laboratories: Toward a performance assessment tool. *Creativity and Innovation Management, 28*(1), 82–100. https://doi.org/10.1111/caim.12301

Osterwalder, A. (2004). The business model ontology: A proposition in a design science approach. *Business, Doctor*, 1–169. https://doi.org/10.1111/j.1467-9310.2010.00605.x

Otto, S. (2019). *Mobilisierung von Wissen: Praktiken der Wissenskodifizierung am Beispiel des Innovationslabors JOSEPHS*. Retrieved from https://eref.uni-bayreuth.de/47147/

Palmié, M., Miehé, L., Oghazi, P., Parida, V., & Wincent, J. (2022). The evolution of the digital service ecosystem and digital business model innovation in retail: The emergence of meta-ecosystems and the value of physical interactions. *Technological Forecasting and Social Change, 177*(January). https://doi.org/10.1016/j.techfore.2022.121496

Parker, G. G., & Van Alstyne, M. W. (2005). Two-sided network effects: A theory of information product design. *Management Science, 51*(10), 1494–1504. https://doi.org/10.1287/mnsc.1050.0400

Parker, G. G., Van Alstyne, M. W., & Choudary, S. P. (2016). *Platform revolution: How networked markets are transforming the economy and how to make them work for you.* Retrieved from https://dl.acm.org/doi/book/10.5555/3002873

Pauwels, K., & Weiss, A. (2008). Moving from free to fee: How online firms market to change their business model successfully. *Journal of Marketing, 72*(3), 14–31. https://doi.org/10.1509/JMKG.72.3.014

Peffers, K., Tuunanen, T., Rothenberger, M. A., & Chatterjee, S. (2007). A design science research methodology for information systems research. *Journal of Management Information Systems, 24*(3), 45–77. https://doi.org/10.2753/MIS0742-1222240302

Perez Mengual, M., Jonas, J., Schmitt-Rüth, S., & Danzinger, F. (June 2018). *Tools for collaborating and interacting in Living Labs: An exploratory case study on JOSEPHS®.* Retrieved from http://www.ep.liu.se/ecp/contents.asp?issue=150

Perscheid, G. (2020). Towards a taxonomy of decentralized platform-based business models. *Twenty-Eighth European Conference on Information Systems (ECIS)*, 1–16.

Peschl, M. F., & Fundneider, T. (2014). Designing and enabling spaces for collaborative knowledge creation and innovation: From managing to enabling innovation as socio-epistemological technology. *Computers in Human Behavior*, *37*, 346–359. https://doi.org/10.1016/j.chb.2012.05.027

Petticrew, M., & Roberts, H. (2005). *Systematic reviews in the social sciences: A practical guide*. John Wiley & Sons.

Piekkari, R., Plakoyiannaki, E., & Welch, C. (2010). 'Good' case research in industrial marketing: Insights from research practice. *Industrial Marketing Management*, *39*(1), 109–117. https://doi.org/10.1016/j.indmarman.2008.04.017

Prahalad, C. K., & Bettis, R. A. (1986). The dominant logic: A new linkage between diversity and performance. *Strategic Management Journal*, *7*, 485–501. https://doi.org/10.1016/S0742-3322(00)17010-X

Prahalad, C. K., & Hamel, G. (1997). The core competence of the corporation. In *Strategische Unternehmungsplanung/Strategische Unternehmungsführung* (pp. 969–987). https://doi.org/10.1007/978-3-662-41482-8_46

Prat, N., Comyn-Wattiau, I., & Akoka, J. (2015). A taxonomy of evaluation methods for information systems artifacts. *Journal of Management Information Systems*, *32*(3), 229–267. https://doi.org/10.1080/07421222.2015.1099390

Pratt, M. (2009). From the editors: For the lack of a boilerplate: Tips on writing up (and reviewing) qualitative research. *Academy of Management Journal*, *52*(5), 856–862. https://doi.org/10.5465/AMJ.2009.44632557

Quartier, K., Claes, S., & Vanrie, J. (2020). A holistic competence framework for (future) retail design and retail design education. *Journal of Retailing and Consumer Services*, *55*(February), 101914. https://doi.org/10.1016/j.jretconser.2019.101914

Ramaswamy, V., & Ozcan, K. (2018). What is co-creation? An interactional creation framework and its implications for value creation. *Journal of Business Research*, *84*, 196–205. https://doi.org/10.1016/j.jbusres.2017.11.027

Rapoport, R. N. (1970). Three dilemmas in action research. *Human Relations*, *23*(6), 499–513.

Reich, Y. (2013). Designing science. *Research in Engineering Design*, *24*(3), 215–218. https://doi.org/10.1007/s00163-013-0157-1

Reichwald, R., & Piller, F. (2009). *Interaktive Wertschöpfung*. Wiesbaden: Gabler.

Reillier, L. C., & Reillier, B. (2017). *Platform strategy: How to unlock the power of communities and networks to grow your business*. Routledge.

Reinartz, W. (2019). Reinventing the retailer: Retaining relevance and customer access. *NIM Marketing Intelligence Review*, *11*(1), 10–17. https://doi.org/10.2478/nimmir-2019-0002

Remane, G., Nickerson, R. C., Hanelt, A., Tesch, J. F., & Kolbe, L. M. (2016). A taxonomy of carsharing business models. *Thirty Seventh International Conference on Information Systems (ICIS 2016)*, 19. Retrieved from https://aisel.aisnet.org/icis2016/Crowdsourcing/Presentations/18/

Ren, C. R., Hu, Y., & Cui, T. H. (2019). Responses to rival exit: Product variety, market expansion, and preexisting market structure. *Strategic Management Journal*, *40*(2), 253–276. https://doi.org/10.1002/smj.2970

Riege, A. M. (2003). Validity and reliability tests in case study research: A literature review with 'hands-on' applications for each research phase. *Qualitative Market Research: An International Journal*, *6*(2), 75–86. https://doi.org/10.1108/13522750310470055

Rietveld, J., & Schilling, M. A. (2020). Platform competition: A systematic and interdisciplinary review of the literature. *Journal of Management*, 1–36. https://doi.org/10.1177/0149206320969791

Ritter, T., & Pedersen, C. L. (2020). Analyzing the impact of the coronavirus crisis on business models. *Industrial Marketing Management*, *88*(May), 214–224. https://doi.org/10.1016/j.indmarman.2020.05.014

Rix, C., Horst, C., Autenrieth, P., Paproth, Y., Frank, J., & Gudergan, G. (2020). Typology of digital platforms in mechanical engineering. *2020 IEEE International Conference on Engineering, Technology and Innovation (ICE/ITMC)*, 1–9. https://doi.org/10.1109/ICE/ITMC49519.2020.9198471

RKI. (2022). COVID-19 in Germany. Retrieved from https://www.rki.de/EN/Home/homepage_node.html;jsessionid=D50B4FDEFE50962AB4A95FD76A95E03F.internet111

Robbins, D. K., & Pearce, J. A. (1993). Entrepreneurial retrenchment among small manufacturing firms. *Journal of Business Ven*, *8*, 301–318.

Rochet, J.-C., & Tirole, J. (2003). Two-sided markets. *Journal of the European Economic Association*, *1*(4), 990–1029.

Roggeveen, A. L., & Sethuraman, R. (2020). How the COVID-19 pandemic may change the world of retailing. *Journal of retailing*, 96(2), 169.

Roth, A., Fritzsche, A., Jonas, J., Danzinger, F., & Möslein, K. M. (2014). Interaktive Kunden als Herausforderung: Die Fallstudie „JOSEPHS® – Die Service-Manufaktur". *HMD Praxis Der Wirtschaftsinformatik*, *51*(6), 883–895. https://doi.org/10.1365/s40702-014-0091-3

Sanchez-Cartas, J. M., & León, G. (2021). Multisided platforms and markets: A survey of the theoretical literature. *Journal of Economic Surveys*, *35*(2), 452–487. https://doi.org/10.1111/joes.12409

Sánchez-Cartas, J. M., & León, G. (May 2018). Multisided platforms and markets: A literature review. Retrieved from https://www.researchgate.net/publication/325225786_Multisided_Platforms_and_Markets_A_Literature_Review

Scheuing, E. E., & Johnson, E. M. (1989). A proposed model for new service development. *Journal of Services Marketing*, *3*(2), 25–34. https://doi.org/10.1108/EUM0000000002484

Schiff, A. (2003). Open and closed systems of two-sided networks. *Information Economics and Policy*, *15*(4), 425–442. https://doi.org/10.1016/S0167-6245(03)00006-4

Schmidt, S., & Brinks, V. (2017). Open creative labs: Spatial settings at the intersection of communities and organizations. *Creativity and Innovation Management*, *26*(3), 291–299. https://doi.org/10.1111/caim.12220

Schneider, S., & Spieth, P. (2013). Business model innovation: Towards an integrated future research agenda. *International Journal of Innovation Management*, *17*(1). https://doi.org/10.1142/S136391961340001X

Schneider, S., & Spieth, P. (2014). Business model innovation and strategic flexibility: Insights from an experimental research design. *International Journal of Innovation Management*, *18*(6), 1–21. https://doi.org/10.1142/S136391961440009X

Scholl, C., & Kemp, R. (2016). City labs as vehicles for innovation in urban planning processes. *Urban Planning*, *1*(4), 89–102. https://doi.org/10.17645/up.v1i4.749

Schreyögg, G., & Kliesch-Eberl, M. (2007). How dynamic can organizational capabilities be? Towards a dual-process model of capability dynamization. *Strategic Management Journal*, *28*(9), 913–933. https://doi.org/10.1002/smj.613

Schuurman, D., & Tõnurist, P. (2017). Innovation in the Public Sector: Exploring the Characteristics and Potential of Living Labs and Innovation Labs. *Technology Innovation Management Review*, *7*(1), 7–14. https://doi.org/10.22215/timreview1045

Sein, M. K., Henfridsson, O., Purao, S., Rossi, M., & Lindgren, R. (2011). Action design research. *MIS Quarterly: Management Information Systems*, *35*(1), 37–56. https://doi.org/10.2307/23043488

Shirahada, K., & Hamazaki, K. (2013). Trial and error mindset of R&D personnel and its relationship to organizational creative climate. *Technological Forecasting and Social Change*, *80*(6), 1108–1118. https://doi.org/10.1016/j.techfore.2012.09.005

Siggelkow, N. (2007). Persuasion with case studies. *Academy of Management Journal*, *50*(1), 20–24. https://doi.org/10.5465/amj.2007.24160882

Simon, H. A. (1996). *The sciences of the artificial*. https://doi.org/10.2307/3102825

Simon, H. A. (1997). *Administrative behaviour* (4th ed.). Free Press.

Sonnenberg, C., & vom Brocke, J. (2012). *Evaluations in the science of the artificial—Reconsidering the build–evaluate pattern in design science research*. https://doi.org/10.1007/978-3-642-29863-9_28

Sosna, M., Trevinyo-Rodríguez, R. N., & Velamuri, S. R. (2010). Business model innovation through trial-and-error learning: The Naturhouse case. *Long Range Planning*, *43*(2–3), 383–407. https://doi.org/10.1016/j.lrp.2010.02.003

Staykova, K. S., & Damsgaard, J. (2015). A typology of multi-sided platforms: The core and the periphery. *Twenty-Third European Conference on Information Systems (ECIS 2015)*, 16. https://doi.org/10.18151/7217486

Steen, K., & van Bueren, E. (2017). The defining characteristics of urban Living Labs. *Technology Innovation Management Review*, *7*(7), 21–33. https://doi.org/10.22215/timreview1088

Stehlin, J., Hodson, M., & McMeekin, A. (2020). Platform mobilities and the production of urban space: Toward a typology of platformization trajectories. *Environment and Planning A: Economy and Space*, *52*(7), 1250–1268. https://doi.org/10.1177/0308518X19896801

Stickdorn, M., Hormess, M., Lawrence, A., & Schneider, J. (2017). *This is service design doing: Applying service design thinking in the real world*. O'Reilly UK Ltd.

Stieglitz, N., Knudsen, T., & Becker, M. C. (2016). Adaptation and inertia in dynamic environments. *Strategic Management Journal*, *37*(9), 1854–1864. https://doi.org/10.1002/smj.2433

Strandvik, T., Holmlund, M., & Edvardsson, B. (2012). Customer needing: A challenge for the seller offering. *Journal of Business and Industrial Marketing*, *27*(2), 132–141. https://doi.org/10.1108/08858621211196994

Stross, R. E. (2007). *The wizard of Menlo Park : How Thomas Alva Edison invented the modern world*. Three Rivers Press.

Sun, Y., & Kantor, P. B. (2006). Cross-evaluation: A new model for information system evaluation. *Journal of the American Society for Information Science and Technology*, *57*(5), 614–628. https://doi.org/10.1002/asi.20324

Suri, H. (2011). Purposeful sampling in qualitative research synthesis. *Qualitative Research Journal*, *11*(2), 63–75. https://doi.org/10.3316/QRJ1102063

Susman, G. I., & Evered, R. D. (1978). An assessment of the scientific merits of action research. *Administrative science quarterly*, 582–603.

Täuscher, K., & Laudien, S. M. (2018). Understanding platform business models: A mixed methods study of marketplaces. *European Management Journal, 36*(3), 319–329. https://doi.org/10.1016/j.emj.2017.06.005

Teece, D. J. (2010). Business models, business strategy and innovation. *Long Range Planning, 43*(2–3), 172–194. https://doi.org/10.1016/j.lrp.2009.07.003

Teece, D. J. (2017). Dynamic capabilities and (digital) platform lifecycles. *Advances in Strategic Management, 37*, 211–225. https://doi.org/10.1108/S0742-332220170000037008

Thomas, M., Le Masson, P., Weil, B., & Legrand, J. (2021). The future of digital platforms: Conditions of platform overthrow. *Creativity and Innovation Management, 30*(1), 80–95. https://doi.org/10.1111/caim.12422

Tiwana, A. (2014). Platform architecture. In *Platform ecosystems* (pp. 73–116). https://doi.org/10.1016/B978-0-12-408066-9.00005-9

To, C. K., Yee, R. W. Y., Mok, P. Y., Chau, K. P., Wong, M. C., & Cheung, N. M. (2018). Collaboration reasoning or social heuristics? Value proposition validity in omnium-gatherum business models. *Journal of Business Research, 88*, 550–559. https://doi.org/10.1016/j.jbusres.2018.01.062

Tudose, M. B., Agafitei, G., & Avasilcai, S. (2020). New research direction on performance and co-creation: A literature review. *IOP Conference Series: Materials Science and Engineering, 898*. https://doi.org/10.1088/1757-899X/898/1/012032

Tura, N., Kutvonen, A., & Ritala, P. (2018). Platform design framework: Conceptualisation and application. *Technology Analysis and Strategic Management, 30*(8), 881–894. https://doi.org/10.1080/09537325.2017.1390220

Van Alstyne, M., & Parker, G. (2017). Platform business: From resources to relationships. *GfK Marketing Intelligence Review, 9*(1), 24–29. https://doi.org/10.1515/gfkmir-2017-0004

Van de Ven, A. H. (2007). *Engaged Scholarship: A guide for organizational and social research*. New York: Oxford University Press.

Van de Ven, A. H. (2018). Information and organization: Academic-practitioner engaged scholarship. *Information and Organization, 28*(1), 37–43. https://doi.org/10.1016/j.infoandorg.2018.02.002

Van De Ven, A. H., & Johnson, P. E. (2006). Knowledge for theory and practice. *Academy of Management Review, 31*(4), 802–821.

Van Holm, E. J. (2015). What are Makerspaces, hackerspaces, and Fab Labs? *SSRN Electronic Journal*. https://doi.org/10.2139/ssrn.2548211

Van Maanen, J., Sørensen, J. B., & Mitchell, T. R. (2007). The interplay between theory and method. *Academy of Management Review, 32*(4), 1145–1154. https://doi.org/10.5465/AMR.2007.26586080

Vandenberg, F., Berghman, M., & Schaap, J. (2021). The 'lonely raver': Music livestreams during COVID-19 as a hotline to collective consciousness? *European Societies, 23*(S1), S141–S152. https://doi.org/10.1080/14616696.2020.1818271

Varadarajan, R., Srinivasan, R., Vadakkepatt, G. G., Yadav, M. S., Pavlou, P. A., Krishnamurthy, S., & Krause, T. (2010). Interactive technologies and retailing strategy: A review, conceptual framework and future research directions. *Journal of Interactive Marketing, 24*(2), 96–110. https://doi.org/10.1016/j.intmar.2010.02.004

Vargo, S. L., & Lusch, R. F. (2004). Evolving to a new dominant logic for marketing. *Journal of Marketing*, *68*(1), 1–17. https://doi.org/10.1509/jmkg.68.1.1.24036

Vargo, S. L., & Lusch, R. F. (2008a). From goods to service(s): Divergences and convergences of logics. *Industrial Marketing Management*, *37*(3), 254–259. https://doi.org/10.1016/j.indmarman.2007.07.004

Vargo, S. L., & Lusch, R. F. (2008b). Service-dominant logic: Continuing the evolution. *Journal of the Academy of Marketing Science*, *36*(1), 1–10. https://doi.org/10.1007/s11747-007-0069-6

Vargo, S. L., & Lusch, R. F. (2011). It's all B2B…and beyond: Toward a systems perspective of the market. *Industrial Marketing Management*, *40*(2), 181–187. https://doi.org/10.1016/j.indmarman.2010.06.026

Vargo, S. L., & Lusch, R. F. (2016). Institutions and axioms: An extension and update of service-dominant logic. *Journal of the Academy of Marketing Science*, *44*(1), 5–23. https://doi.org/10.1007/s11747-015-0456-3

Vargo, S. L., & Lusch, R. F. (2017). Service-dominant logic 2025. *International Journal of Research in Marketing*, *34*(1). https://doi.org/10.1016/j.ijresmar.2016.11.001

Vargo, S. L., Maglio, P. P., & Akaka, M. A. (2008). On value and value co-creation: A service systems and service logic perspective. *European Management Journal*, *26*(3), 145–152. https://doi.org/10.1016/j.emj.2008.04.003

Venable, J. (2006). The role of theory and theorising in design science research. *Proceedings of the 1st International Conference on Design Science in Information Systems and Technology (DESRIST 2006)*, 1–18.

Venable, J., Pries-Heje, J., & Baskerville, R. (2012). A comprehensive framework for evaluation in design science research: Advances in theory and practice (DESRIST 2012). *Proceedings of the 7th International Conference on Design Science Research in Information Systems*, 423–438. https://doi.org/10.1007/978-3-642-29863-9_31

Venable, J., Pries-Heje, J., & Baskerville, R. (2016). FEDS: A framework for evaluation in design science research. *European Journal of Information Systems*, *25*(1), 77–89. https://doi.org/10.1057/ejis.2014.36

vom Brocke, J., Simons, A., Niehaves, B., Riemer, K., Plattfaut, R., & Cleven, A. (2009). Reconstructing the giant: On the importance of rigour in documenting the literature search process. *ECIS 2009 Proceedings*. Retrieved from https://aisel.aisnet.org/ecis2009/161

Wahyuni, D. (2012). The research design maze. *Journal of Applied Management Accounting Research*, *10*(1), 69–80.

Walls, J. G., Widmeyer, G. R., & El Sawy, O. A. (1992). Building an information system design theory for vigilant EIS. *Information Systems Research*, *3*(1), 36–59.

Walravens, N. (2014). Smart city as a service platform: Identification and validation of city platform roles in mobile service provision. In *Mobile Electronic Commerce* (pp. 434–467). CRC Press.

Walsham, G. (2006). Doing interpretive research. *European Journal of Information Systems*, *15*(3), 320–330. https://doi.org/10.1057/palgrave.ejis.3000589

Wand, Y., Monarchi, D. E., Parsons, J., & Woo, C. C. (1995). Theoretical foundations for conceptual modelling in information systems development. *Decision Support Systems*, *15*(4), 285–304. https://doi.org/10.1016/0167-9236(94)00043-6

Warnaby, G., & Shi, C. (2019). Changing customer behaviour : Changing retailer response? The potential for pop-up retailing. *Journal of Customer Behaviour, 18*(1), 7–16. https://doi.org/10.1362/147539219X15633616548489

Webster, J., & Watson, R. T. (2002). Analyzing the past to prepare for the future: Writing a literature review. *MIS Quarterly, 26*(2), xiii–xxiii. https://doi.org/10.1.1.104.6570

Weiblen, T., & Chesbrough, H. W. (2015). Engaging with startups to enhance corporate innovation. *California Management Review, 57*(2), 66–90. https://doi.org/10.1525/cmr.2015.57.2.66

Weking, J., Hein, A., Böhm, M., & Krcmar, H. (2020). A hierarchical taxonomy of business model patterns. *Electronic Markets, 30*, 447–468. https://doi.org/10.1007/s12525-018-0322-5

Wenzel, M., Cornelissen, J. P., Koch, J., Hartmann, M., & Rauch, M. (2020). (Un)Mind the gap: How organizational actors cope with an identity–strategy misalignment. *Strategic Organization, 18*(1), 212–244. https://doi.org/10.1177/1476127019856524

Wenzel, M., Stanske, S., & Lieberman, M. B. (2021). Strategic responses to crisis. *Strategic Management Journal, 42*(2), O16–O27. https://doi.org/10.1002/smj.3161

Westerlund, M., Leminen, S., & Rajahonka, M. (2018). A Topic Modelling Analysis of Living Labs Research. *Technology Innovation Management Review, 8*(7), 40–51. https://doi.org/10.22215/timreview/1170

Westley, F., Laban, S., Rose, C., McGowan, K., Robinson, K., Tjornbo, O., … M. (2014). *No Social Innovation Lab Guide*. Retrieved from http://networkingaction.net/wp-content/uploads/10_silabguide_final.pd

Wetter-Edman, K. (2014). *Design for Service: A framework for articulating designers' contribution as interpreter of users' experience.*

Weyrauch, T., & Herstatt, C. (2017). What is frugal innovation? Three defining criteria. *Journal of Frugal Innovation, 2*(1), 1–17. https://doi.org/10.1186/s40669-016-0005-y

Williams, K., Chatterjee, S., & Rossi, M. (2008). Design of emerging digital services: A taxonomy. *European Journal of Information Systems, 17*(5), 505–517. https://doi.org/10.1057/ejis.2008.38

Wolpert, S., & Roth, A. (2020). Development of a classification framework for technology based retail services: A retailers' perspective. *International Review of Retail, Distribution and Consumer Research, 30*(5), 498–538. https://doi.org/10.1080/09593969.2020.1768575

Wycoff, J., & Snead, L. (1999). Stimulating innovation with collaboration rooms. *The Journal for Quality and Participation, 22*(2), 55–57. Retrieved from https://search.proquest.com/docview/219179724

Wynn, D. C., Eckert, C. M., & Clarkson, P. J. (2007). Modelling iteration in engineering design. *Proceedings of ICED 2007, the 16th International Conference on Engineering Design, DS 42*(August), 1–12.

Yablonsky, S. (2018). A multidimensional framework for digital platform innovation and management: From business to technological platforms. *Systems Research and Behavioral Science, 35*(4), 485–501. https://doi.org/10.1002/sres.2544

Yin, R. K. (2003). Design and methods. *Case study research, 3*(9.2).

Yin, R. K. (2013). Validity and generalization in future case study evaluations. *Evaluation, 19*(3), 321–332. https://doi.org/10.1177/1356389013497081

Yoffie, D. B., Gawer, A., & Cusumano, M. A. (2019). A study of more than 250 platforms a reveal why most fail. *Harvard Business Review*. Retrieved June 23, 2022, from https://openresearch.surrey.ac.uk/esploro/outputs/journalArticle/A-study-of-more-than-250/99514445602346

You, W., Chen, W., Agyapong, M., & Mordi, C. (2020). The business model of do-it-yourself (DIY) laboratories: A triple-layered perspective. *Technological Forecasting and Social Change, 159*, 120205. https://doi.org/10.1016/j.techfore.2020.120205

You, X., & Hands, D. (2019). A reflection upon Herbert Simon's vision of design in the sciences of the artificial. *Design Journal, 22*(sup1), 1345–1356. https://doi.org/10.1080/14606925.2019.1594961

Yu, E., & Sangiorgi, D. (2018). Service design as an approach to implement the value cocreation perspective in new service development. *Journal of Service Research, 21*(1), 40–58. https://doi.org/10.1177/1094670517709356

Zavratnik, V., Superina, A., & Duh, E. S. (2019). Living Labs for rural areas: Contextualization of Living Lab frameworks, concepts and practices. *Sustainability (Switzerland), 11*(14). https://doi.org/10.3390/su11143797

Zhang, T., Lu, C., Torres, E., & Cobanoglu, C. (2020). Value co-creation and technological progression: A critical review. *European Business Review, 32*(4), 687–707. https://doi.org/10.1108/EBR-08-2019-0149

MIX
Papier aus verantwortungsvollen Quellen
Paper from responsible sources
FSC® C105338

If you have any concerns about our products,
you can contact us on
ProductSafety@springernature.com

In case Publisher is established outside the EU,
the EU authorized representative is:
Springer Nature Customer Service Center GmbH
Europaplatz 3, 69115 Heidelberg, Germany

Printed by Libri Plureos GmbH
in Hamburg, Germany